Fodor's
Seattle &
Vancouver

"When it comes to information on regional history, what to see and do, and shopping, these guides are exhaustive."

—USAir Magazine

"Usable, sophisticated restaurant coverage, with an emphasis on good value."
—Andy Birsh, *Gourmet Magazine* columnist

"Valuable because of their comprehensiveness."
—Minneapolis Star-Tribune

"Fodor's always delivers high quality...thoughtfully presented...thorough."

—Houston Post

"An excellent choice for those who want everything under one cover."

—Washington Post

Reprinted from *Fodor's Pacific North Coast*

Fodor's Travel Publications, Inc.
New York • Toronto • London • Sydney • Auckland

Fodor's Seattle & Vancouver

Editors: Chelsea S. Mauldin, Nancy van Itallie

Contributors: Steven K. Amsterdam, Robert Andrews, Robert Blake, Tom Barr, Susan Brown, Janet Foley, Tom Gaunt, Jeff Kuechle, Melissa Rivers, Linda K. Schmidt, Mary Ellen Schultz, M. T. Schwartzman (Gold Guide editor), Glenn W. Sheehan, Dinah Spritzer, Loralee Wenger, Adam Woog

Creative Director: Fabrizio La Rocca

Cartographer: David Lindroth

Cover Photograph: Eddie Hironaka/Image Bank

Text Design: Between the Covers

Copyright

Special Sales

CONTENTS

ON THE ROAD WITH FODOR'S

A GOOD TRAVEL GUIDE is like a wonderful traveling companion. It's charming, it's brimming with sound recommendations and solid ideas, it pulls no punches in describing lodging and dining establishments, and it's consistently full of fascinating facts that make you view what you've traveled to see in a rich new light. In the creation of this third edition of *Fodor's Seattle & Vancouver,* we at Fodor's have gone to great lengths to provide you with the very best of all possible traveling companions—and to make your trip the best of all possible vacations.

About Our Writers

The information in these pages is a collaboration of a number of extraordinary writers.

Travel junkie **Melissa Rivers,** updater of the Vancouver chapter, lives in Oregon and travels throughout the Pacific Northwest and eastern Mexico on assignments for Fodor's.

A principal investigator at SJS Archaeological Services, Inc., in Bridgeport, Pennsylvania, **Glenn W. Sheehan** has worked extensively in the Pacific Northwest and Arctic regions.

Loralee Wenger is the former travel editor for *Pacific Northwest* magazine and a freelance writer whose articles have appeared in the *San Francisco Examiner, Washington Post, Parade* magazine, and *Glamour* magazine.

Adam Woog is a Seattle-based freelance writer whose works have appeared in the *Village Voice, Seattle Times,* and *Japan Times.*

What's New

A New Design

If this is not the first Fodor's guide you've purchased, you'll immediately notice our new look. More readable and easier to use than ever? We think so—and we hope you do, too.

Let Us Do Your Booking

Our writers have scoured Seattle and Vancouver to come up with an extensive and well-balanced list of the best B&Bs, inns, and hotels, both small and large, new and old. But you don't have to beat the bushes to come up with a reservation. Now we've teamed up with an established hotel-booking service to make it easy for you to secure a room at the property of your choice. It's fast, it's free, and confirmation is guaranteed. If your first choice is booked, the operators can line up your second right away. Just call 800/FODORS-1 or 800/363-6771 (0800-89-1030 in Great Britain; 0014-800-12-8271 in Australia; 1-800/55-9101 in Ireland).

Travel Updates

In addition, just before your trip, you may want to order a Fodor's Worldview Travel Update. From local publications all over the Pacific North Coast, the lively, cosmopolitan editors at Worldview gather information on concerts, plays, opera, dance performances, gallery and museum shows, sports competitions, and other special events that coincide with your visit. See the order blank at the back of this book, call 800/799-9609, or fax 800/799-9619.

How to Use This Book

Organization

Up front is the **Gold Guide,** comprising two sections on gold paper that are full of practical information listed in alphabetical order by topic. **Important Contacts A to Z** gives addresses and telephone numbers of organizations and companies that offer destination-related services, detailed information, or useful publications. This is also where you'll find information about how to get to Seattle and Vancouver from wherever you are. **Smart Travel Tips A to Z,** the Gold Guide's second section, gives specific tips on how to get the most out of traveling, as well as hints for having a (relatively) hassle-free trip to Seattle and Vancouver.

Each chapter ends with a section called Essentials, which tells you how to get there and get around and lists important local addresses and telephone numbers.

At the back of the book you'll find a wonderful **Portrait** that provides an overview of Northwest Coast archaeology, followed by suggestions for pretrip reading and viewing.

Stars

Stars in the margin are used to denote highly recommended sights, attractions, hotels, and restaurants.

Restaurant and Hotel Criteria and Price Categories

Restaurants and accommodations are chosen with a view to giving you the cream of the crop in each location and in each price range. In all restaurant price charts, costs are per person, excluding drinks, tip, and tax. We note a dress code only when men are required to wear a jacket or a jacket and tie.

In hotel price charts, rates are for standard double rooms, excluding city and state sales taxes. Note that in general you incur charges when you use many hotel facilities. We wanted to let you know what facilities a hotel has to offer, but we don't always specify whether or not there's a charge, so when planning a vacation that entails a stay of several days, it's wise to ask what's included in the rate.

Credit Cards

The following abbreviations are used: **AE,** American Express; **D,** Discover; **DC,** Diners Club; **MC,** MasterCard; and **V,** Visa.

Please Write to Us

Everyone who has contributed to *Fodor's Seattle & Vancouver* has worked hard to make the text accurate. All prices and opening times are based on information supplied to us at press time, and Fodor's cannot accept responsibility for any errors that may have occurred. The passage of time will bring changes, so it's always a good idea to call ahead and confirm information when it matters—particularly if you're making a detour to visit specific sights or attractions. When making reservations at a hotel or inn, be sure to mention if you have a disability or are traveling with children, if you prefer a private bath or a certain type of bed, or if you have specific dietary needs or any other concerns.

Were the restaurants we recommended as described? Did our hotel picks exceed your expectations? Did you find a museum we recommended a waste of time? We would love your feedback, positive and negative. If you have complaints, we'll look into them and revise our entries when the facts warrant it. If you've happened upon a special place that we haven't included, we'll pass the information along to the writers so they can check it out. So please send us a letter or postcard—you can address it to Seattle & Vancouver Editor, 201 East 50th Street, New York, NY 10022. We'll look forward to hearing from you. And in the meantime, have a wonderful trip!

Karen Cure

Karen Cure
Editorial Director

World Time Zones

Numbers below vertical bands relate each zone to Greenwich Mean Time (0 hrs.).
Local times frequently differ from these general indications,
as indicated by light-face numbers on map.

Pacific North Coast

PACIFIC

IMPORTANT CONTACTS A TO Z

An Alphabetical Listing of Publications, Organizations, and Companies That Will Help You Before, During, and After Your Trip

No single travel resource can give you every detail about every topic that might interest or concern you at the various stages of your journey—when you're planning your trip, while you're on the road, and after you get back home. The following organizations, books, and brochures will supplement the information in *Fodor's Seattle & Vancouver.* For related information, including both basic tips on visiting the Pacific North Coast and background information on many of the topics below, study Smart Travel Tips A to Z, the section that follows Important Contacts A to Z.

A

AIR TRAVEL

Nonstop flying time from New York to Seattle is approximately five hours; flights from Chicago are about 4–4½ hours; flights between Los Angeles and Seattle take 2½ hours. Flights from New York to Vancouver take about eight hours with connections; from Chicago, about 4½ hours nonstop; and from Los Angeles, about three hours nonstop.

CARRIERS

MAJOR AIRLINES➣ Flying into Seattle from points throughout the United States are **Alaska** (☎ 800/426–0333), **American** (☎ 800/433–7300), **Continental** (☎ 800/525–0280), **Delta** (☎ 800/221–1212), **Northwest** (☎ 800/225–2525), **TWA** (☎ 800/221–2000), **United** (☎ 800/241–6522), and **USAir** (☎ 800/428–4322). Flying into Vancouver from U.S. points are **American Airlines, Delta,** and **United.** Flying into Vancouver from Canadian cities are **Air Canada** (☎ 800/663–8868) and **Canadian Airlines International** (☎ 800/426–7000).

For inexpensive, no-frills flights, contact **MarkAir** (☎ 800/627–5247), based in Anchorage, Alaska, or **Southwest Airlines** (☎ 800/444–5660), based in Salt Lake City and serving Oregon and Washington.

From the United Kingdom, **British Airways** (☎ 0181/897–4000 in London or 0345/222111 in all other areas) services Seattle and Vancouver from Heathrow. **KLM** (☎ 0181/751–9000; in U.S. ☎ 800/777–5553) travels to Vancouver from 25 U.K. and Irish airports via Amsterdam. **Air Canada** (☎ 0181/759–2636 in London or 0345/181313 elsewhere) flies from Heathrow and Glasgow to Vancouver; **Canadian Airlines International** (☎ 0181/577–7722 or 0345/616767 outside London) services Vancouver from Heathrow.

For budget-priced flights into Vancouver, contact **Globespan Ltd.** (☎ 0141/332–6600) and **Bluebird Express** (☎ 01444/235–678). At press time, prices began at £400 round-trip. You can also find good deals through specialized ticket agencies (*see* Tour Operators, *below*).

REGIONAL AIRLINES➣ Leading regional carriers in the Pacific North Coast are **Horizon Air** (☎ 800/547–9308) and **United Express** (☎ 800/241–6522). The two airlines provide frequent service between cities in Washington and Oregon. Horizon Air also flies internationally from Seattle to Vancouver and Victoria and Calgary, Alberta.

The two major regional carriers in Canada are **Air BC** (☎ 800/663–8868 or 800/776–3000) and **Canadian Partner** (☎ 800/426–7000). They serve communities throughout western Canada and have daily flights from Vancouver and Victoria into Seattle. **Air BC** also has several daily flights between Vancouver and Portland. **Helijet Airways** (☎ 604/273–

1414) provides jet helicopter service from Vancouver to Victoria.

In addition to its regular airport service, Air BC has floatplane service between Vancouver and Victoria harbors. **Kenmore Air** (☎ 206/486–8400 or 800/543–9595) has scheduled flights from Seattle's Lake Union to Victoria and points in the San Juan Islands. Along with several other floatplane companies, Kenmore provides fly-in service to remote fishing resorts along the coast of British Columbia.

COMPLAINTS

To register complaints about charter and scheduled airlines, contact the U.S. Department of Transportation's **Office of Consumer Affairs** (400 7th St. NW, Washington, DC 20590, ☎ 202/366–2220 or 800/322–7873).

CONSOLIDATORS

An established consolidator selling to the public is **TFI Tours International** (34 W. 32nd St., New York, NY 10001, ☎ 212/736–1140 or 800/745–8000). **FLY-ASAP** (3824 E. Indian School Rd., Phoenix, AZ 85018, ☎ 800/359–2727) isn't a discounter, but gets good deals from among published fares, and gets discount tickets from consolidators.

PUBLICATIONS

For general information about charter carriers, ask for the Office of Consumer Affairs' brochure **"Plane Talk:**

Public Charter Flights." The Department of Transportation also publishes a 58-page booklet, **"Fly Rights"** ($1.75; Consumer Information Center, Dept. 133B, Pueblo, CO 81009).

For other tips and hints, consult the Consumers Union's monthly **"Consumer Reports Travel Letter"** ($39 a year; Box 53629, Boulder, CO 80322, ☎ 800/234–1970) and the newsletter **"Travel Smart"** ($37 a year; 40 Beechdale Rd., Dobbs Ferry, NY 10522, ☎ 800/327–3633); *The Official Frequent Flyer Guidebook,* by Randy Petersen ($14.99 plus $3 shipping; 4715-C Town Center Dr., Colorado Springs, CO 80916, ☎ 719/597–8899 or 800/487–8893); *Airfare Secrets Exposed,* by Sharon Tyler and Matthew Wonder (Universal Information Publishing; $16.95 plus $3.75 shipping from Sandcastle Publishing, Box 3070-A, South Pasadena, CA 91031, ☎ 213/255–3616 or 800/655–0053); and *202 Tips Even the Best Business Travelers May Not Know,* by Christopher McGinnis ($10 plus $3 shipping; Irwin Professional Publishing, 1333 Burr Ridge Pkwy., Burr Ridge, IL 60521, ☎ 800/634–3966).

B

BETTER BUSINESS BUREAU

Contact the **Washington Better Business Bureau** (Box 68926, Sea-Tac 98168-0926, ☎ 206/431–2222). For other

local contacts, consult the **Council of Better Business Bureaus** (4200 Wilson Blvd., Arlington, VA 22203, ☎ 703/276–0100).

BUS TRAVEL

Contact **Greyhound Lines** (☎ 800/231–2222) for bus service to Seattle and Vancouver from various points in the United States and Canada.

WITHIN THE PACIFIC NORTH COAST

SCHEDULED SERVICE➤ **Greyhound Lines** (☎ 800/231–2222) operates regular intercity bus routes to points throughout the region. **Gray Line of Seattle** (☎ 206/624–5077) has daily bus service between Seattle and Victoria via the Washington State ferry at Anacortes. Smaller bus companies provide service within local areas. One such service, **Pacific Coach Lines** (☎ 800/661–1725), runs from downtown Vancouver to Victoria (via the British Columbia ferry system). **Quick Coach Lines** (☎ 604/244–3744; 800/665–2122 in the U.S.) provides bus service between Seattle's Sea-Tac Airport and Vancouver's major hotels and cruise terminal.

CHARTERS➤ Several companies operate charter bus service and scheduled sightseeing tours that last from a few hours to several days. Most tours can be booked locally and provide a good way for visitors to see the sights comfortably within a short period of time. **Gray Line** companies in Seattle (☎ 206/624–5077) and Vancouver (☎ 604/681–8687) run such sightseeing trips.

C

CAR RENTAL

Major car-rental companies represented in Seattle and Vancouver include **Avis** (☎ 800/331–1212, 800/879–2847 in Canada), **Budget** (☎ 800/527–0700, 0800/181–181 in the U.K.), **Dollar** (known as Eurodollar outside North America; ☎ 800/800–4000, 0181/952–6565 in the U.K.), **Hertz** (☎ 800/654–3131, 800/263–0600 in Canada, 0181/679–1799 in the U.K.), and **National** (☎ 800/227–7368, 0181/950–5050 in the U.K., where it is known as Europcar). Rates in Seattle begin at $22 a day and $139 a week. Rates in Vancouver begin at $23 a day and $130 a week.

CHILDREN AND TRAVEL

FLYING

Look into **"Flying With Baby"** ($5.95 plus $1 shipping; Third Street Press, Box 261250, Littleton, CO 80126, ☎ 303/595–5959), cowritten by a flight attendant. **"Kids and Teens in Flight,"** free from the U.S. Department of Transportation's Office of Consumer Affairs, offers tips for children flying alone. Every two years the February issue of **Family Travel Times** (*see* Know-How, *below*) details children's ser-

vices on three dozen airlines.

GAMES

The gamemeister, Milton Bradley, has games to help keep little (and not so little) children from getting fidgety while riding in planes, trains, and automobiles. Try packing the Travel Battleship sea battle game ($7), Travel Connect Four, a vertical strategy game ($8), the Travel Yahtzee dice game ($6), the Travel Trouble dice and board game ($7), and the Travel Guess Who mystery game ($8).

KNOW-HOW

Family Travel Times, published four times a year by Travel With Your Children (TWYCH, 45 W. 18th St., New York, NY 10011, ☎ 212/206–0688; annual subscription $40), covers destinations, types of vacations, and modes of travel.

The **Family Travel Guides** catalogue ($1 postage; Box 6061, Albany, CA 94706, ☎ 510/527–5849) lists about 200 books and articles on family travel. Also check **Take Your Baby and Go! A Guide for Traveling with Babies, Toddlers and Young Children,** by Sheri Andrews, Judy Bordeaux, and Vivian Vasquez ($5.95 plus $1.50 shipping; Bear Creek Publications, 2507 Minor Ave., Seattle, WA 98102, ☎ 206/322–7604 or 800/326–6566). Also from Globe Pequot are **The 100 Best Family Resorts in North Amer-**

ica, by Jane Wilford with Janet Tice ($12.95), and the two-volume (eastern section and western editions) set of **50 Great Family Vacations in North America** ($18.95 each plus $3 shipping).

TOUR OPERATORS

Contact **Grandtravel** (6900 Wisconsin Ave., Suite 706, Chevy Chase, MD 20815, ☎ 301/986–0790 or 800/247–7651), which has tours for people traveling with grandchildren ages 7–17; or **Rascals in Paradise** (650 5th St., Suite 505, San Francisco, CA 94107, ☎ 415/978–9800 or 800/872–7225).

If you're outdoorsy, look into the Conservation Summits, nature camps sponsored by the **National Wildlife Federation** (8925 Leesburg Pike, Vienna, VA 22184-0001, ☎ 703/790–4000 or 800/245–5484); **Ecology Tours** (c/o the Audubon Center of the North Woods, Box 530, Sandstone, MN 55072, ☎ 612/245–2648), which mix travel and nature study; as well as programs from **American Wilderness Experience** (Box 1486, Boulder, CO 80306, ☎ 303/444–2622 or 800/444–0099) and the **American Museum of Natural History** (79th St. and Central Park W, New York, NY 10024, ☎ 212/769–5700 or 800/462–8687).

CUSTOMS

U.S. CITIZENS

The **U.S. Customs Service** (Box 7407, Washington, DC 20044, ☎ 202/

927–6724) can answer questions on duty-free limits and publishes a helpful brochure, "Know Before You Go." For information on registering foreign-made articles, call 202/927–0540.

CANADIAN CITIZENS

Contact **Revenue Canada** (2265 St. Laurent Blvd. S, Ottawa, Ontario K1G 4K3, ☎ 613/993–0534) for a copy of the free brochure **"I Declare/Je Déclare"** and for details on duties that exceed the standard duty-free limit.

U.K. CITIZENS

HM Customs and Excise (Dorset House, Stamford St., London SE1 9NG, ☎ 0171/202–4227) can answer questions about U.K. customs regulations and publishes **"A Guide for Travellers,"** detailing standard procedures and import rules.

D
FOR TRAVELERS WITH DISABILITIES

COMPLAINTS

To register complaints under the provisions of the Americans with Disabilities Act, contact the U.S. Department of Justice's **Public Access Section** (Box 66738, Washington, DC 20035, ☎ 202/514–0301, FAX 202/307–1198, TTY 202/514–0383).

ORGANIZATIONS

The **Canadian Paraplegic Association** (780 S.W. Marine Dr., Vancouver, BC V6P 5Y7,

604/324–3611) provides information on touring British Columbia. Information for people with hearing impairments is available from the **Western Institute for the Deaf** (2125 W. 7th Ave., Vancouver, BC V6K 1X9, ☎ 604/736–7391, TTY 604/736–2527). The annual *British Columbia Accommodation Guide* (☎ 800/663–6000) includes a list of hotel facilities for individuals with disabilities.

FOR TRAVELERS WITH HEARING IMPAIRMENTS➤ Contact the **American Academy of Otolaryngology** (1 Prince St., Alexandria, VA 22314, ☎ 703/836–4444, FAX 703/683–5100, TTY 703/519–1585).

FOR TRAVELERS WITH MOBILITY PROBLEMS➤ Contact the **Information Center for Individuals with Disabilities** (Fort Point Pl., 27–43 Wormwood St., Boston, MA 02210, ☎ 617/727–5540, 800/462–5015 in MA, TTY 617/345–9743); **Mobility International USA** (Box 10767, Eugene, OR 97440, ☎ and TTY 503/343–1284, FAX 503/343–6812), the U.S. branch of an international organization based in Belgium (*see below*) that has affiliates in 30 countries; **MossRehab Hospital Travel Information Service** (1200 W. Tabor Rd., Philadelphia, PA 19141, ☎ 215/456–9603, TTY 215/456–9602); the **Society for the Advancement of Travel for the Handicapped** (347 5th Ave., Suite 610, New York, NY

10016, ☎ 212/447–7284, FAX 212/725–8253); the **Travel Industry and Disabled Exchange** (TIDE, 5435 Donna Ave., Tarzana, CA 91356, ☎ 818/344–3640, FAX 818/344–0078); and **Travelin' Talk** (Box 3534, Clarksville, TN 37043, ☎ 615/552–6670, FAX 615/552–1182).

FOR TRAVELERS WITH VISION IMPAIRMENTS➤ Contact the **American Council of the Blind** (1155 15th St. NW, Suite 720, Washington, DC 20005, ☎ 202/467–5081, FAX 202/467–5085) or the **American Foundation for the Blind** (15 W. 16th St., New York, NY 10011, ☎ 212/620–2000, TTY 212/620–2158).

IN THE U.K.

Contact the **Royal Association for Disability and Rehabilitation** (RADAR, 12 City Forum, 250 City Rd., London EC1V 8AF, ☎ 0171/250–3222) or **Mobility International** (Rue de Manchester 25, B1070 Brussels, Belgium, ☎ 00–322–410–6297), an international clearinghouse of travel information for people with disabilities.

PUBLICATIONS

The Easter Seal Society (521 2nd Ave. W, Seattle, WA 98119, ☎ 206/281–5700) publishes *Access Seattle,* a free guide to the city's services for people with disabilities.

Several publications for travelers with disabilities are available from the **Consumer Information Center** (Box 100, Pueblo, CO 81009, ☎ 719/948–3334). Call or write for a free catalogue of current titles.

Fodor's **Great American Vacations for Travelers with Disabilities** ($18; available in bookstores, or call 800/533–6478) details accessible attractions, restaurants, and hotels in U.S. destinations. The 500-page **Travelin' Talk Directory** ($35; Box 3534, Clarksville, TN 37043, ☎ 615/552–6670) lists people and organizations who help travelers with disabilities. For specialist travel agents worldwide, consult the **Directory of Travel Agencies for the Disabled,** by Helen Hecker ($19.95 plus $3.50 handling; Disability Bookshop, Box 129, Vancouver, WA, 98666, ☎ 206/694–2462). The Sierra Club publishes **Easy Access to National Parks** ($16 plus $3 shipping; 730 Polk St., San Francisco, CA 94109, ☎ 415/776–2211 or 800/935–1056).

TRAVEL AGENCIES AND TOUR OPERATORS

The Americans with Disabilities Act requires that travel firms serve the needs of all travelers. However, some agencies and operators specialize in making group and individual arrangements for travelers with disabilities, among them **Access Adventures** (206 Chestnut Ridge Rd., Rochester, NY 14624,

☎ 716/889–9096), run by a former physical-rehab counselor; and **Travel Trends** (2 Allan Plaza, 4922 51st Ave., Box 3581, Leduc, Alberta T9E 6X2, ☎ 403/986–9000 or 800/661–2109 in Canada), which has group tours and is especially good for cruises. In addition, many operators and agencies (*see* Tour Operators, *below*) can also arrange vacations for travelers with disabilities.

FOR TRAVELERS WITH MOBILITY IMPAIRMENTS➤ A number of operators specialize in working with travelers with mobility impairments: **Accessible Journeys** (35 W. Sellers Ave., Ridley Park, PA 19078, ☎ 610/521–0339 or 800/846–4537, FAX 610/521–6959), a registered nursing service that arranges vacations; **Hinsdale Travel Service** (201 E. Ogden Ave., Suite 100, Hinsdale, IL 60521, ☎ 708/325–1335 or 800/303–5521), a travel agency that will give you access to the services of wheelchair traveler Janice Perkins; and **Wheelchair Journeys** (16979 Redmond Way, Redmond, WA 98052, ☎ 206/885–2210), which can handle arrangements worldwide.

FOR TRAVELERS WITH DEVELOPMENTAL DISABILITIES➤ Contact the nonprofit **New Directions** (5276 Hollister Ave., Suite 207, Santa Barbara, CA 93111, ☎ 805/967–2841) as

well as the general-interest operations above.

Options include **Entertainment Travel Editions** (fee $28–$53, depending on destination; Box 1068, Trumbull, CT 06611, ☎ 800/445–4137), **Great American Traveler** ($49.95 annually; Box 27965, Salt Lake City, UT 84127, ☎ 800/548–2812), **Moment's Notice Discount Travel Club** ($25 annually, single or family; 163 Amsterdam Ave., Suite 137, New York, NY 10023, ☎ 212/486–0500), **Privilege Card** ($74.95 annually; 3391 Peachtree Rd. NE, Suite 110, Atlanta, GA 30326, ☎ 404/262–0222 or 800/236–9732), **Travelers Advantage** ($49 annually, single or family; CUC Travel Service, 49 Music Sq. W, Nashville, TN 37203, ☎ 800/548–1116 or 800/648–4037), and **Worldwide Discount Travel Club** ($50 annually for family, $40 single; 1674 Meridian Ave., Miami Beach, FL 33139, ☎ 305/534–2082).

The **AlaskaPass Travelpass** (Box 351, Vashon Island, WA 98070, ☎ 800/248–7598) provides transportation aboard any British Columbia ferry as well as many connecting bus and train services. Passes of varying lengths enable the independent traveler to exercise a high degree of flexibility in choosing an itinerary.

VIA Rail Canada (☎ 800/665–0200) offers a **Canrailpass** that is good for 30 days. System-wide passes cost $282 (Jan. 6–June 6 and Oct. 1–Dec. 14) and $420 (June 7–Sept. 30). Youth passes (age 24 and under) are $377 in peak season and $257 during the off-season. Prices are quoted in U.S. dollars. Tickets can be purchased in the United States or the United Kingdom from a travel agent, from **Long Haul Leisurail** (Box 113, Peterborough PE1 1LE, ☎ 0733/51780), or upon arrival in Canada. This offer does not apply to Canadian citizens.

F

BRITISH COLUMBIA

The **British Columbia Ferry Corporation** (1112 Fort St., Victoria, BC V8V 4V2, ☎ 604/386–3431 in Victoria or 604/669–1211 in Vancouver; for recorded schedule information, ☎ 604/656–0757 in Victoria or 604/277–0277 in Vancouver) operates one of the largest and most modern ferry fleets in the world, with 38 ships serving 42 ports of call along the coast of British Columbia. More than 15 million passengers ride this fleet each year.

Clipper Navigation (2701 Alaskan Way, Pier 69, Seattle, WA 98121, ☎ 800/888–2535) operates three passenger-only jet catamarans between Seattle and Victoria; the largest holds 300 peo-

ple, the smallest 250. Each boat makes the scenic crossing in just under three hours.

Black Ball Transport's (430 Belleville St., Victoria, BC V8V 1W9, ☎ 604/386–2202 in Victoria or 360/457–4491 in Port Angeles) MV *Coho* makes daily crossings year-round, from Port Angeles to Victoria. The *Coho* can carry 800 passengers and 100 cars across the Strait of Juan de Fuca in 1½ hours. Advance reservations are not accepted.

Victoria Line (185 Dallas Rd., Victoria, BC V8V 1A1, ☎ 604/480–5555) operates a car/passenger ferry, the *Royal Victorian,* from mid-May to late September between Seattle and Victoria with one round-trip daily. Sailing time is 4½ hours.

WASHINGTON

The **Washington State Ferry System** (Colman Dock, Seattle, WA 98104, ☎ 206/464–6400 or 800/843–3779 in WA) has 25 ferries in its fleet, which carries more than 23 million passengers a year between points on Puget Sound and the San Juan Islands. Reservations are not available on any domestic routes.

G

ORGANIZATIONS

The **International Gay Travel Association** (Box 4974, Key West, FL 33041, ☎ 800/448–

8550), a consortium of 800 businesses, can supply names of travel agents and tour operators.

PUBLICATIONS

The premier international travel magazine for gays and lesbians is **Our World** ($35 for 10 issues; 1104 N. Nova Rd., Suite 251, Daytona Beach, FL 32117, ☎ 904/441–5367). The 16-page monthly **"Out & About"** ($49 for 10 issues; ☎ 212/645–6922 or 800/929–2268) covers gay-friendly resorts, hotels, cruise lines, and airlines.

TOUR OPERATORS

Cruises and resort vacations are handled by **R.S.V.P. Travel Productions** (2800 University Ave. SE, Minneapolis, MN 55414, ☎ 800/328–7787) for gays, **Olivia** (4400 Market St., Oakland, CA 94608, ☎ 800/631–6277) for lesbian travelers. For mixed gay and lesbian travel, contact **Toto Tours** (1326 W. Albion, Suite 3W, Chicago, IL 60626, ☎ 312/274–8686 or 800/565–1241).

TRAVEL AGENCIES

The largest agencies serving gay travelers are **Advance Travel** (10700 Northwest Freeway, Suite 160, Houston, TX 77092, ☎ 713/682–2002 or 800/695–0880), **Islanders/ Kennedy Travel** (183 W. 10th St., New York, NY 10014, ☎ 212/242–3222 or 800/988–1181), **Now Voyager** (4406 18th St., San Francisco, CA 94114, ☎ 415/626–1169 or 800/255–6951), and

THE GOLD GUIDE / IMPORTANT CONTACTS

Yellowbrick Road (1500
W. Balmoral Ave.,
Chicago, IL 60640,
☎ 312/561–1800
or 800/642–2488).
Skylink Women's Travel
(746 Ashland Ave.,
Santa Monica, CA
90405, ☎ 310/452–
0506 or 800/225-5759)
works with lesbians.

I
INSURANCE

Travel insurance cover-
ing baggage, health,
and trip cancellation or
interruptions is avail-
able from Access Amer-
ica (Box 90315,
Richmond, VA 23286,
☎ 804/285–3300 or
800/284–8300), Care-
free Travel Insurance
(Box 9366, 100 Garden
City Plaza, Garden City,
NY 11530, ☎ 516/
294–0220 or 800/323–
3149), Near Travel
Services (Box 1339,
Calumet City, IL
60409, ☎ 708/868–
6700 or 800/654–
6700), Tele-Trip (Mutual
of Omaha Plaza, Box
31716, Omaha, NE
68131, ☎ 800/228–
9792), Travel Insured
International (Box
280568, East Hartford,
CT 06128-0568,
☎ 203/528–7663
or 800/243–3174),
Travel Guard Interna-
tional (1145 Clark St.,
Stevens Point, WI
54481, ☎ 715/345–
0505 or 800/826–
1300), and Wallach &
Company (107 W.
Federal St., Box 480,
Middleburg, VA 22117,
☎ 703/687–3166 or
800/237–6615).

IN THE U.K.

The Association of
British Insurers (51
Gresham St., London
EC2V 7HQ, ☎ 0171/
600–3333; 30 Gordon
St., Glasgow G1 3PU,
☎ 0141/226–3905;
Scottish Provident Bldg.,
Donegall Sq. W, Belfast
BT1 6JE, ☎ 01232/
249176; and other
locations) gives advice
by phone and publishes
the free "Holiday Insur-
ance," which sets out
typical policy provisions
and costs.

L
LODGING

APARTMENT AND
VILLA RENTALS

Among the companies
to contact are Property
Rentals International
(1008 Mansfield Cross-
ing Rd., Richmond, VA
23236, ☎ 804/378–
6054 or 800/220–
3332), Rent-a-Home
International (7200
34th Ave. NW, Seattle,
WA 98117, ☎ 206/
789–9377 or 800/
488–7368), and Vaca-
tion Home Rentals
Worldwide (235 Kens-
ington Ave., Norwood,
NJ 07648, ☎ 201/
767–9393 or 800/
633–3284). Members
of the travel club
Hideaways Interna-
tional ($99 annually;
767 Islington St.,
Portsmouth, NH
03801, ☎ 603/430–
4433 or 800/843–
4433) receive two
annual guides plus
quarterly newsletters
and arrange rentals
among themselves.

BED-AND-
BREAKFASTS

Reservation services for
Seattle and Vancouver
include Best Canadian
Bed & Breakfast Net-
work (1090 W. King
Edward Ave., Vancou-
ver, BC V6H 1Z4,
☎ 604/738–7207),

Hometours Interna-
tional, Inc. (1170 Broad-
way, Suite 614, New
York, NY 10001,
☎ 212/689–0851 or
800/367–4668), North-
west Bed & Breakfast
Travel Unlimited (610
S.W. Broadway, Port-
land, OR 97205,
☎ 503/243–7616), and
Traveller's Bed & Break-
fast (Box 492, Mercer
Island, WA 98040,
☎ 206/232–2345).
Before leaving the
United Kingdom, you
can book a B&B
through American Bed
& Breakfast, Inter-Bed
Network (31 Ernest
Rd., Colchester, Essex
CO7 9LQ, ☎ 0206/
223162).

HOME EXCHANGE

Principal clearinghouses
include HomeLink Inter-
national/Vacation Ex-
change Club ($60
annually; Box 650,
Key West, FL 33041,
☎ 305/294–1448 or
800/638–3841), which
gives members four
annual directories, with
a listing in one, plus
updates; Intervac Inter-
national ($65 annually;
Box 590504, San Fran-
cisco, CA 94159,
☎ 415/435–3497),
which has three annual
directories; and Loan-a-
Home ($35–$45 annu-
ally; 2 Park La., Apt.
6E, Mount Vernon, NY
10552-3443, ☎ 914/
664–7640), which
specializes in long-term
exchanges.

HOTELS

Vancouver and Seattle
have experienced major
hotel building booms
during the past 10 years.
Most of the major
chains have properties in
one or all of these cities.
For more information,

contact **Canadian Pacific** (☎ 800/828–7447), **Delta** (☎ 800/877–1133), **Doubletree** (☎ 800/528–0444), **Four Seasons** (☎ 800/332–3442), **Hilton** (☎ 800/445–8667), **Holiday Inn** (☎ 800/465–4329), **Hyatt** (☎ 800/233–1234), **Marriott** (☎ 800/228–9290), **Ramada** (☎ 800/228–2828), **Red Lion Hotels and Inns** (☎ 800/547–8010), **Sheraton** (☎ 800/325–3535), **Stouffer** (☎ 800/468–3571), **West Coast Hotels/Coast Hotels** (☎ 800/426–0670), and **Westin** (☎ 800/228–3000).

Examples of all-suite hotels are **Courtyard By Marriott** (☎ 800/321–2211) and **Embassy Suites Hotels** (☎ 800/362–2779).

MOTELS/MOTOR INNS

Nationally recognized chains include **Best Western** (☎ 800/528–1234), **Days Inn** (☎ 800/325–2525), **La Quinta Inns** (☎ 800/531–5900), **Motel 6** (☎ 800/440–6000), **Quality Inns** (☎ 800/228–5151), and **Super 8 Motels** (☎ 800/848–8888). **Travelodge** (☎ 800/255–3050), **Nendel's** (☎ 800/547–0106), **Sandman Inns** (☎ 800/726-3626), and **Shilo Inns** (☎ 800/222–2244) are regional chains.

M
MONEY MATTERS

ATMS

For specific **Cirrus** locations in the United States and Canada, call 800/424–7787. For U.S. **Plus** locations, call

800/843–7587 and enter the area code and first three digits of the number you're calling from (or of the calling area where you want an ATM).

WIRING FUNDS

Funds can be wired via **American Express MoneyGram**^{SM} (☎ 800/926–9400 from the U.S. and Canada for locations and information) or **Western Union** (☎ 800/325–6000 for agent locations or to send using MasterCard or Visa, 800/321–2923 in Canada).

P
PASSPORTS
AND VISAS

Canadian and U.S. citizens do not need a passport to travel between the United States and Canada.

U.K. CITIZENS

For fees, documentation requirements, and to get an emergency passport, call the **London Passport Office** (☎ 0171/271–3000). For visa information, call the **U.S. Embassy Visa Information Line** (☎ 0891/200–290; calls cost 48p per minute or 36p per minute cheap rate) or write the **U.S. Embassy Visa Branch** (5 Upper Grosvenor St., London W1A 2JB). If you live in Northern Ireland, write the **U.S. Consulate General** (Queen's House, Queen St., Belfast BTI 6EO).

PHOTO HELP

The **Kodak Information Center** (☎ 800/242–2424) answers consumer questions about

film and photography. Fodor's also publishes the *Kodak Guide to Shooting Great Travel Pictures* ($16.50; available at bookstores or from Fodor's Travel Publications, ☎ 800/533–6478), which has hundreds of tips and photos on everything from how to shoot common travel subjects—markets, beaches, architectural details, and so on—to how to compensate for various light and weather conditions.

R
RAIL TRAVEL

Amtrak (☎ 800/872–7245), the U.S. passenger rail system, has daily service to Seattle from the Midwest and California. The *Empire Builder* takes a northern route from Chicago to Seattle. The *Coast Starlight* begins in Los Angeles, makes stops throughout western Oregon and Washington, and terminates its route in Seattle. At present, there are no trains that cross the border from Seattle into Canada.

Canada's passenger service, **VIA Rail Canada** (☎ 800/665–0200), operates transcontinental routes on the *Canadian* three times weekly between eastern Canada and Vancouver.

WITHIN THE PACIFIC NORTH COAST

The Pacific North Coast has a number of scenic train routes in addition to those operated by Amtrak and VIA Rail Canada. The **Rocky Mountaineer** (Great

THE GOLD GUIDE / IMPORTANT CONTACTS

Canadian Railtour Co., Ltd., 340 Brooksbank Ave., Suite 104, North Vancouver, BC V7J 2C1, ☎ 800/665–7245) is a two-day rail cruise between Vancouver and the Canadian Rockies, May–October. There are two routes—one to Banff/Calgary and the other to Jasper—through landscapes considered to be the most spectacular in the world. An overnight hotel stop is made in Kamloops.

On Vancouver Island, VIA Rail (☎ 604/383–4324) runs the *E&N Railway* daily from Victoria north to Nanaimo. **BC Rail** (Box 8770, Vancouver, BC V6B 4X6, ☎ 604/631–3500) operates daily service from its North Vancouver terminal to the town of Prince George. At Prince George, it is possible to connect with VIA Rail's *Skeena* service east to Jasper and Alberta or west to Prince Rupert. BC Rail also operates a summertime excursion steam train, the *Royal Hudson*, between North Vancouver and Squamish, at the head of Howe Sound.

DISCOUNTS➤ The AlaskaPass (*see* Discount Passes, *above*) offers one-price travel on bus and other modes of transportation in British Columbia.

S

EDUCATIONAL TRAVEL

The nonprofit **Elderhostel** (75 Federal St., 3rd Floor, Boston, MA 02110, ☎ 617/426–7788), for people 60 and older, has offered inexpensive study programs since 1975. The nearly 2,000 courses cover everything from marine science to Greek myths and cowboy poetry. Fees for programs in the United States and Canada, which usually last one week, run about $300, not including transportation.

ORGANIZATIONS

Contact the **American Association of Retired Persons** (membership $8 per person or couple annually; 601 E St. NW, Washington, DC 20049, ☎ 202/434–2277). Its Purchase Privilege Program gets members discounts on lodging, car rentals, and sightseeing, and the AARP Motoring Plan furnishes domestic trip-routing information and emergency road-service aid for an annual fee of $39.95 per person or couple ($59.95 for a premium version).

For other discounts on lodgings, car rentals, and other travel products, along with magazines and newsletters, contact the **National Council of Senior Citizens** (membership $12 annually; 1331 F St. NW, Washington, DC 20004, ☎ 202/347–8800) and **Mature Outlook** (subscription $9.95 annually; 6001 N. Clark St., Chicago, IL 60660, ☎ 312/465–6466 or 800/336–6330).

PUBLICATIONS

The 50+ Traveler's Guidebook: Where to Go, Where to Stay, What to Do, by Anita Williams and Merrimac Dillon ($12.95; St. Martin's Press, 175 5th Ave., New York, NY 10010, ☎ 212/674–5151 or 800/288–2131), offers many useful tips. **"The Mature Traveler"** ($29.95; Box 50400, Reno, NV 89513, ☎ 702/786–7419), a monthly newsletter, covers travel deals.

BICYCLING

Bicycling is a popular sport in Seattle and Vancouver, appealing to both families out for a leisurely ride and avid cyclists seeking a challenge on rugged mountain trails.

Several cycling organizations sponsor trips of various lengths and degrees of difficulty, both on- and off-road. For further information, contact **Cascade Bicycle Club** (☎ 206/522–2453) and **Bicycling Association of British Columbia** (332–1367 W. Broadway, Vancouver, BC V6H 4A9, ☎ 604/737–3034.

Rentals are available from bicycle shops in Seattle and Vancouver.

BOATING

The **Trade Association of Sea Kayaking (TASK)** (Box 84144, Seattle, WA 98124, ☎ 206/621–1018) provides information on outfitters, rentals, seminars, and safety.

CLIMBING/ MOUNTAINEERING

For information, contact **The Mountaineers** (300 3rd Ave. W,

Seattle, WA 98119, ☎ 206/284–6310).

FISHING

For information on fishing regulations, contact **Washington Department of Fisheries** (Administration Bldg., Room 115, Olympia, WA 98504, ☎ 206/586–1425 for Washington salmon fishing or marine licenses) or **Washington State Department of Wildlife** (600 Capitol Way N, Olympia, WA 98501, ☎ 206/753–5700 for freshwater fishing). In British Columbia, separate licenses are required for saltwater and freshwater fishing. Information and licenses for saltwater fishing can be obtained from the **Department of Fisheries and Oceans** (555 W. Hastings St., Suite 400, Vancouver, BC V6B 5G3, ☎ 604/666–0384). For freshwater fishing, contact the **Ministry of Environment, Fish and Wildlife Information** (Parliament Bldgs., Victoria, BC V8V 1X5, ☎ 604/387–9740).

HIKING

There are many trails in the Pacific North Coast that are geared to both beginning and experienced hikers. The **National Parks and Forests Outdoor Recreation Information Center** (915 2nd Ave., Room 442, Seattle, WA 98174, ☎ 206/220–7450) can provide maps of trails that are well marked and well maintained. Guidebooks that describe the best trails in the area are readily available in local bookstores. The *Footsore*

series of books, published by the Mountaineers (306 2nd Ave. W, Seattle, WA 98119, ☎ 206/285–2665), are among the best.

HUNTING

For information on hunting facilities and licenses, contact **Washington State Department of Wildlife** (600 Capitol Way N, Olympia, WA 98501, ☎ 206/753–5700) or **British Columbia Ministry of Environment, Wildlife Branch** (810 Blanshard St., Victoria, BC V8W 2H1, ☎ 604/387–9740).

SCUBA DIVING

The crystal-clear waters of Puget Sound present excellent opportunities for scuba diving and underwater photography. For information on dive shops, equipment rentals, and charter boats in British Columbia, contact **Dive B.C.** (707 Westminster Ave., Powell River, BC V8A 1C5, ☎ 604/485–6267).

SKIING

CROSS-COUNTRY➤ Cross-country skiing is a popular and relatively inexpensive way to enjoy the winter wilderness. Many downhill ski resorts also have well-marked and well-groomed cross-country trails. Washington operates a system of more than 40 **SnoParks** (Office of Winter Recreation, Parks and Recreation Commission, 7150 Cleanwater La., KY-11, Olympia, WA 98504, ☎ 206/586–0185) that are a series of groomed cross-country trails within state parks in

which, for the price of a one-day ($7), three-day ($10), or seasonal ($20) pass, skiers have access to trails in 70 locations statewide.

STUDENTS

GROUPS

A major tour operator is **Contiki Holidays** (300 Plaza Alicante, Suite 900, Garden Grove, CA 92640, ☎ 714/740–0808 or 800/466–0610).

HOSTELING

Contact **Hostelling International–American Youth Hostels** (733 15th St. NW, Suite 840, Washington, DC 20005, ☎ 202/783–6161) in the United States, **Hostelling International–Canada** (205 Catherine St., Suite 400, Ottawa, Ontario K2P 1C3, ☎ 613/237–7884) in Canada, and the **Youth Hostel Association of England and Wales** (Trevelyan House, 8 St. Stephen's Hill, St. Albans, Hertfordshire AL1 2DY, ☎ 01727/855215 and 01727/845047) in the United Kingdom. Membership ($25 in the U.S., C$26.75 in Canada, and £9 in the U.K.) gets you access to 5,000 hostels worldwide that charge $7–$20 nightly per person.

I.D. CARDS

To get discounts on transportation and admissions, get the **International Student Identity Card** (ISIC) if you're a bona fide student or the **Go 25 Card** if you're under 26. In the United States, the ISIC and Go 25 cards cost $18 each and include basic travel accident and illness coverage, plus a toll-free travel hot line. Apply through the Council on International Educational Exchange (*see* Organizations, *below*). Cards are available for $15 each in Canada from **Travel Cuts** (187 College St., Toronto, Ontario M5T 1P7, ☎ 416/979–2406 or 800/667–2887) and in the United Kingdom for £5 each at student unions and student travel companies.

ORGANIZATIONS

A major contact is the **Council on International Educational Exchange** (CIEE, 205 E. 42nd St., 16th Floor, New York, NY 10017, ☎ 212/661–1450) with locations in Boston (729 Boylston St., 02116, ☎ 617/266–1926), Miami (9100 S. Dadeland Blvd., 33156, ☎ 305/670–9261), Los Angeles (10904 Lindbrook Dr., 90024, ☎ 310/208–3551), 43 other college towns nationwide, and the United Kingdom (28A Poland St., London W1V 3DB, ☎ 0171/437–7767). Twice a year, it publishes *Student Travels* magazine. The CIEE's Council Travel Service offers domestic air passes for bargain travel within the United States and is the exclusive U.S. agent for several student-discount cards.

Campus Connections (325 Chestnut St., Suite 1101, Philadelphia, PA 19106, ☎ 215/625–8585 or 800/428–3235) specializes in discounted accommoda-

tions and airfares for students. The **Educational Travel Centre** (438 N. Frances St., Madison, WI 53703, ☎ 608/256–5551) offers rail passes and low-cost airline tickets, mostly for flights departing from Chicago.

In Canada, also contact **Travel Cuts** (*see above*).

PUBLICATIONS

See the *Berkeley Guide to the Pacific North Coast & Alaska* ($16.95; available in bookstores or through Fodor's Travel Publications, ☎ 800/533–6478).

T
TOUR OPERATORS

Among the companies selling tours and packages to Seattle and Vancouver, the following have a proven reputation, are nationally known, and offer plenty of options.

GROUP TOURS

For a deluxe escorted tour, contact **Maupintour** (Box 807, Lawrence, KS 66044, ☎ 913/843–1211 or 800/255–4266) and **Tauck Tours** (11 Wilton Rd., Westport, CT 06880, ☎ 203/226–6911 or 800/468–2825). Another operator falling between deluxe and first class is **Globus** (5301 S. Federal Circle, Littleton, CO 80123, ☎ 303/797–2800 or 800/221–0090). In the first-class and tourist range, try **Collette Tours** (162 Middle St., Pawtucket, RI 02860, ☎ 401/728–3805 or 800/832–4656), **Gad-**

about Tours (700 E. Tahquitz Canyon Way, Palm Springs, CA 92262, ☎ 619/325–5556 or 800/952–5068), and **Mayflower Tours** (1225 Warren Ave., Downers Grove, IL 60515, ☎ 708/960–3430 or 800/323–7604), **Trieloff Tours** (24301 El Toro Rd., Suite 140, Laguna Hills, CA 92653, ☎ 800/248–6877 or 800/432–7125 in CA). For budget and tourist class programs, contact **Cosmos** (*see* Globus, *above*).

PACKAGES

Independent vacation packages to Seattle and Vancouver are available from major tour operators and airlines. Contact **American Airlines Fly AAway Vacations** (☎ 800/321–2121), **SuperCities** (139 Main St., Cambridge, MA 02142, ☎ 617/621–0099 or 800/333–1234), **Continental Airlines' Grand Destinations** (☎ 800/634–5555), **Delta Dream Vacations** (☎ 800/872–7786), **Certified Vacations** (Box 1525, Fort Lauderdale, FL 33302, ☎ 305/522–1414 or 800/233–7260), **United Vacations** (☎ 800/328–6877), **Kingdom Tours** (300 Market St., Kingston, PA 18704, ☎ 717/283–4241 or 800/872–8857), and **USAir Vacations** (☎ 800/455–0123). For rail packages, try **Amtrak** (☎ 800/872–7245).

FROM THE U.K.

Travel agencies that offer cheap fares to Seattle and Vancouver include **Trailfinders** (42–50 Earl's Court Rd., London W8 6FT, ☎ 0171/937–5400), **Travel Cuts** (295a Regent St., London W1R 7YA, ☎ 0171/637–3161; see Students, *above*), and **Flightfile** (49 Tottenham Court Rd., London W1P 9RE, ☎ 0171/700–2722).

THEME TRIPS

For information on themed tours of Seattle and Vancouver, *see* Guided Tours *in* the Essentials section at the end of each chapter.

ORGANIZATIONS

The **National Tour Association** (546 E. Main St., Lexington, KY 40508, ☎ 606/226–4444 or 800/755–8687) and **United States Tour Operators Association** (USTOA, 211 E. 51st St., Suite 12B, New York, NY 10022, ☎ 212/750–7371) can provide lists of member operators and information on booking tours.

PUBLICATIONS

Consult the brochure **"On Tour"** and ask for a current list of member operators from the National Tour Association (*see* Organizations, *above*). Also get a copy of the **"Worldwide Tour & Vacation Package Finder"** from the USTOA (*see* Organizations, *above*) and the

Better Business Bureau's **"Tips on Travel Packages"** (publication No. 24-195, $2; 4200 Wilson Blvd., Arlington, VA 22203).

For names of reputable agencies in your area, contact the **American Society of Travel Agents** (1101 King St., Suite 200, Alexandria, VA 22314, ☎ 703/739–2782).

The U.S. Department of State's Overseas Citizens Emergency Center (Room 4811, Washington, DC 20520; enclose SASE) issues **Consular Information Sheets,** which cover crime, security, political climate, and health risks as well as embassy locations, entry requirements, currency regulations, and other routine matters. For the latest information, stop in at any U.S. passport office, consulate, or embassy; call the interactive hot line (☎ 202/647–5225 or ℻ 202/647-3000); or, with your PC's modem, tap into the Bureau of Consular Affairs' computer bulletin board (☎ 202/647–9225).

IN THE U.S.

Washington Tourism Development Division (Box 45213, Olympia, WA 98504, ☎ 206/586–2088, 206/586–2102, or 800/544–1800).

IN CANADA

Tourism British Columbia (1117 Wharf St., Victoria, BC V8W 2Z2, ☎ 800/663–6000).

IN THE U.K.

For touring tips and brochures, contact the **United States Travel and Tourism Administration** (Box 1EN, London WIA 1EN, ☎ 0171/495–4466), **Canadian High Commission, Tourism Division** (Canada House, Trafalgar Sq., London SW1Y 5BJ, ☎ 0171/930–6857), or **Tourism British Columbia** (1 Regent St., London SW1Y 4NS, ☎ 0171/930–6857).

For current conditions and forecasts, plus the local time and helpful travel tips, call the **Weather Channel Connection** (☎ 900/932–8437; 95¢ per minute) from a touch-tone phone.

SMART TRAVEL TIPS A TO Z

Basic Information on Traveling in Seattle and Vancouver and Savvy Tips to Make Your Trip a Breeze

The more you travel, the more you know about how to make trips run like clockwork. To help make your travels hassle-free, Fodor's editors have rounded up dozens of tips from our contributors and travel experts all over the world, as well as basic information on visiting the Pacific North Coast. For names of organizations to contact and publications that can give you more information, *see* Important Contacts A to Z, *above.*

A

AIR TRAVEL

If time is an issue, **always look for nonstop flights,** which require no change of plane. If possible, **avoid connecting flights,** which stop at least once and can involve a change of plane, although the flight number remains the same; if the first leg is late, the second waits.

CUTTING COSTS

The Sunday travel section of most newspapers is a good source of deals.

MAJOR AIRLINES➤ The least-expensive airfares from the major airlines are priced for round-trip travel and are subject to restrictions. You must usually **book in advance and buy the ticket within 24 hours** to get cheaper fares, and you may have to **stay over a Saturday night.** The lowest fare is subject to availability, and only a small percentage of the plane's total seats are sold at that price. It's good to **call a number of airlines, and when you are quoted a good price, book it on the spot**—the same fare on the same flight may not be available the next day. Airlines generally allow you to change your return date for a $25 to $50 fee, but most low-fare tickets are nonrefundable. However, if you don't use it, you can apply the cost toward the purchase price of a new ticket, again for a small charge.

Fares on scheduled flights from the United Kingdom vary considerably. January to March are the cheapest months to fly, and midweek flights nearly always offer some reductions.

CONSOLIDATORS➤ Consolidators, who buy tickets at reduced rates from scheduled airlines, sell them at prices below the lowest available from the airlines directly—usually without advance restrictions. Sometimes you can even get your money back if you need to return the ticket. Carefully read the fine print detailing penalties for changes and cancellations. If you doubt the reliability of a consolidator, **confirm your reservation with the airline.**

ALOFT

AIRLINE FOOD➤ If you hate airline food, **ask for special meals when booking.** These can be vegetarian, low cholesterol, or kosher, for example; commonly prepared to order in smaller quantities than standard catered fare, they can be tastier.

JET LAG

To avoid this syndrome, which occurs when travel disrupts your body's natural cycles, try to maintain a normal routine. At night, **get some sleep.** By day, move about the cabin to **stretch your legs, eat light meals, and drink water—not alcohol.**

SMOKING➤ Smoking is banned on all flights within the United States of less than six hours' duration and on all Canadian flights; the ban also applies to domestic segments of international flights aboard U.S. and foreign carriers. Delta has banned smoking system-wide. On U.S. carriers flying to Canada and other destinations abroad, a seat in a no-smoking section must be provided for every passenger who requests one, and the section must be enlarged to accommodate such passengers if necessary as long as they have complied with the airline's deadline for check-in and seat assignment. If smoking bothers you, request a seat far from the smoking section.

Foreign airlines are exempt from these rules but do provide no-smoking sections (British Airways has banned smoking; some nations have banned smoking on all domestic flights, and others may ban smoking on some flights). Talks continue on the feasibility of broadening no-smoking policies.

B
BUS TRAVEL

Bus service in North America—though fairly economical—has not been a first-class means of travel in recent years. But Greyhound and other bus companies are taking great pains to improve service. New amenities may include an onboard host/hostess, meals, and VCRs.

BUSINESS HOURS

SEATTLE

Most retail stores in Washington are open 9:30–6 seven days a week in downtown locations and later at suburban shopping malls. Downtown stores sometimes stay open late Thursday and Friday nights. Normal banking hours are weekdays 9–6; some branches are also open on Saturday morning.

VANCOUVER

In British Columbia, many stores close on

Sunday. Outlets that cater to tourists are the notable exception. Normal banking hours in Canada are 10–3 on weekdays, with extended hours in many locations. Some banks in major cities are now open on Saturday morning.

C
CAMERAS, CAMCORDERS, AND COMPUTERS

LAPTOPS

Before you depart, **check your portable computer's battery,** because you may be asked at security to turn on the computer to prove that it is what it appears to be. At the airport, you may prefer to **request a manual inspection,** although security X-rays do not harm hard-disk or floppy-disk storage. Also, **register your foreign-made laptop with U.S. Customs.** If your laptop is U.S.-made, call the consulate of the country you'll be visiting to find out whether or not it should be registered with local customs upon arrival. You may want to **find out about repair facilities at your destination** in case you need them.

PHOTOGRAPHY

If your camera is new or if you haven't used it for a while, **shoot and develop a few rolls of film** before you leave. Always **store film in a cool, dry place**—never in the car's glove compartment or on the shelf under the rear window.

Every pass through an X-ray machine increases film's chance of clouding. To protect it, carry it in a clear plastic bag and **ask for hand inspection at security.** Such requests are virtually always honored at U.S. airports, and are usually accommodated abroad. Don't depend on a lead-lined bag to protect film in checked luggage—the airline may increase the radiation to see what's inside.

VIDEO

Before your trip, **test your camcorder, invest in a skylight filter to protect the lens, and charge the batteries.** (Airport security personnel may ask you to turn on the camcorder to prove that it's what it appears to be.)

Videotape is not damaged by X-rays, but it may be harmed by the magnetic field of a walk-through metal detector, so **ask that videotapes be hand-checked.**

CHILDREN AND TRAVEL

Many local organizations, such as public libraries, museums, parks and recreation departments, and YMCA/YWCAs, have special events throughout the year for children of all ages. Check local newspaper listings for such activities as plays, storytelling, sporting events, and so forth.

BABY-SITTING

For recommended local sitters, **check with your hotel desk.**

DRIVING

If you are renting a car, **arrange for a car seat when you reserve.** Sometimes they're free.

FLYING

Always **ask about discounted children's fares.** On international flights, the fare for infants under age two not occupying a seat is generally either free or 10% of the accompanying adult's fare; children ages 2–11 usually pay half to two-thirds of the adult fare. On domestic flights, children under two not occupying a seat travel free, and older children currently travel on the lowest applicable adult fare. Some routes are considered neither international nor domestic and have still other rules.

BAGGAGE➤ In general, the adult baggage allowance applies for children paying half or more of the adult fare. Before departure, **ask about carry-on allowances,** if you are traveling with an infant. In general, those paying 10% of the adult fare are allowed one carry-on bag, not to exceed 70 pounds or 45 inches (length + width + height) and a collapsible stroller; you may be allowed less if the flight is full.

SAFETY SEATS➤ According to the Federal Aviation Administration, it's a good idea to **use safety seats aloft.** Airline policy varies. U.S. carriers allow FAA-approved models, but airlines usually require that you buy a ticket, even if your child would otherwise ride free, because the seats must be strapped into regular passenger seats. Foreign carriers may not allow infant seats, may charge the child's rather than the infant's fare for their use, or may require you to hold your baby during takeoff and landing, thus defeating the seat's purpose.

FACILITIES➤ When making your reservation, **ask for children's meals or freestanding bassinets** if you need them; the latter are available only to those with seats at the bulkhead, where there's enough legroom. If you don't need a bassinet, **think twice before requesting bulkhead seats**—the only storage for in-flight necessities is in the inconveniently distant overhead bins.

LODGING

Most hotels allow children under a certain age to stay in their parents' room at no extra charge, while others charge them as extra adults; be sure to **ask about the cutoff age.**

CRUISES

Cruise ships travel the Inside Passage and Gulf of Alaska from mid-May through late September. The most popular ports of embarkation are Vancouver and Seward (port city for Anchorage), but cruises also leave from San Francisco and Seattle. One of the best ways to see the state is to **combine your cruise with a land tour.**

To get the best deal on a cruise, **consult a cruise-only travel agency.** For a low-priced cruise alternative, **consider traveling by ferry.**

CUSTOMS AND DUTIES

IN THE U.S.

RESIDENTS➤ You may bring home $400 worth of foreign goods duty-free if you've been out of the country for at least 48 hours and haven't already used the $400 exemption, or any part of it, in the past 30 days.

Travelers 21 or older may bring back 1 liter of alcohol duty-free, provided the beverage laws of the state through which they reenter the United States allow it. In addition, 100 non-Cuban cigars and 200 cigarettes are allowed, regardless of your age. Antiques and works of art more than 100 years old are duty-free.

Duty-free, travelers may mail packages valued at up to $200 to themselves and up to $100 to others, with a limit of one parcel per addressee per day (and no alcohol or tobacco products or perfume valued at more than $5); outside, identify the package as being for personal use or an unsolicited gift, specifying the contents and their retail value. Mailed items do not count as part of your exemption.

VISITORS➤ Visitors aged 21 or over may import the following into the United States: 200 cigarettes or 50 cigars or 2 kilograms of tobacco; 1 U.S. liter of alcohol; gifts to the value of $100. Restricted items include meat products, seeds, plants, and fruits. Never carry illegal drugs.

IN CANADA

RESIDENTS➤ Once per calendar year, when you've been out of Canada for at least seven days, you may bring in C$300 worth of goods duty-free. If you've been away less than seven days but more than 48 hours, the duty-free exemption drops to C$100 but can be claimed any number of times (as can a C$20 duty-free exemption for absences of 24 hours or more). You cannot combine the yearly and 48-hour exemptions, use the C$300 exemption only partially (to save the balance for a later trip), or pool exemptions with family members. Goods claimed under the C$300 exemption may follow you by mail; those claimed under the lesser exemptions must accompany you.

Alcohol and tobacco products may be included in the yearly and 48-hour exemptions but not in the 24-hour exemption. If you meet the age requirements of the province through which you reenter Canada, you may bring in, duty-free, 1.14 liters (40 imperial ounces) of wine or liquor *or* 24 12-ounce cans or bottles of beer or ale. If you are 16 or older, you may bring in, duty-free, 200 cigarettes, 50 cigars or cigarillos, and 400

tobacco sticks or 400 grams of manufactured tobacco. Alcohol and tobacco must accompany you on your return.

An unlimited number of gifts valued up to C$60 each may be mailed to Canada duty-free. These do not count as part of your exemption. Label the package "Unsolicited Gift— Value Under $60." Alcohol and tobacco are excluded.

VISITORS➤ American and British visitors may bring in the following items duty-free: 200 cigarettes, 50 cigars, and 2 pounds of tobacco; one bottle (1.1 liters or 40 imperial ounces) of liquor or wine, or 24 355-milliliter (12-ounce) bottles or cans of beer for personal consumption; gifts up to the value of C$60 per gift. A deposit is sometimes required for trailers (refunded upon return). Cats and dogs must have a certificate issued by a licensed veterinarian that clearly identifies the animal and certifies that it has been vaccinated against rabies during the preceding 36 months. Plant material must be declared and inspected. With certain restrictions (some fruits and vegetables), visitors may bring food with them for their own use, providing the quantity is consistent with the duration of the visit.

Canada's firearms laws are significantly stricter than those of the United States. All handguns, semi-automatic, and

fully automatic weapons are prohibited and cannot be brought into the country. Sporting rifles and shotguns may be imported provided they are to be used for sporting, hunting, or competition while in Canada. All firearms must be declared to Canada Customs at the first point of entry. Failure to declare firearms will result in their seizure and criminal charges may be made. (New legislation has just been introduced in Parliament to further tighten Canada's gun laws.)

IN THE U.K.

From countries outside the European Union, including the United States and Canada, you may import duty-free 200 cigarettes, 100 cigarillos, 50 cigars or 250 grams of tobacco; 1 liter of spirits or 2 liters of fortified or sparkling wine; 2 liters of still table wine; 60 milliliters of perfume; 250 milliliters of toilet water; plus £136 worth of other goods, including gifts and souvenirs.

D
FOR TRAVELERS WITH DISABILITIES

When discussing accessibility with an operator or reservationist, **ask hard questions.** Are there any stairs, inside *or* out? Are there grab bars next to the toilet *and* in the shower/tub? How wide is the doorway to the room? To the bathroom? For the most extensive facilities, meeting the latest legal specifications, **opt for** newer facilities, which more often have been designed with access in mind. Older properties or ships must usually be retrofitted and may offer more limited facilities as a result. Be sure to **discuss your needs before booking.**

DISCOUNT CLUBS

Travel clubs offer members unsold space on airplanes, cruise ships, and package tours at as much as 50% below regular prices. Membership may include a regular bulletin or access to a toll-free hot line giving details of available trips departing from three or four days to several months in the future. Most also offer 50% discounts off hotel rack rates. Before booking with a club, **make sure the hotel or other supplier isn't offering a better deal.**

DRIVING

FROM THE U.S.

The U.S. interstate highway network provides quick and easy access to the Pacific North Coast in spite of imposing mountain barriers. From the south, I–5 runs from the U.S.–Mexican border through California, into Oregon and Washington, and ends at the U.S.–Canadian border. Most of the population is clustered along this corridor. From the east, I–90 stretches from Boston to Seattle. I–84 runs from the midwestern states to Portland.

The main entry point into Canada by car is on I–5 at Blaine, Washington, 30 miles south

of Vancouver. Two major highways enter British Columbia from the east: the Trans-Canada Highway (the longest highway in the world, running more than 5,000 miles from St. John's, Newfoundland, to Victoria, British Columbia) and the Yellowhead Highway, which runs through northern British Columbia from the Rocky Mountains to Prince Rupert.

Border-crossing procedures are usually quick and simple (*see* Passports and Visas *and* Customs, *above*). The I–5 border crossing at Blaine, Washington, is open 24 hours a day and is one of the busiest border crossings anywhere between the United States and Canada. Peak traffic times at the border northbound into Canada are daily at 4 PM. Southbound, delays can be expected evenings and weekend mornings. Try to plan on reaching the border at off-peak times. There are smaller highway border stations at various other points between Washington and British Columbia but they may be closed at night.

WITHIN THE PACIFIC NORTHWEST

Except for a short distance north of Vancouver, there are no roads along the rugged mainland coast of British Columbia.

AUTO CLUBS

The American Automobile Association (AAA) and the Canadian

Automobile Association (CAA) provide full services to members of any of the Commonwealth Motoring Conference (CMC) clubs, including the Automobile Association, the Royal Automobile Club, and the Royal Scottish Automobile Club. Services are also available to members of the Alliance Internationale de l'Automobile (AIT), the Federation Internationale de l'Automobile (FIA), and the Federation of Interamerican Touring and Automobile Clubs (FITAC). Members receive travel information, itineraries, maps, tour books, information about road and weather conditions, emergency road services, and travel-agency services.

INSURANCE

Vehicle insurance is compulsory in the United States and Canada. Motorists are required to produce evidence of insurance if they become involved in an accident. Upon arrival, visitors from foreign countries should contact an insurance agent or broker to obtain the necessary insurance for North America.

SPEED LIMITS

The speed limit on U.S. interstate highways is 65 miles per hour in rural areas and 55 miles per hour in urban zones and on secondary highways. In Canada (where the metric system is used), the speed limit is usually 100 kilometers (62 miles) per hour on expressways and 80 kilometers (50 miles) per hour on secondary roads.

WINTER DRIVING

Winter driving in the Pacific North Coast can sometimes present some real challenges. In coastal areas, the mild, damp climate contributes to roadways that are frequently wet. Winter snowfalls are not common (generally only once or twice a year), but when snow does fall, traffic grinds to a halt and the roadways become treacherous and stay that way until the snow melts.

Tire chains, studs, or snow tires are essential equipment for winter travel in mountain areas. If you're planning to drive into high elevations, be sure to check the weather forecast beforehand. Even the main-highway mountain passes can be forced to close because of snow conditions. During the winter months, state and provincial highway departments operate snow advisory telephone lines that give pass conditions.

F
FERRIES

Ferries play an important part in the transportation network of the Pacific North Coast. In some areas, ferries provide the only form of access into and out of communities. In other places, ferries transport thousands of commuters a day to and from work in the cities. For visitors, ferries are one of the best ways to

get a feel for the region and its ties to the sea.

BRITISH COLUMBIA

The British Columbia Ferry Corporation's busiest ferries operate between the mainland and Vancouver Island, carrying passengers, cars, campers, RVs, trucks, and buses. Peak traffic times are Friday afternoon, Saturday morning, and Sunday afternoon, especially during summer months and holiday weekends.

WASHINGTON

If you are planning to use the Washington State Ferry System, try to **avoid peak commuter hours.** The heaviest traffic flows are eastbound in the mornings and on Sunday evening, and westbound on Saturday morning and weekday afternoons. The best times for travel are 9–3 and after 7 PM on weekdays. In July and August, you may have to wait up to two hours to take a car aboard one of the popular San Juan Islands ferries. Walk-on space is always available; if possible, **leave your car behind.**

I
INSURANCE

Travel insurance can protect your investment, replace your luggage and its contents, or provide for medical coverage should you fall ill during your trip. Most tour operators, travel agents, and insurance agents sell specialized health-and-accident, flight, trip-cancellation, and luggage insurance

as well as comprehensive policies with some or all of these features. Before you make any purchase, **review your existing health and home-owner policies** to find out whether they cover expenses incurred while traveling.

BAGGAGE

Airline liability for your baggage is limited to $1,250 per person on domestic flights. On international flights, the airlines' liability is $9.07 per pound or $20 per kilogram for checked baggage (roughly $640 per 70-pound bag) and $400 per passenger for unchecked baggage. Insurance for losses exceeding the terms of your airline ticket can be bought directly from the airline at check-in for about $10 per $1,000 of coverage; note that it excludes a rather extensive list of items, shown on your airline ticket.

FLIGHT

You should **think twice before buying flight insurance.** Often purchased as a last-minute impulse at the airport, it pays a lump sum when a plane crashes, either to a beneficiary if the insured dies or sometimes to a surviving passenger who loses eyesight or a limb. Supplementing the airlines' coverage described in the limits-of-liability paragraphs on your ticket, it's expensive and basically unnecessary. Charging an airline ticket to a major credit card often automatically entitles you to coverage and may also embrace travel by bus, train, and ship.

HEALTH

If your own health insurance policy does not cover you outside the United States, **consider buying supplemental medical coverage.** It can provide $1,000 to $150,000 worth of medical and/or dental expenses incurred as a result of an accident or illness during a trip. These policies also may include a personal-accident, or death-and-dismemberment, provision, which pays a lump sum ranging from $15,000 to $500,000 to your beneficiaries if you die or to you if you lose one or more limbs or your eyesight, and a medical-assistance provision, which may either reimburse you for the cost of referrals, evacuation, or repatriation and other services, or may automatically enroll you as a member of a particular medical-assistance company.

FOR U.K. TRAVELERS

According to the Association of British Insurers, a trade association representing 450 insurance companies, it's wise to **buy extra medical coverage when you visit the United States.** You can buy an annual travel-insurance policy valid for most vacations during the year in which it's purchased. If you go this route, make sure it covers you if you have a preexisting medical condition or are pregnant.

TRIP

Without insurance, you will lose all or most of your money if you must cancel your trip due to illness or any other reason. Especially if your airline ticket, cruise, or package tour is nonrefundable and cannot be changed, it's essential that you **buy trip-cancellation-and-interruption insurance.** When considering how much coverage you need, look for a policy that will cover the cost of your trip plus the nondiscounted price of a one-way airline ticket should you need to return home early. Read the fine print carefully, especially sections defining "family member" and "preexisting medical condition." Also **consider default or bankruptcy insurance,** which protects you against a supplier's failure to deliver. However, such policies often do not cover default by a travel agency, tour operator, airline, or cruise line if you bought your tour and the coverage directly from the firm in question.

L

LANGUAGE

Canada is officially a bilingual country (English and French). You will see many signs and services offered in both languages; however, little French is spoken on Canada's west coast.

LODGING

Although the hotel and motel price categories are standard, the prices listed under each may vary from one area to another. This variation reflects local price standards. In all cases, price ranges for each category are clearly stated before each listing.

APARTMENT AND VILLA RENTALS

If you want a home base that's roomy enough for a family and comes with cooking facilities, **consider a furnished rental.** It's generally cost-wise, too, although not always—some rentals are luxury properties (economical only when your party is large). Home-exchange directories do list rentals—often second homes owned by prospective house swappers—and some services search for a house or apartment for you and handle the paperwork. Some send an illustrated catalogue and others send photographs of specific properties, sometimes at a charge; up-front registration fees may apply.

BED-AND-BREAKFASTS

Bed-and-breakfasts are private homes that reflect the personalities and tastes of their owners. Generally, B&Bs have 2–10 rooms, some with private baths and others with shared facilities. Breakfast is always included in the price of the room.

B&Bs have flourished in recent years. Some homes advertise to the public, while others maintain a low profile. Most belong to a reservation system through which you can book a room.

CAMPING

Camping is a popular and inexpensive way to tour the area. Washington and British Columbia have networks of excellent government-run parks that offer camping and organized activities. A few state and provincial parks will accept advance camping reservations, but most do not. Privately operated campgrounds sometimes have extra amenities such as laundry rooms and swimming pools. For more information, contact the local state or provincial tourism department.

HOME EXCHANGE

If you would like to find a house, an apartment, or other vacation property to exchange for your own while on vacation, **become a member of a home-exchange organization,** which will send you its annual directories listing available exchanges and will include your own listing in at least one of them. Arrangements for the actual exchange are made by the two parties to it, not by the organization.

HOTELS

Most big-city hotels cater primarily to business travelers, with such facilities as restaurants, cocktail lounges, swimming pools, exercise equipment, and meeting rooms. Room rates often reflect the range of amenities offered. Most cities also have less-expensive hotels, which are clean and comfortable but have fewer upscale facilities. A new accommodations trend is all-suite hotels, which offer more intimate facilities and are gaining popularity with business travelers.

Many properties offer special weekend rates, sometimes up to 50% off regular prices. However, these deals are usually not extended during peak summer months, when hotels are normally full.

INNS

These establishments generally are located outside cities and have anywhere from eight to 20 rooms. Lodging is often in an old restored building with some historical or architectural significance. Inns are sometimes confused with bed-and-breakfasts because they may include breakfast in their basic rate.

MOTELS/MOTOR INNS

The familiar roadside motel of the past is fast disappearing from the landscape. In its place are economical chain-run motor inns that are strategically located at highway intersections. Some of these establishments offer very basic facilities; others provide restaurants, swimming pools, and other amenities.

YMCAS/YWCAS

YMCAs or YWCAs are usually a good bet for clean, no-frills, reliable lodging in large towns and cities. These buildings are often centrally located, and their rates are significantly lower than those at city hotels. Nonmembers are welcome, but they may pay slightly more than members. A few very large Ys have accommodations for couples, but sleeping arrangements are usually segregated.

M

MAIL

Postage rates vary for different classes of mail and destinations. Check with the local post office for rates before mailing a letter or parcel. At press time, it cost 32¢ to mail a standard letter anywhere within the United States. Mail to Canada costs 40¢ per first ounce, and 23¢ for each additional ounce; mail to Great Britain and other foreign countries costs 50¢ per half ounce.

First-class rates in Canada are 46¢ for up to 30 grams of mail delivered within Canada, 52¢ for up to 30 grams delivered to the United States, 70¢ for up to 50 grams. International mail and postcards run 92¢ for up to 20 grams, $1.26 for 20–50 grams.

RECEIVING MAIL

Visitors can have letters or parcels sent to them while they are traveling by using the following address: Name of addressee, c/o General Delivery, Main Post Office, City and State/Province, U.S./Canada, Zip Code (U.S.) or Postal Code (Canada). Contact the nearest post office for further details. Any item mailed to "General

Delivery" must be picked up by the addressee in person within 15 days or it will be returned to the sender.

MONEY MATTERS

The United States and Canada both use the same currency denominations—dollars and cents—although each currency has a different value on the world market. In the United States, the most common paper currency comes in $1, $5, $10, and $20 bills. Common notes in Canada include the $2, $5, $10, and $20 bills. (Canada recently phased out its $1 bill, replacing it with a $1 gold-color coin nicknamed the "loonie" by Canadians because it contains a picture of a loon on one side.) Coins in both countries come in denominations of 1¢ (penny), 5¢ (nickel), 10¢ (dime), 25¢ (quarter), and 50¢.

ATMS

Cirrus, Plus and many other networks connecting automated-teller machines operate internationally. Chances are that you can **use your bank card at ATMs** to withdraw money from an account and get cash advances on a credit-card account if your card has been programmed with a personal identification number, or PIN. Before leaving home, **check on frequency limits** for withdrawals and cash advances. Also **ask whether your card's PIN must be reprogrammed** for use in Canada. Four digits are commonly used overseas. Note that Discover is ac-

cepted only in the United States.

On cash advances you are charged interest from the day you receive the money from ATMs as well as from tellers. Transaction fees for ATM withdrawals outside your home turf may be higher than for withdrawals at home. Although transaction fees for ATM withdrawals abroad may be higher than fees for withdrawals at home, Cirrus and Plus exchange rates are excellent because they are based on wholesale rates only offered by major banks.

COSTS

Prices for meals and accommodations in Seattle and Vancouver are generally lower than in other major North American regions. Prices for first-class hotel rooms range from $100 to $200 a night, although you can still find some "value" hotel rooms for $65 to $90 a night. Most hotels have weekend packages that offer discounts of up to 50%. Don't look for these special deals during the peak summer season, however, when hotels are nearly filled to capacity.

As a rule, costs outside the major cities are lower, but prices for rooms and meals at some of the major deluxe resorts can rival those at the best big-city hotels.

Prices in Canada are always quoted in Canadian dollars. When comparing prices with those in the United

States, costs should be calculated via the current rate of exchange. At press time (fall 1995), the Canadian dollar was worth US$.75, but this exchange rate can vary considerably. Check with a bank or other financial institution for the current rate. A good way to be sure you're getting the best exchange rate is by using your credit card. The issuing bank will convert your bill at the current rate.

Sales tax varies among areas. The sales tax in Washington is 7%–8.2%. Seattle adds 5% to the rate for hotel rooms. Canada's 7% Goods & Services Tax (GST) is added to hotel bills but will be rebated to foreign visitors. In British Columbia, consumers pay an 8%–10% provincial and municipal tax. The percentage varies from one municipality to another.

EXCHANGING CURRENCY

American money is readily accepted in much of Canada (especially in communities near the border). For the most favorable rates, **change money at banks.** You won't do as well at exchange booths in airports, rail, and bus stations, or in hotels, restaurants, and stores, although you may find their hours more convenient. To avoid lines at airport exchange booths, **get a small amount of currency before you leave home.**

TAXES

GST➤ Canada's Goods and Services Tax (GST) is 7%, applicable on virtually every purchase except basic groceries and a small number of other items. Visitors to Canada may claim a full rebate of the GST on any goods taken out of the country as well as on short-term accommodations. Rebates can be claimed either immediately on departure from Canada at participating duty-free shops or by mail. Rebate forms can be obtained at most stores and hotels in Canada or by writing to Revenue Canada (Visitor's Rebate Program, Ottawa, Ontario K1A 1J5, ☎ 613/991–3346 or 800/668–4748 in Canada). Claims must be for a minimum of $7 worth of tax and can be submitted up to a year from the date of purchase. Purchases made during multiple visits to Canada can be grouped together for rebate purposes.

SALES➤ Washington's tax is 7%–8.2%, depending on municipality; provincial sales tax in British Columbia is 7%.

TRAVELER'S CHECKS

Whether or not to buy traveler's checks depends on where you are headed; **take cash to rural areas and small towns, traveler's checks to cities.** The most widely recognized are American Express, Citicorp, Thomas Cook, and Visa, which are sold by major commercial banks for 1% to 3% of the checks' face value—it pays to **shop around.** Both American Express and Thomas Cook issue checks that can be countersigned and used by you or your traveling companion, and they both provide checks, at no extra charge, denominated in Canadian dollars. You can cash them in banks without paying a fee (which can be as much as 20%) and use them as readily as cash in many hotels, restaurants, and shops. So you won't be left with excess foreign currency, **buy a few checks in small denominations** to cash toward the end of your trip. Record the numbers of the checks, cross them off as you spend them, and keep this information separate from your checks.

WIRING MONEY

You don't have to be a cardholder to send or receive funds through MoneyGram[SM] from American Express. Just go to a MoneyGram agent, located in retail and convenience stores and in American Express Travel Offices. Pay up to $1,000 with cash or a credit card, anything over that in cash. The money can be picked up within 10 minutes in the form of U.S. dollar traveler's checks or local currency at the nearest Money-Gram agent or, abroad, the nearest American Express Travel Office (in Vancouver, ☎ 604/687–7686). There's no limit, and the recipient need only present photo identification. The cost, which includes a free long-dis... call wir... States... to 10... the a... destination, ... you pay.

You can also send money using Western Union. Money sent from the United States or Canada will be available for pickup at agent locations in 100 countries within 15 minutes. Once the money is in the system, it can be picked up at any one of 25,000 locations. Fees range from 4% to 10%, depending on the amount you send.

P
PACKAGES
AND TOURS

A package or tour to Seattle or Vancouver can make your vacation less expensive and more convenient. Firms that sell tours and packages purchase airline seats, hotel rooms, and rental cars in bulk and pass some of the savings on to you. In addition, the best operators have local representatives to help you out at your destination. Arctic tours are particularly good for travelers who would otherwise move about independently.

A GOOD DEAL?

The more your package or tour includes, the better you can predict the ultimate cost of your vacation. Make sure you know exactly what is included, and **beware of hidden costs.** Are taxes, tips, and service charges luded? Transfers and baggage handling? Entertainment and excursions? These can add up.

Most packages and tours are rated deluxe, first-class superior, first class, tourist, and budget. The key difference is usually accommodations. If the package or tour you are considering is priced lower than in your wildest dreams, **be skeptical.** Also, **make sure your travel agent knows the hotels** and other services. Ask about location, room size, beds, and whether it has a pool, room service, or programs for children, if you care about these. Has your agent been there or sent others you can contact?

BUYER BEWARE

Each year consumers are stranded or lose their money when operators go out of business—even very large ones with excellent reputations. If you can't afford a loss, take the time to **check out the operator**—find out how long the company has been in business, and ask several agents about its reputation. Next, **don't book unless the firm has a consumer-protection program.** Members of the United States Tour Operators Association and the National Tour Association are required to set aside funds exclusively to cover your payments and travel arrangements in case of default. Nonmember operators may instead carry insurance; look for the details in the

operator's brochure— and the name of an underwriter with a solid reputation. Note: When it comes to tour operators, **don't trust escrow accounts.** Although there are laws governing those of charter-flight operators, no governmental body prevents tour operators from raiding the till.

Next, **contact your local Better Business Bureau and the attorney general's office** in both your own state and the operator's; have any complaints been filed? Last, **pay with a major credit card.** Then you can cancel payment, provided that you can document your complaint. Always **consider trip-cancellation insurance** (*see* Insurance, *above*).

BIG VS. SMALL➤ An operator that handles several hundred thousand travelers annually can use its purchasing power to give you a good price. Its high volume may also indicate financial stability. But some small companies provide more personalized service; because they tend to specialize, they may also be experts on an area.

USING AN AGENT

Travel agents are an excellent resource. In fact, large operators accept bookings only through travel agents. But it's good to **collect brochures from several agencies,** because some agents' suggestions may be skewed by promotional relationships with tour and package firms that reward them

for volume sales. If you have a special interest, **find an agent with expertise in that area;** the American Society of Travel Agents can give you leads in the United States. (Don't rely solely on your agent, though; agents may be unaware of small niche operators, and some special-interest travel companies only sell direct.)

SINGLE TRAVELERS

Prices are usually quoted per person, based on two sharing a room. If traveling solo, you may be required to pay the full double-occupancy rate. Some operators eliminate this surcharge if you agree to be matched up with a roommate of the same sex, even if one is not found by departure time.

PACKING FOR SEATTLE AND VANCOUVER

Residents of the Pacific North Coast are generally informal by nature and wear clothing that reflects their disposition. Summer days are warm but evenings can cool off substantially. Your best bet is to **dress in layers**—sweatshirts, sweaters, and jackets are removed or put on as the day progresses. If you plan to explore the region's cities on foot, or if you choose to hike along mountain trails or beaches, bring comfortable walking shoes.

Dining out is usually an informal affair, although some restaurants require a jacket and tie for men and dresses for women. Residents tend to dress conservatively when going to the theater or symphony, but it's not uncommon to see some patrons wearing jeans. In other words, almost anything is acceptable for most occasions.

If you plan on hiking or camping during the summer, insect repellent is a must. Bring an extra pair of eyeglasses or contact lenses in your carry-on luggage, and if you have a health problem, **pack enough medication** to last the trip or have your doctor write a prescription using the drug's generic name, because brand names vary from country to country (you'll then need a prescription from a doctor in the country you're visiting). **Don't put prescription drugs or valuables in luggage to be checked,** for it could go astray. To avoid problems with customs officials, carry medications in original packaging. Also don't forget the addresses of offices that handle refunds of lost traveler's checks.

LUGGAGE

Free airline baggage allowances depend on the airline, the route, and the class of your ticket; ask in advance. In general, on domestic flights and on international flights between the United States and foreign destinations, you are entitled to check two bags—neither exceeding 62 inches, or 158 centimeters (length + width + height), or weighing more than 70 pounds

(32 kilograms). A third piece may be brought aboard; its total dimensions are generally limited to less than 45 inches (114 centimeters), so it will fit easily under the seat in front of you or in the overhead compartment. In the United States, the FAA gives airlines broad latitude to limit carry-on allowances and tailor them to different aircraft and operational conditions. Charges for excess, oversize, or overweight pieces vary.

If you are flying between two foreign destinations, note that baggage allowances may be determined not by piece but by weight—generally 88 pounds (40 kilograms) in first class, 66 pounds (30 kilograms) in business class, and 44 pounds (20 kilograms) in economy. If your flight between two cities abroad *connects* with your transatlantic or transpacific flight, the piece method still applies.

SAFEGUARDING YOUR LUGGAGE➤ Before leaving home, **itemize your bags' contents** and their worth, and label them with your name, address, and phone number. (If you use your home address, cover it so that potential thieves can't see it.) Inside your bag, **pack a copy of your itinerary.** At check-in, **make sure that your bag is correctly tagged** with the airport's three-letter destination code. If your bags arrive damaged or not at all, file a

written report with the airline before leaving the airport.

PASSPORTS
AND VISAS

U.S. AND CANADIAN CITIZENS

Citizens and permanent residents of the United States and Canada are not required to have passports or visas to visit each other's country. However, native-born citizens should carry identification showing proof of citizenship, such as a birth certificate, a voter-registration card, or a valid passport. Naturalized citizens should carry a naturalization certificate or some other proof of citizenship. Individuals under the age of 18 who are not accompanied by their parents should bring a letter from a parent or guardian giving them permission to travel in another country. Permanent residents of the United States who are not U.S. citizens should carry their Alien Registration Receipt Cards. U.S. citizens interested in visiting Canada for more than 90 days may apply for a visa that allows them to stay for six months.

U.K. CITIZENS

British citizens need a valid passport. If you are staying fewer than 90 days and traveling on a vacation, with a return or onward ticket, you will probably not need a visa. However, you will need to fill out the Visa Waiver Form, 1-94W, supplied by the airline. British visitors are not required to have a visa to enter Canada. Their stay in Canada, however, cannot exceed six months without authorization from Canadian immigration.

While traveling, **keep one photocopy of your passport's data page** separate from your wallet and leave another copy with someone at home. If you lose your passport, promptly call the nearest embassy or consulate, and the local police; having the data page can speed replacement.

R
RENTING A CAR
CUTTING COSTS

To get the best deal, **book through a travel agent and shop around.** When pricing cars, **ask where the rental lot is located.** Some off-airport locations offer lower rates—even though their lots are only minutes away from the terminal via complimentary shuttle. You may also want to **price local car-rental companies,** whose rates may be lower still, although service and maintenance standards may not be up to those of a national firm. Also **ask your travel agent about a company's customer-service record.** How has it responded to late plane arrivals and vehicle mishaps? Are there often lines at the rental counter, and, if you're traveling during a holiday period, does a confirmed reservation guarantee you a car?

Always **find out what equipment is standard**

at your destination before specifying what you want; **do without automatic transmission or air-conditioning** if they're optional.

INSURANCE

When you drive a rented car, you are generally responsible for any damage or personal injury that you cause as well as damage to the vehicle. Before you rent, **see what coverage you already have** under the terms of your personal auto-insurance policy and credit cards. For about $14 a day, rental companies sell insurance, known as a collision damage waiver (CDW), that eliminates your liability for damage to the car; it's always optional and should never be automatically added to your bill.

REQUIREMENTS

In Canada your own driver's license is acceptable. An International Driver's Permit, available from the American or Canadian Automobile Association, is a good idea.

FOR U.K. CITIZENS

In the United States you must be 21 to rent a car; rates may be higher for those under 25. Extra costs cover child seats, compulsory for children under five (about $3 per day), and additional drivers (about $1.50 per day). To pick up your reserved car you will need the reservation voucher, a passport, a U.K. driver's license, and a travel policy covering each driver.

SURCHARGES

Before picking up the car in one city and leaving it in another, **ask about drop-off charges or one-way service fees,** which can be substantial. Note, too, that some rental agencies charge extra if you return the car before the time specified on your contract. To avoid a hefty refueling fee, **fill the tank just before you turn in the car.**

S
SENIOR-CITIZEN DISCOUNTS

To qualify for age-related discounts, **mention your senior-citizen status up front** when booking hotel reservations, not when checking out, and before you're seated in restaurants, not when paying your bill. Note that discounts may be limited to certain menus, days, or hours. When renting a car, **ask about promotional car-rental discounts**—they can net lower costs than your senior-citizen discount.

STUDENTS ON THE ROAD

To save money, **look into deals available through student-oriented travel agencies.** To qualify, you'll need to have a bona fide student I.D. card. Members of international student groups also are eligible. *See* Students *in* Important Contacts A to Z, *above.*

T
TELEPHONES

The telephone area codes are 206 for the

metropolitan Seattle area and 604 for British Columbia.

Pay telephones cost 25¢ for local calls. Charge phones are also found in many locations. These phones can be used to charge a call to a telephone-company credit card, your home phone, or the party you are calling: You do not need to deposit 25¢. For directory assistance, dial 1, the area code, and 555–1212. For local directory assistance, dial 1 followed by 555–1212. You can dial most international calls direct. Dial 0 to reach an operator.

Many hotels place a surcharge on local calls made from your room and include a service charge on long-distance calls. It may be cheaper for you to make your calls from a pay phone in the hotel lobby rather than from your room.

LONG DISTANCE

The long-distance services of AT&T, MCI, and Sprint make calling home relatively convenient and let you avoid hotel surcharges; typically, you dial a local number. Before you go, **find out the local access codes** for your destinations.

TIPPING

Tips and service charges are usually not automatically added to a bill in the United States or Canada. If service is satisfactory,

customers generally give waiters, waitresses, taxi drivers, barbers, hairdressers, and so forth, a tip of 15%–20% of the total bill. Bellhops, doormen, and porters at airports and railway stations are generally tipped $1 for each item of luggage.

W
WHEN TO GO

The Pacific North Coast's mild, pleasant climate is best from June through September. Hotels in the major tourist destinations are often filled in July and August, so it's important to book reservations in advance. Summer temperatures generally range in the 70s, and rainfall is usually minimal. Nights, however, can be cool, so if you're going to enjoy the nightlife, take along a sweater or jacket.

Spring and fall are also excellent times to visit. The weather usually remains quite good, and the prices for accommodations, transportation, and tours can be lower (and the crowds much smaller!) in the most popular destinations.

In winter, the coastal rain turns to snow in the nearby mountains, making the region a skier's dream.

CLIMATE

Tempered by a warm Japan current and protected by the mountains from the extreme

weather conditions found inland, the coastal regions of Washington and British Columbia experience a uniformly mild climate.

Average daytime summer highs are in the 70s; winter temperatures are generally in the 40s. Snow is uncommon in the lowland areas. If it does snow (usually in December or January), everything grinds to a halt—but children love it!

The area's reputation for rain is somewhat misleading, as the amount of rainfall in the Pacific North Coast varies greatly from one locale to another. In the coastal mountains, for example, 160 inches of rain falls annually, creating temperate rain forests. In Washington and British Columbia, near-desert conditions prevail, with rainfall as low as 6 inches per year.

Seattle has an average of only 36 inches of rainfall a year—less than New York, Chicago, or Miami. The wetness, however, is concentrated during the winter months, when cloudy skies and drizzly weather persist. More than 75% of Seattle's annual precipitation occurs from October through March.

The following are average daily maximum and minimum temperatures for Seattle and Vancouver.

Climate in Seattle and Vancouver

SEATTLE

Jan.	45F	7C	May	66F	19C	Sept.	69F	20C
	35	2		47	8		52	11
Feb.	50F	10C	June	70F	21C	Oct.	62F	16C
	37	3		52	11		47	8
Mar.	53F	12C	July	76F	24C	Nov.	51F	10C
	38	3		56	13		40	4
Apr.	59F	13C	Aug.	75F	24C	Dec.	47F	8C
	42	5		55	13		37	3

VANCOUVER

Jan.	41F	5C	May	63F	17C	Sept.	64F	18C
	32	0		46	8		50	10
Feb.	46F	8C	June	66F	19C	Oct.	57F	14C
	34	1		52	11		43	6
Mar.	48F	9C	July	72F	22C	Nov.	48F	9C
	36	2		55	13		37	3
Apr.	55F	13C	Aug.	72F	22C	Dec.	45F	7C
	41	5		55	13		34	1

1 Destination: Seattle and Vancouver

TWO CHAIRS ARE BETTER THAN THREE

THE FIRST TIME I VISITED SEATTLE, I took with me preconceived ideas about the Pacific Northwest. A friend who had moved here recently was full of stories about camping on the weekends, biking after work, and theater tickets that cost the same as movie tickets in New York. Articles in the national press raved about the region's natural beauty, cultural vibrancy, and healthy economy. "America's Most Livable City," they touted, referring to Seattle. So I arrived with high expectations.

The weather was ideal. We went to Orcas Island—a short drive and ferry ride from Seattle—and camped on a bluff overlooking Puget Sound. My friend fell asleep, and I lay on my back in front of a dying fire, beneath stellar patterns I had rarely noticed before, and considered how inadequate my life in New York was, how suited I was to the natural, more wholesome lives people led in the Great Northwest. All of what I had heard seemed true: I felt I had found the ideal blend of natural splendor and urban sophistication, where a rain forest could mingle in perfect harmony with a modern metropolis. The next day we drove to the top of Mt. Constitution, the highest peak on the island. From this privileged perspective, I surveyed virtually the whole pristine region, including Puget Sound, Vancouver Island, and the Olympic Mountains. I decided to move west.

Needless to say, I suffered some disillusionment. I can remember waiting for a taxi at Sea-Tac Airport on my first day in Seattle, trying to decide if the mist demanded an umbrella and wondering why everything suddenly looked so dreary. Two days later I made my first major purchase in Seattle—a mountain bike. Eager to prove myself an outdoorsman, that evening I pedaled to a party on Queen Anne Hill; the terrain—typical for Seattle—was a little steeper than I had expected. Cursing every step, I ended up climbing the arduous hill, with bike alongside me. I was beginning to learn that, while the image of the great outdoors

meeting the great metropolis evokes drama, if not romance, the two forces don't always create the most comfortable situations.

Last December, for instance, a snowstorm hit Seattle, leaving the steep hills sheathed in ice. As a New York native, I expected salt on the sidewalks, sand on the streets, and a fairly active city the next day. Not a chance. Many of the busiest streets hadn't been plowed, cars were abandoned by the side of the road, and businesses and schools were shut down. The message was clear: If you live on the Pacific North Coast, you must accept nature's tendency to disrupt and inconvenience you. Houses slide down eroded slopes into Puget Sound, volcanoes erupt, and it rains and rains and rains. Rigidity, outrage, obstinate determination, or any other form of hubris can get you into trouble. I was the only passenger on a bus one night, and the bus driver drove three blocks off his route to drop me at the door of my destination. Sure, he was being kind, but it's more than that. Native northwesterners are used to adjustments, and they make them without thinking twice.

My enchanted experience on Orcas Island was no fluke. If nature disrupts, its grace and power also inspires. On a clear day in Seattle, Mt. Rainier floats, dreamlike, over the industrial southern end of the city; the Cascade Mountains reign in the east, looming over Lake Washington; in the west, the Olympics rise over Bainbridge Island and Elliott Bay, and ragged clouds turn an evening sky into an explosion of color. Standing at the seawall in Vancouver's Stanley Park, the mountains rest at what seems like just an arm's reach across Burrard Inlet. Take just a few steps onto one of the park trails and you feel as though you're lost in a virgin forest, with no sign of city life.

If the weather has been especially depressing, I seize the first clear day and rent a canoe at the University of Washington waterfront in Seattle. The channels at the University Arboretum give way to Lake Washington, fringed by the Cascade Mountains. Inevitably, I feel serene, as I did on Orcas Island, and the Northwest once again becomes the ideal place to live.

But residents of Seattle and Vancouver don't just paddle away their days. Politics run hot here, and local leaders work hard to maintain legislation that has helped to protect the environment of the cities and their surroundings. Likewise, advocates deserve kudos for their efforts to restore some of the history that went into the makings of Seattle and Vancouver. In 1971, the Canadian Government bought Granville Island, which was originally used to store logging supplies. Today, only businesses that deal with maritime activities, the arts, and a public market are permitted to set up shop on the island. A walk around the island will lead you past produce stalls, crafts merchants, food vendors, and artists' studios. Around the same time as the Granville Island purchase, Vancouver embarked on the restoration of Gastown, a historic area by the waterfront and named for "Gassy" Jack Deighton, who opened the settlement's first saloon. By the time Deighton died in 1875, a bawdy and sometimes lawless townsite had sprouted in the vicinity of his saloon. In one way, the area remained faithful to his vision, as it proceeded for the next 100 years to attract an abundance of drunks. In 1960, more than two-thirds of all arrests in Vancouver were made in the vicinity of the old Deighton House. Some of the old buildings remain, but until the rehabilitation the squalor of the neighborhood was more prominent than its history. Today boutiques, galleries, restaurants, and a steam-powered clock line the cobblestone streets of this touted tourist spot—a worthy tribute to the old codger.

Vancouver's history predates Gassy Jack Deighton and the first white entourage. When the settlers arrived in Vancouver, there were, according to one witness, 10 Suquamish villages in the area. A few years later, most of the land had been claimed by the newcomers, and the villages had vanished. Fortunately, the native culture survived, and today Vancouver is the center for producing and selling native Pacific Coast crafts. Local Haida carver Bill Reid has his studio on Granville Island; galleries display the works of Inuit, Tlingit, Tsimshian, Kwakiutl, Haida, and Salish artisans; students can study the craft

at the University of British Columbia; and the university's Museum of Anthropology houses one of the finest collections of native art in the world. Western techniques have been studied and incorporated into the works, but the dominant styles and the mythological references—usually related to the animal wildlife of the region—are firmly rooted in Pacific Coast cultures.

SEATTLE'S EARLY HISTORY began with the native Suquamish people, and the city has devoted much energy to preserving its historic neighborhoods. In the late 1800s, Seattle began to expand around a steam-powered lumber mill at the foot of a hill, in the area of what is now called Pioneer Square. Loggers cut the trees near the hilltop and skidded them down to the mill along a road that came to be known as "skid road." "Road" soon became "row," and the term lost its original significance.

By the early 1960s, Pioneer Square had lost its historic character, going the same sordid route as Gastown had in Vancouver. So Seattle undertook a massive rehabilitation of its own. Historic buildings were restored, shops and galleries moved in, and, in keeping with the theme, the city put 1890s-style uniforms on the police officers who walked the local beat.

Fortunately, Pioneer Square hasn't become overly sanitized. On my first visit to Seattle, a friend took me to a small bar on the block between the square and the waterfront. A quiet place to have a beer, she said. Soon after we sat down, a man with a gruff voice broke into a chorus of "Barnacle Bill the Sailor." When a younger man dressed in black told him to be quiet, a fight broke out. So much for the quiet beer. Most urban rehabilitations leave only the pure and clean, but Pioneer Square retains its old rowdiness, lending authenticity to the restoration. A church that feeds the homeless is right across the street from the Elliott Bay Bookstore, where well-known writers read from their latest works. On weekend nights, the OK Hotel (not really a hotel) may have slam dancing that appeals to a young, leather-adorned crowd, and just a few blocks away the busy Trattoria Mitchelli offers late-night pasta to a mixed-bag clientele. Seattle's unrefined elements nicely balance all the historical charm, making this part of town feel lived-in and real.

The city's other major restoration project was the Pike Place Market, which was originally built in 1907. The complex of lofts and stalls overlooking Elliott Bay nearly faced the demolition ball in the 1960s, but was saved by a voter referendum. Amid a maze of ramps and hallways, today's visitors shop for gourmet foods, spices, posters, jewelry, crafts, clothes, fish, and produce.

I go down to the market to get my hair cut. On my way, I pass a fish stall that's on the first level. A seller—I call him the fish-thrower—stands before an array of sea creatures displayed on beds of ice. Hoarsely, the man calls out the specials and jokes with a few potential customers. No takers, yet. Now the man is discussing a particular salmon with an older woman. He holds up the fish and lets it fly, over the heads of potential customers and into a piece of wax paper held by one of the counter merchants. Successful completion, as usual.

Now I walk down to the barbershop. Kim, my barber of choice, raises the radio volume, prattles for a while about her love life, and needles the owner, who is tending to the customer in the only other chair. He takes her ribbing in stride. The cut costs $7, and without fail there's a line out the door. My impulse is to ask the owner why he doesn't expand—get a bigger shop, with room for a new chair and another assistant. Clearly, there's a demand for it. But I can imagine his response: "You transplants are all the same, all bent on expansion." In this city, I remind myself, two chairs can be better than three. It's the same message that the Pike Place merchants are now sending to the Preservation and Development Authority, which manages the complex and nearly allowed it to slip into the control of a New York investor group. The mar-

ket remains in the hands of the PDA, but merchants still worry about the future of the complex.

Of course, no one can deny that both cities have reaped at least some economic and cultural benefits from all the growth and renewal of the past few decades. Vancouver is among the busiest ports in North America, and Seattle—recognized in the past as the home of airline manufacturer Boeing—is now a center for computer technology as well, thanks to Bill Gates's Microsoft company. You can go to the theater for less than $10 in Seattle and, while a chandelier may not fall from the ceiling à la *Phantom of the Opera,* the performance is generally first-rate. Vancouver's Jazz Festival ranks among the best in the world.

All the success is also making people think. Highways are more crowded; sprawling suburbs encroach on the forests; and homelessness, drugs, and street gangs are on the rise. In Seattle, some locals have responded by forming a group called Lesser Seattle, devoted to discouraging people from moving here. "Keep the Bastards Out," they say, only half-jokingly. But beneath the tough talk lies a simple wish they share with Vancouverites: to maintain at least some control over the recent changes in their cities. If you plan on spending some time in either Seattle or Vancouver, don't be too concerned with this talk. No one will blame you outright for all the congestion and untrammelled growth; folks out here are too polite for that. They may instead hint at it, or bait you into a statement that you'll later regret. "This rain can be depressing, huh?" A resident might feel you out with this kind of question, to see what kind of appreciation you really have. Keep your answers short, and remember that out here, two chairs are often better than three.

By Philip Joseph

A native New Yorker, Phil has found his way to Seattle where he is a free-lance writer and editor.

WHAT'S WHERE

Seattle

In the Pacific North Coast's hippest city, the green hills and bay views are best appreciated from a coffee bar, and the music and art scenes seem to change with the tides. But Seattle has more to offer than steaming lattes and hot bands—you can wander historic neighborhoods, browse amidst the sights and smells of the Pike Place Market, explore the lakes and islands of this port city, or just eat, eat, eat—Seattle enjoys a spectrum of restaurants that is one of the nation's most innovative and diverse.

Vancouver

Cosmopolitan Vancouver, Canada's answer to San Francisco, enjoys a spectacular setting. Tall fir trees stand practically downtown, rock spires tower close by, the ocean is at your doorstep, and residents who have come from every corner of the earth create a young and vibrant atmosphere.

PLEASURES & PASTIMES

Beaches

The beaches of Washington are more remote from the major centers of population. Seattle is a two- to three-hour drive from the nearest ocean beaches. Even in summer, the beaches are never crowded.

Most of the west coast of Vancouver Island is totally isolated. Pacific Rim National Park is one of the few places where ocean beaches are accessible. On the eastern coast of Vancouver Island, there are a number of good swimming beaches around the town of Parksville.

The gravel beaches of the Puget Sound attract few swimmers or sunbathers, but the beaches are popular for beachcombing and viewing abundant marine life.

Boating

The sheltered waters of Puget Sound make boating one of the most popular outdoor activities in the area. On sunny days, a virtual fleet of boats dots the waterways; in

fact, some experts say that there are more boats per capita in the Puget Sound area than anywhere else in the world. For charters, outfitters, and information, see the boating section in each chapter.

Because of the region's mild climate, it is possible to enjoy boating throughout the year. Charters, which are available with or without a skipper and crew, can be rented for a period of a few hours to several days. The calm waterways are also rated among the best in the world for sea kayaking, an appealing way to explore the intertidal regions.

Climbing and Mountaineering

The mountains of the Pacific North Coast have given many an adventurer quite a challenge. It is no coincidence that many members of the U.S. expedition teams to Mt. Everest have come from this region.

With expert training and advanced equipment, mountaineering can be a safe sport, but you should never go climbing without an experienced guide. Classes are available from qualified instructors.

Dining

Many restaurants in the Pacific North Coast serve local specialties such as salmon, crab, oysters, and other seafood delicacies. Seattle's Pike Place Market and Vancouver's Granville Island Market display bountiful supplies of local seafood and produce, and these are good places to scan what you might find on restaurant menus. Ethnic foods are also becoming increasingly popular, especially Asian cuisines such as Japanese, Korean, and Thai.

There is tremendous emphasis on and enjoyment of the hearty and savory fare available in this area. Chefs of all stripes key their menus to the seasonal availability of local produce. In June strawberries are in season, July brings in Walla Walla Sweets (a softball-size mild onion and a local delicacy), blackberries (which grow wild, and can be picked from the roadside) take the forefront in August, and the Washington apple crop comes in in the fall.

Portions of Washington and British Columbia are major wine-producing regions. Local wines are often featured in the best restaurants. Beer, too, is a popular local product, and microbreweries have enjoyed increasing popularity throughout the Northwest. Often located in or connected with a local pub, some of these breweries produce only enough specialty beers (called microbrews) for their own establishments. Some, however, such as Red Hook Ale, Ballard Bitter, and Anchor Ale, are also available from regular beer outlets. Some wineries and microbreweries offer tours and tastings.

Coffee has become a passion in Seattle. Lattés (the local version of café au lait), cappuccinos, and espressos are the beverages of choice in the finer—and even not so fine—restaurants around town (you can get a latté at the downtown McDonald's). Espresso stands do a brisk business on almost every other downtown corner. The latest phenomena are drive-through espresso stands that are popping up in suburban areas. The coffee craze is also spreading to Vancouver. Enjoy!

As a general rule, restaurants in metropolitan areas are more expensive than those outside the city. But many city establishments, especially those that feature foreign cuisines, are surprisingly inexpensive. Because of space limitations, we have listed only restaurants recommended as the best within each price range.

Fishing

The coastal regions and inland lakes and rivers of the Pacific Northwest are known for their excellent fishing opportunities. Fishing lodges, many of which are accessible only by floatplane, cater to anglers in search of the ultimate fishing experience.

Visiting sportsmen must possess a nonresident license for the state or province in which they plan to fish. Licenses are easily obtainable at sporting-goods stores, bait shops, and other outlets in popular fishing areas.

Golf

The Pacific North Coast has many excellent golf courses, but not all of them are open to the public. Consequently, visitors may find it difficult to arrange a tee time at a popular course. If you are a member of a golf club at home, check to see if your club has a reciprocal playing arrangement with any of the private clubs in the areas that you will be visiting.

Sailboarding

Puget Sound and some of the inland lakes are popular sailboarding venues. Sailboard rentals and lessons are available from local specialty shops.

Shopping

The Pacific North Coast offers shoppers quite a selection of locally made crafts and souvenirs. Some of the most distinctive items are produced by Native American artists, who manufacture prints, wood carvings, boxes, masks, and other items. Shops in Seattle and Vancouver carry a wide variety of these objects, but collectors can find the best selection and prices in the small communities located on Vancouver Island.

Another popular "souvenir" for visitors is freshly caught salmon. Fish vendors can pack a recent catch in a special airlines-approved box that will keep the fish fresh for a couple of days. A package of smoked salmon—which will keep even longer—is another alternative.

Public markets are among the best places to purchase salmon and other gifts. Seattle's historic Pike Place Market and Vancouver's Granville Island Market offer a wonderful array of fish stalls, fresh fruit and vegetable stands, arts and crafts vendors, and small shops that sell practically everything.

Because residents of the Pacific North Coast have such an active lifestyle, many leading manufacturers and retailers of outdoor equipment and apparel have their headquarters here. Recreation Equipment Inc. (REI) has several stores in the Seattle area that sell everything from high-quality sleeping bags and backpacks to freeze-dried food and mountain-climbing equipment. Eddie Bauer, the famous recreational clothing and equipment catalogue distributor and retailer, was founded in Seattle and still has outlets here.

Skiing

Skiing is by far the most popular winter activity in the area. Moist air off the Pacific Ocean dumps snow on the coastal mountains, providing excellent skiing from November through the end of March and sometimes into April. Local newspapers regularly list snow conditions for ski areas throughout the region during the winter season. Resort and lift-ticket prices tend to be less expensive here than at the internationally known ski destinations. Most Washington ski resorts cater to those who've come for a day of skiing rather than a longer stay.

The Whistler and Blackcomb mountains, north of Vancouver, comprise the biggest ski area in the region. Whistler Village resort boasts the longest and second-longest vertical drops (more than a mile each) of any ski area in North America. Aside from Whistler/Blackcomb, British Columbia has many other excellent ski resorts scattered throughout the province, including several that are only minutes from downtown Vancouver.

Washington has 20 ski areas, several of which are located just east of Seattle in the Cascade Mountains. Snoqualmie Pass, the ski area closest to Seattle—about 45 minutes east—contains three ski areas: Snoqualmie, Ski Acres, and Alpental.

Swimming

Despite all the water surrounding the region, there is not as much swimming as one might expect along the Pacific North Coast. While the sandy ocean beaches attract throngs of people during the summer, most sun worshipers spend little time in the water—it's just too cold!

FODOR'S CHOICE

Seattle

Sights & Attractions

★ **Ballard Locks.** Follow the fascinating progress of fishing boats and pleasure craft through the locks, part of the Lake Washington Ship Canal, then watch as salmon and trout make the same journey from salt water to fresh: Several seaquarium-like viewing rooms run alongside a fish ladder that allows migrating fish to swim upstream on a gradual incline.

★ **Museum of Flight.** Boeing Field is home to the city's top museum. Exhibits on the history of human flight fill the Red Barn, Boeing's original airplane factory, and the Great Gallery contains more than 20 classic airplanes, dating from the Wright brothers to the jet era.

★ **Pike Place Market.** Read the hundreds of names etched into the floor tiles as you wander among the stalls selling fresh seafood, produce, cheese, Northwest wines, bulk spices, tea, coffee, and arts and crafts.

★ **Space Needle.** There's nothing like the view of the city at night from the observation deck of this Seattle landmark.

Restaurants

★ **Campagne.** The snowy linens, fresh flowers, white walls, and picture windows at this intimate French restaurant evoke Provence, as does the menu: French cuisine here means the robust flavors of the Midi, not the more polished tastes of Paris. $$–$$$

★ **Painted Table.** Sand-colored walls and warm mahogany paneling provide an elegant backdrop for the Northwest cuisine of chef Tim Kelly, who selects from the freshest produce available from nearby small vendors, farms, and the Pike Place Market. $$–$$$

★ **Wild Ginger.** This restaurant near the Pike Place Market specializes in seafood and Southeast Asian fare, ranging from mild Cantonese to spicier Vietnamese, Thai, and Korean dishes. The satay bar, where you can sip local brews and eat tangy, elegantly seasoned skewered tidbits until 2 AM, has quickly become a favorite local hangout. $$

★ **Saigon Gourmet.** This small café in the International District is about as plain as it gets, but the Vietnamese food is superb and the prices are incredibly low. $

Hotels & Inns

★ **Four Seasons Olympic Hotel.** Seattle's most elegant hotel has a 1920s Renaissance Revival–style grandeur; public rooms are appointed with marble, wood paneling, potted plants, and thick rugs, and furnished with plush armchairs. $$$$

★ **Sorrento.** Sitting high on First Hill, this deluxe European-style hotel, designed to look like an Italian villa, has wonderful views overlooking downtown and the waterfront. $$$

★ **Inn at the Market.** This sophisticated but unpretentious hotel, located right up the street from the Pike Place Market, combines the best aspects of a small French country inn with the informality of the Pacific Northwest. *$$–$$$*

☆ **Meany Tower Hotel.** Built in 1931 and remodeled many times since, this pleasant hotel just a few blocks from the University of Washington has managed to retain much of its old-fashioned charm. *$$*

Vancouver

Sights & Attractions

☆ **Granville Island.** This small sandbar, once a derelict factory district, was redeveloped—now the refurbished industrial buildings and tin sheds, painted in upbeat primary colors, house restaurants, a public market, marine activities, and artisans' studios.

☆ **Museum of Anthropology.** Vancouver's most spectacular museum displays aboriginal art from the Pacific Northwest and around the world. See dramatic totem poles, ceremonial archways, and dugout canoes; exquisite carvings of gold, silver, and argillite; and masks, tools, and costumes from many cultures.

☆ **Stanley Park.** An afternoon in this 1,000-acre wilderness park, just blocks from downtown, can include beaches, the ocean, the harbor, Douglas fir and cedar forests, and a good look at the North Shore mountains.

Restaurants

☆ **Chartwell.** Named after Sir Winston Churchill's country home, the flagship dining room at the Four Seasons Hotel offers robust, inventive Continental food in a British-club atmosphere. *$$$–$$$$*

☆ **Star Anise.** Pacific Rim cuisine with French flair shines in this intimate restaurant on the west side of town. *$$$*

☆ **Chez Thierry.** This cozy, unpretentious bistro knows how to add pizzazz to a celebration: Charming owner Thierry Damilano stylishly slashes open champagne bottles with a cavalry sabre on request. For the past 18 years, he has also worked with chef Francois Launay to create delicious country-style French fare. *$$*

☆ **Phnom Penh Restaurant.** Part of a small cluster of Southeast Asian shops on the fringes of Chinatown, Phnom Pehn serves unusually robust Vietnamese and Cambodian fare. *$*

Hotels & Inns

☆ **Sutton Place.** This property feels more like an exclusive guest house than a large hotel: Its lobby has sumptuously thick carpets, enormous displays of flowers, and elegant European furniture; rooms are even better. *$$$$*

☆ **Hotel Vancouver.** The copper roof of this grand château-style hotel dominates Vancouver's skyline. The hotel itself, opened in 1939 by the Canadian National Railway, commands a regal position in the center of town across from the art gallery and Cathedral Place. *$$$*

☆ **English Bay Inn.** In this renovated 1930s Tudor house a block from the ocean, the guest rooms have wonderful sleigh beds with matching armoires. A small, sunny English country garden brightens the back of the inn. *$$*

FESTIVALS AND SEASONAL EVENTS

WINTER

JAN.➤ The **Polar Bear Swim** on New Year's Day in Vancouver is said to bring good luck all year; **skiing competitions** take place at most alpine ski resorts throughout the province (through Feb.).

MAR.➤ **Pacific Rim Whale Festival** on Vancouver Island's west coast celebrates the spring migration of gray whales with guided tours by whale experts and accompanying music and dancing; the **Vancouver International Wine Festival** is held.

SPRING

MID-MAY➤ **Vancouver Children's Festival**, the largest event of its kind in the world, presents dozens of performances in mime, puppetry, music, and theater (☎ 604/687–7697).

LATE MAY➤ **Northwest Folklife Festival** lures musicians and artists to Seattle for one of the largest folkfests in the United States (☎ 206/684–7300).

LATE MAY➤ **Swiftsure Race Weekend** draws more than 300 competitors to Victoria's harbor for an international yachting event (☎ 604/592–2441). **Victoria Day,** a

national holiday, is usually celebrated throughout Canada on the penultimate weekend in May.

SUMMER

LATE JUNE➤ **Canadian International Dragon Boat Festival,** in Vancouver, features races between long, slender boats decorated with huge dragon heads, an event based on a Chinese "awakening the dragons" ritual; the festival also includes community and children's activities, dance performances, and arts exhibits (☎ 604/684–5151). **Du Maurier International Jazz Festival** celebrates a broad spectrum of jazz, blues, and related improvised music, with more than 200 performances in 20 locations in Vancouver (☎ 604/682–0706).

LATE JUNE–EARLY JULY➤ **Fort Vancouver Days** in Vancouver is a citywide celebration with a rodeo, a bluegrass festival, a chili cook-off, and the largest fireworks display west of the Mississippi (☎ 206/693–1313).

JULY 1➤ **Canada Day** inspires celebrations around the country in honor of Canada's birthday.

MID-JULY➤ **Bite of Seattle** serves up sumptuous specialties from the city's finest restaurants (☎ 206/232–2982).

MID-JULY➤ **Vancouver Sea Festival** celebrates the city's nautical heritage with the World Championship Bathtub Race, sailing regattas, and windsurfing races, plus a parade, fireworks, entertainment, and a carnival (☎ 604/684–3378).

MID-JULY–EARLY AUG.➤ **Seafair,** Seattle's biggest event of the year, kicks off with a torchlight parade through downtown and culminates in the Blue Angels air show and hydroplane races on Lake Washington (☎ 206/728–0123).

MID-AUG.–EARLY SEPT.➤ **Pacific National Exhibition,** western Canada's biggest annual fair, brings top-name entertainment and a variety of displays to Vancouver (☎ 604/253–2311).

LATE AUG.–EARLY SEPT.➤ **Bumbershoot,** a Seattle festival of the arts, presents more than 400 performers in music, dance, theater, comedy, and the visual and literary arts (☎ 206/684–7200).

AUTUMN

SEPT.➤ Cars speed through downtown Vancouver in the **Molson Indy Formula 1 race.**

OCT.➤ The **Vancouver International Film Festival** is held.

2 Seattle

In the Pacific North Coast's hippest city, the green hills and bay views are best appreciated from a coffee bar, and the music and art scenes seem to change with the tides. But Seattle has more to offer than steaming lattes and hot bands—you can wander historic neighborhoods, browse amidst the sights and smells of the Pike Place Market, explore the lakes and islands of this port city, or just eat, eat, eat— Seattle enjoys a spectrum of restaurants that is one of the nation's most innovative and diverse.

By Adam
Woog and
Loralee
Wenger

SEATTLE IS DEFINED BY WATER. There's no use denying the city's damp weather, or the fact that its skies are cloudy for much of the year. Residents of Seattle don't tan—goes the joke—they rust. But Seattle is also defined by a different kind of water. A variety of rivers, lakes, and canals bisect steep hills, creating a series of distinctive areas along the water's edge that provide for a wide range of activities. Funky fishing boats, floating homes, swank yacht clubs, and waterfront restaurants exist side by side.

But a city is defined by its people as well as by its geography, and the people of Seattle—some half million within the city proper, another 2 million in the surrounding Puget Sound region—are a diversified bunch. Seattle has long had an active Asian and Asian-American population, as well as well-established communities of Scandinavians, African-Americans, Jews, Native Americans, Latinos, and other ethnic groups.

Although it's impossible to accurately generalize about such a varied group, the prototypical Seattleite was once pithily summed up by a *New Yorker* cartoon in which one arch-eyebrowed East Coast matron says to another, "They're backpacky, but nice." Aided by the proximity of high mountains—the Cascades to the east, the Olympics to the west—and all that water, Seattle's vigorous outdoor sports are indeed perennial favorites. And the city's extensive park system (designed by Frederick Law Olmsted, creator of New York City's Central Park) and miles of secluded walking and bicycling paths add to one's appreciation of the city's surroundings.

At the same time, the climate fosters an easygoing, indoor lifestyle as well. Overcast days and long winter nights help make Seattle a haven for moviegoers and book readers. The city is often used by Hollywood as a testing ground for new films, and according to independent bookstore sales and per-capita book purchases, the city ranks in the highest category. The town that Sir Thomas Beacham once described as a "cultural wasteland" now has all the artistic trappings of a full-blown big city, with ad agencies and artists' co-ops, symphonies and ballet companies. Several magazines compete with the two daily newspapers. There's an innovative new convention center, a covered dome for professional sports, a world-renowned theater scene, an excellent opera company, and a strong music community.

Other signs that Seattle is shedding its sleepy-town image abound. For years, giant aerospace manufacturer Boeing was the only major factor in the area's economy besides lumber and fishing—the staples of the Northwest. But just as the 1962 World's Fair (and its enduring symbol, the Space Needle) signaled a change from small town to medium-size city, so the 1990 Goodwill Games announced the city's new role as a respected international hub. Seattle, one of the fastest-growing communities in the United States, is now a major seaport and a vital link in Pacific Rim trade. Evidence of this internationalism is everywhere, from the discreet Japanese script identifying downtown department stores (i.e., "Nordstrom" written as "Katakana") to the multilingual recorded messages at Seattle-Tacoma International Airport.

As the city grows, though, it is also beginning to display full-blown big-city problems. Increases in crime, drug abuse, homelessness, and poverty are coupled with a decline in the quality of the public schools. Suburban growth is also rampant; nearby Bellevue, the largest suburb, has swollen in just a few years from a quiet farming community to the second-largest city in the state. Furthermore, the area is plagued with one of the worst traffic problems in the country. But Seattleites are an active political bunch with a great love for their city and a firm commitment to maintaining its reputation as one of the most livable in the country.

EXPLORING

Tour 1: Downtown

Downtown Seattle is bounded by the Kingdome to the south, the Seattle Center to the north, I–5 to the east, and the waterfront to the west. You can reach most points of interest by foot, bus, or the monorail. Bear in mind that Seattle is a city of hills, so comfortable walking shoes are a must.

Numbers in the margin correspond to points of interest on the Downtown Seattle map.

❶ Start at the **Visitor Information Center** on the street level of the Washington State Convention and Trade Center to pick up maps, brochures, and listings of events. *800 Convention Pl. (at 8th Ave. and Pike St.),* ☎ *206/461–5840.* ☉ *Labor Day–Memorial Day, weekdays 8:30–5; summer, daily 8:30–5.*

❷ From the Information Center, proceed west three blocks on Pike Street to 5th Avenue, turn right, and head one block north to **Westlake Center** (*see* Shopping, *below*), a complex completed in 1989 in spite of the controversy surrounding its construction. Some city residents objected to plans for the structure—a 27-story office tower and three-story shopping structure with enclosed walkways—and favored, instead, a large grassy park without commercial buildings. While the center was built, the block of Pine Street between 4th and 5th avenues is now a pedestrian mall and outdoor plaza. *1601 5th Ave.,* ☎ *206/467–1600.* ☉ *Weekdays 9:30–9.*

Beyond its commercial purpose, the center is also a major terminus for buses and for the monorail. If you head up to the monorail terminal (on the Pine Street and 5th Avenue corner), you can take a short jaunt over to **Seattle Center.** Like the monorail itself, this 74-acre complex was built for the 1962 Seattle World's Fair. It includes an amusement park, theaters, the Coliseum, exhibition halls, museums, shops, and the popular Space Needle with its restaurants and observation deck.

★ ❸ The distinctive silhouette of the **Space Needle** (rather like something from the old "Jetsons" cartoon show) can be seen from almost any spot in the downtown area. The view from the inside out, however, is even better—at over 500 feet high, the observation deck offers panoramic vistas of the entire region. Have a drink at the Space Needle Lounge or a latte at the adjacent coffee bar and take in Elliott Bay, Queen Anne Hill, and on a clear day, the peaks of the Cascades. The needle also houses two revolving restaurants. ☛ *Observation deck: $7 adults, $6.50 senior citizens, $3.50 children 5–12.* ☉ *Daily 8 AM–midnight.*

❹ Take the monorail back downtown and head west on Pine Street. From the corner of Pine and 2nd Avenue, you can head three blocks south on 2nd to the **Seattle Art Museum.** The five-story building, completed in 1991, was designed by postmodern theorist Robert Venturi and is a work of art in itself. The building features a limestone exterior with large-scale vertical fluting, accented by terra-cotta, cut granite, and marble. The museum displays an extensive collection of Asian,

Native American, African, Oceanic, and pre-Columbian art and has a café and gift shop. *1320 2nd Ave., ☎ 206/625–8900. ☛ $6 adults, $4 senior citizens and students, free for children under 12 and 1st Tues. of month. ⊙ Tues.–Sun. 10–5 (Thurs. until 9); call for tour schedule.*

★ ❺ From 2nd Avenue, you can go west on Pine or Pike streets to the **Pike Place Historical District,** home of the **Pike Place Market,** a Seattle institution. It began in 1907 when the city issued permits to farmers allowing them to sell produce from their wagons parked at Pike Place. Later the city built stalls that were allotted to the farmers on a daily basis. At one time the market was a madhouse of vendors hawking their produce, haggling over prices; some of the fishmongers still carry on this kind of frenzied banter, but chances are you won't get them to waver on their prices. Urban renewal almost killed the market, but city voters, led by the late architect Victor Steinbreuck, rallied and voted it a historical asset. Many of the buildings have been restored, and the project is now connected to the waterfront by stairs and elevators. Besides a number of restaurants, you'll find booths selling fresh seafood—which can be packed in dry ice for your flight home—produce, cheese, Northwest wines, bulk spices, tea, coffee, and arts and crafts. *Pike Place, between Pike and Pine Sts., ☎ 206/682–7453. ⊙ Mon.–Sat. 9–6, Sun. 11–5.*

TIME OUT If the weather is nice, gather a picnic of market foods—fresh fruit and smoked salmon, of course, but soups, sandwiches, pastries, and various ethnic snacks are also available in the market or from the small shops facing it along Pike Place. Carry your bounty north to just past the market buildings, where you'll find **Victor Steinbreuk Park,** a small green gem named for Pike Place's savior.

From the market, take a set of stairs or an elevator down to the waterfront. In the early days, the waterfront was the center of activity in Seattle. Today it stretches some 19 blocks, from Pier 70 (a converted warehouse with shops and restaurants) and Myrtle Edwards Park in the north, down to Pier 51 in Pioneer Square. A vintage trolley runs the length of the waterfront before turning inland and continuing on to Pioneer Square and the International District (*see below*).

❻ At the base of the Pike Street Hillclimb at Pier 59 is the **Seattle Aquarium,** showcasing Northwest marine life. The Discovery Lab offers visitors a chance to see baby barnacles, minute jellyfish, and other "invisible" creatures through high-resolution video microscopes. The Tide Pool exhibit re-creates Washington's rocky coast and sandy beaches at low tide; there's even a 6,000-gallon wave that sweeps in over the underwater life—spectators standing close by may get damp from the simulated sea spray. Sea otters and seals swim and dive in their pools, and the "State of the Sound" exhibit shows the aquatic life and ecology of Puget Sound. *Pier 59, ☎ 206/386–4320. ☛ $6.95 adults, $5.50 senior citizens, $4.50 children 6–18, $2.25 children 3–5; call for group rates. ⊙ Daily 10–5, 10–8 in summer.*

❼ Next to the aquarium is the **Omnidome Film Experience,** where short films on such subjects as the eruption of Mt. St. Helens, mountain gorillas, and the Great Barrier Reef play on a large curved screen. *Pier 59, ☎ 206/622–1868. ☛ $6 adults, $5 senior citizens and youths 13–18, $4 children 3–12; call for prices of combination tickets to the Omnidome and aquarium. ⊙ Daily 10–5.*

North of the aquarium, at Pier 66 along Alaskan Way, is the site of the **Odyssey Contemporary Maritime Museum,** scheduled to open in

14

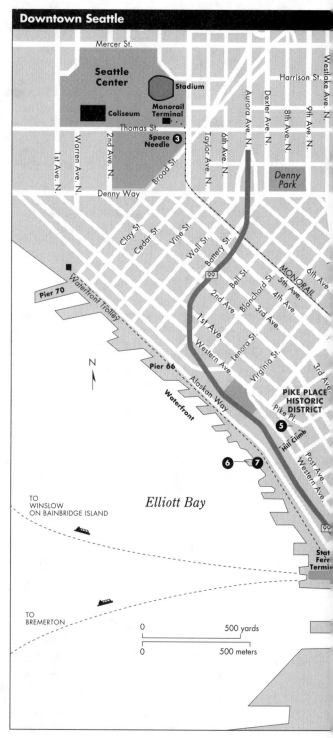

Downtown Seattle

Mercer St.

Seattle Center

Stadium

Harrison St.

Coliseum

Monorail Terminal

Thomas St.

Space Needle ❸

Broad St.

Denny Park

Denny Way

Westlake Ave. N.
Aurora Ave. N.
Dexter Ave. N.
8th Ave. N.
9th Ave. N.
6th Ave. N.
Taylor Ave. N.
2nd Ave. N.
1st Ave. N.
Warren Ave. N.

Clay St.
Cedar St.
Vine St.
Wall St.
Battery St.

Pier 70

Waterfront Trolley

99

Bell St.

Blanchard St.

2nd Ave.
3rd Ave.
4th Ave.
5th Ave.

MONORAIL

6th Ave.

Lenora St.

Virginia St.

1st Ave.
Western Ave.

N

Pier 66

Alaskan Way

Waterfront

PIKE PLACE HISTORIC DISTRICT

Pike Pl.

❺

Hill Climb

Post Ave.
Western Ave.

❻ ❼

3rd Ave.

Elliott Bay

TO WINSLOW ON BAINBRIDGE ISLAND

99

State Ferry Terminal

TO BREMERTON

0   500 yards

0   500 meters

1996–97. This new center will feature cultural and educational maritime exhibits on Puget Sound and ocean trade, and offer visitors tours of ships and boats docked nearby. The development will also include a conference center, short-stay boat basin, fish-processing and fisheries-support terminals, and a restaurant.

Catch the waterfront trolley in front of the aquarium and ride it three stops to the area now known as **Pioneer Square.** Two blocks north of the trolley line, at the corner of 1st Avenue and Yesler Way, an ornate iron-and-glass pergola stands in **Pioneer Park.** This was the site of the pier and sawmill owned by Henry Yesler, one of Seattle's first businessmen. Timber logged off the hills was sent to the sawmill on a "skid road"—now Yesler Way—made of small logs laid crossways and greased so that the freshly cut trees would slide down to the mill. The area grew into Seattle's first business center; in 1889, a fire destroyed many of the district's wood-frame buildings, but the industrious residents and businesspeople rebuilt them with brick and mortar.

With the 1897 Klondike gold rush, however, this area became populated with saloons and brothels; businesses gradually moved north, and the old pioneering area deteriorated. Eventually, only drunks and bums hung out in the neighborhood that had become known as Skid Row, and the name became synonymous with "down and out." Today's Pioneer Square encompasses about 18 blocks and includes restaurants, bars, shops, and the city's largest concentration of art galleries, but it is once again known as a hangout for those down on their luck. Incidents of crime in the neighborhood have increased lately, especially after dark.

If you'd like to know more about the city's pioneer days, visit the interpretive center of the **Klondike Gold Rush National Historical Park,** near the trolley stop on Main Street. The center provides insight into the story of Seattle's role in the 1897–98 gold rush through film presentations, permanent exhibits, and gold-panning demonstrations. *117 S. Main St.,* ☎ *206/553–7220.* ☛ *Free.* ⊙ *Daily 9–5; closed major holidays.*

Half a block east on Main Street, and two blocks south on Occidental Avenue, is the **Kingdome,** where the Seattle Seahawks NFL team and the Seattle Mariners baseball team play. The 650-foot-diameter covered stadium was built in 1976 and has the world's largest self-supporting roof, which sits 250 feet high. If you're interested in the inner workings, take the one-hour guided tour offered in summer. *201 S. King St.,* ☎ *206/296–3663 for information.* ☛ *Tour: $4 adults, $2 senior citizens and children.*

To the east is a 40-square-block area known as the **International District** (the ID), as about ⅓ of the area's residents are Chinese, ⅓ are Filipino, and another ⅓ come from elsewhere in Asia. The ID began as a haven for Chinese workers who had immigrated to the United States to work on the Transcontinental Railroad. The community has remained largely intact despite anti-Chinese riots in Seattle during the 1880s and the internment of Japanese-Americans during World War II.

The district, which includes many Chinese, Japanese, and Korean restaurants, also houses herbalists, massage parlors, acupuncturists, and about 30 private clubs for gambling and socializing. The most notorious club is the **Wah Mee Club,** on Canton Avenue, where a multiple murder linked to gangs and gambling occurred in 1983. You'll find **Uwajimaya** (519 6th Ave. S, ☎ 206/624–6248), one of the—if not *the*—largest Japanese stores on the West Coast, on the corner of 6th Avenue

South and King Street; besides housing a complete supermarket with an array of Asian foods, the store carries a wide selection of affordable china, gifts, fabrics, and housewares.

TIME OUT   If you need to rest your feet a bit by now, stop in at **Okazuya** (519 6th Ave. S, ☎ 206/624–6248), the Asian snack bar in Uwajimaya. You can get noodle dishes, sushi, tempura, *humbow,* and other Asian dishes for carry-out or to eat in.

From Uwajimaya, continue east on King Street to 7th Avenue and turn
⑫ left. The final stop on your downtown Seattle tour will be at the **Wing Luke Museum,** named for the first Asian person to be elected to a Seattle city office, where you'll find displays on various aspects of Asian history and culture. An acupuncture exhibit demonstrates how needles are inserted into parts of the body to release blocked energy and promote healing. Other elements of the permanent collection include costumes, fabrics, crafts, basketry, and Chinese traditional medicines. *407 7th Ave. S, ☎ 206/623–5124. ☛ $2.50 adults, $1.50 senior citizens and students, 75¢ children. ☉ Tues.–Fri. 11–4:30, weekends noon–4.*

Tour 2: North of Downtown

Numbers in the margin correspond to points of interest on the Northern Seattle map.

North of downtown Seattle are a number of attractions that juxtapose the natural world with the urban—from landscaped gardens and a working fish ladder to a habitat zoo and a natural-history museum. From downtown follow Elliott Avenue (which runs along the waterfront from just north of Pike Place Market) north until it turns into 15th Avenue West; continue on 15th over the Ballard Bridge to Northwest Market Street. Turn left on Market and continue until it jogs to the left and turns into Northwest 54th Street.

Here you'll find the Hiram M. Chittenden Locks, more commonly called
★ ① the **Ballard Locks,** part of the 8-mile Lake Washington Ship Canal linking lakes Washington and Union with the salt water of Shilshole Bay and Puget Sound. Completed in 1917, the locks currently service some 100,000 boats yearly by raising and lowering water levels anywhere from 6 to 26 feet. On the north side of the locks is a fine 7-acre **ornamental garden** of native and exotic plants, shrubs, and trees. Also on the north side are a staffed visitor center with displays on the history and operation of the locks and several fanciful sculptures by local artists. Along the south side is a lovely 1,200-foot promenade with a footbridge, fishing pier, and an observation deck.

Take some time to watch the fascinating progress of fishing boats and pleasure craft through the locks, then check out how the marine population makes the same journey from saltwater to fresh: The **fish ladder** has 21 levels that allow fish to swim upstream on a gradual incline. Several seaquarium-like viewing rooms run alongside the ladder below the waterline and allow visitors to watch various types of salmon and trout—an estimated half million fish yearly—struggle against the current as they migrate upstream to their spawning grounds. Most of the migration takes place from late June through October. (The fish ladder, by the way, is where various attempts are being carried out to prevent sea lions, including the locally notorious Herschel, from depleting the salmon population.) *North entrance, 3015 N.W. 54th St., Locks ☎ 206/783–7001, visitor center ☎ 206/783–7059. ☉ Locks: year-*

Northern Seattle

round, dawn–dusk; visitor center: summer, daily 10–7; winter, Thurs.–Mon. 11–5; call for info on tours.

Head back east on N.W. Market Street, past 15th Avenue Northwest, to Phinney Avenue North, and turn left. At North 55th Street, you'll find the west gate of the 92-acre **Woodland Park Zoo,** where many of the animals roam free in climate-specific habitat areas. The African savanna, the elephant house, and the tropical rain forest are particularly interesting. Wheelchairs and strollers can be rented. *5500 Phinney Ave. N,* ☎ *206/684–4800.* ☛ *$7 adults, $5.25 senior citizens and students, $4.50 children 6–17, $2.25 children 3–5.* ☼ *Summer, daily 9:30–6; winter, daily 10–4.*

From the Woodland Park Zoo, follow Phinney south to North Market Street and turn left. Take Market east for 2 miles as it crosses Highway 99 (Aurora Ave. N), becomes N. 45th Street, and crosses I–5. A few blocks east of 15th Avenue Northeast is the entrance to the 33,500-student **University of Washington.** Founded in 1861, the university is familiarly known as U-Dub.

On the northwestern corner of the beautifully landscaped campus is the **Thomas Burke Memorial Washington State Museum,** Washington's natural-history and anthropological museum. The museum features exhibits on cultures of the Pacific region and the state's 35 Native American tribes. *17th Ave. NE and N.E. 45th St.,* ☎ *206/543–5590.* ☛ *Free (donation requested).* ☼ *Daily 10–5 (Thurs. until 8).*

Going south, on the west side of the campus is the **Henry Art Gallery,** which displays paintings from the 19th and 20th centuries, textiles, and traveling exhibits. The museum was closed at press time for remodeling and expansion, but is scheduled to reopen in early 1997. *15th Ave. NE and N.E. 41st St.,* ☎ *206/543–2280.*

South of the channel linking Portage and Union bays, off Montlake and Lake Washington boulevards, is the **Museum of History and Industry.** An 1880s-era room and a Seattle time line depict the city's earlier days. Other displays from the permanent collection are shown on a rotating basis, along with traveling exhibits. *2700 24th Ave. E,* ☎ *206/324–1125.* ☛ *$5.50 adults, $3.50 senior citizens and children 6–12.* ☉ *Daily 10–5.*

At the museum pick up a brochure of self-guided walking tours of the nearby **Washington Park Arboretum.** The arboretum's Rhododendron Glen and Azalea Way are in full bloom from March through June. During the rest of the year, other plants and wildlife flourish. A visitor center at the north end of the park is open to instruct you on the species of flora and fauna you'll see here. *2300 Arboretum Dr. E,* ☎ *206/325–4510.* ☛ *Free.* ☉ *Park: daily 7 AM–sunset; visitor center: weekdays 10–4, weekends noon–4.*

On the Trail of Ale

A visit to a brew pub—as drinking establishments attached to actual breweries are called—is a congenial and educational alternative to usual city attractions. Seattle, as well as a good portion of the Pacific Northwest, has become a hotbed for microbrews, high-quality beers made for local distribution. All the pubs listed below also serve food and nonalcoholic beverages. If live music is performed, a cover charge may be required; otherwise admission is free.

The **Pacific Northwest Brewing Co.,** located in the heart of Pioneer Square, offers six mild beers that reflect the taste of its British owner. The elegantly decorated interior—a smooth high-tech design, with antiques and brewing equipment in full view—fits not only the personality of proprietor Richard Wrigley, but the upscale downtown location as well. *322 Occidental Ave. S,* ☎ *206/621–7002.* ☉ *Tues.–Fri. 11:30 AM–midnight, Sat. 10:30–2 AM, Sun. 11 AM–9 PM.*

The **Trolleyman,** found near the north end of the Fremont Bridge, 8 miles from downtown, is the birthplace of local favorites Ballard Bitter and Red Hook Ale. The pub mixes Northwest style—whitewashed walls and a no-smoking policy—with a cozy atmosphere that includes a fireplace and ample armchairs. Redhook Brewery is right next door—take a 45-minute tour for $1 before you pop in for a pint. *3400 Phinney Ave. N,* ☎ *206/548–8000.* ☉ *Mon.–Thurs. 8:30 AM–11 PM, Fri. 8:30 AM–midnight, Sat. 11 AM–midnight, Sun. noon–7; call for tour times.*

Big Time Brewery caters to the nearby university crowd and resembles an archetypal college-town pub, what with a moose head on the wall and bits of vintage memorabilia scattered about. Pale ale, amber, and porter are always on tap; specialty brews change monthly. *4133 University Way NE,* ☎ *206/545–4509.* ☉ *Daily 11:30 AM–1 AM.*

While technically not a brew pub, **Cooper's Northwest Alehouse,** located north of the University District, nonetheless deserves mention for featuring the products of so many regional microbreweries. Its stock of more than 20 brews comes from all over the West Coast, and the staff is incredibly knowledgeable about the subtle distinctions between each brew. If you don't come for the drink, come for the dart tournaments that are played on a regular basis. *8065 Lake City Way NE,* ☎

206/522–2923. ✆ *Weekdays 3* PM*–2* AM*, Sat. 1* PM*–2* AM*, Sun. 1*
PM*–midnight.*

Around Town: Wine, Wings, and Hallowed Ground

If your preference is for the grape, not the hop, visit **Ste. Michelle Winery,** one of the oldest wineries in the state. It's located 15 miles northeast of Seattle, nestled on 87 wooded acres that were once part of the estate of lumber baron Fred Stimson. Some of the original 1912 buildings are still on the property, including the family home—the manor house—which is on the National Register of Historic Places. Trout ponds, a carriage house, a caretaker's cottage, and formal gardens are part of the original estate. The landscaping, created by New York's Olmsted family (designers of New York City's Central Park), has been restored, and the gardens feature hundreds of trees, shrubs, and plants. Visitors are invited to picnic and explore the grounds. Delicatessen items, wines, and wine-related gifts are available at the winery shop. In the summer, the company hosts a series of nationally known performers and arts events in the amphitheater. *14111 N.E. 145th St., Woodinville,* ✆ *206/488–1133. From downtown Seattle take I–90 east, then go north on I–405. Take Exit 23 east (S.R. 522) to the Woodinville exit. Complimentary wine tastings and cellar tours available daily 10–4:30, except holidays.*

Pilot your way to **Boeing Field** for a fascinating look at the world of aviation. As Boeing, the world's largest builder of airplanes, is based
★ in Seattle, it's not surprising that the **Museum of Flight** is one of the city's best museums. The Red Barn, Boeing's original airplane factory, houses an exhibit on the history of human flight. The Great Gallery, a dramatic structure designed by Seattle architect Ibsen Nelson, contains more than 20 vintage airplanes—suspended from the ceiling and on the ground—dating from the Wright brothers to the jet era. *9404 E. Marginal Way S (take I–5 south to exit 158; turn right on Marginal),* ✆ *206/764–5720.* ✒ *Museum: $6 adults and senior citizens, $3 children 6–15.* ✆ *Daily 10–5 (Thurs. until 9).*

Two legendary performers—rock guitarist Jimi Hendrix and kung-fu movie star Bruce Lee—are buried in the Seattle area. Their graves are popular sites with fans who wish to pay their respects. In addition, there is a memorial to Hendrix, a Seattle native, overlooking the African savanna exhibit at Woodland Park Zoo; appropriately enough, it's a big rock.

Jimi Hendrix's grave site is at the Greenwood Cemetery, in Renton. *From Seattle, take I–5 south to Renton exit, then I–405 past Southcenter to Exit 4B. Bear right under freeway, take right along Sunset Blvd. 1 block and right again up 3rd St. Continue 1 mi and go right at 3rd light; cemetery is on the corner of 3rd and Monroe Sts.,* ✆ *206/255–1511.* ✆ *Daily until dusk. Inquire at the office; a counselor will direct you to the site.*

Bruce Lee's grave site is at the Lakeview Cemetery on the north slope of Capitol Hill. *1554 15th Ave. E, directly north of Volunteer Park,* ✆ *206/322–1582.* ✆ *Weekdays 9–4:30. Inquire at the office for a map.*

What to See and Do with Children

Burke-Gilman Trail (*see* Sports and the Outdoors, *below*) offers good bike trails for children.

Elliott Bay Book Company (*see* Books *in* Shopping, *below*) hosts a children's story hour at 11 AM on the first Saturday of the month.

Green Lake (*see* Sports and the Outdoors, *below*).

Museum of Flight (*see* Around Town, *above*).

Myrtle Edwards Park (*see* Sports and the Outdoors, *below*).

Seattle Aquarium (*see* Tour 1, *above*).

Seattle Children's Museum has tripled its colorful, spacious facility at the Seattle Center's Center House. A global village introduces children to everything from housing and shops to cooking pots and clothing from areas of Ghana, Japan, and the Philippines. The mountain wilderness poking up through one level of the museum educates kids about climbing, camping, and the Northwest environment and features a slide and waterfall. Cog City is a giant maze of pipes and pulleys. The pretend neighborhood provides a post office, café, fire station, grocery store, and more for imaginative play. An infant/toddler area is well padded for climbing and sliding. A large arts-and-crafts area, special exhibits, and workshops are also offered. *Fountain level of Seattle Center House, 305 Harrison St.,* ☎ *206/441–1768.* ☛ *$3.50 adults and children.* ⊙ *Tues.–Sun. 10–5.*

Seattle Children's Theatre performs in the $10 million Charlotte Martin Theatre, which opened in the fall of 1993, and the more intimate 280-seat Eve Alvord Theatre, which opened in 1995. SCT, the second-largest resident, professional children's theater company in the United States, has developed a national reputation for its high-quality and innovative productions and has commissioned more than 55 new plays, adaptations, and musicals, many of which have gone on to be produced by theater companies across the nation. Their season runs September–June. *Charlotte Martin Theatre at Seattle Center, Box 9640, 2nd Ave. N and Thomas St.,* ☎ *206/441–3322.*

Thomas Burke Memorial Washington State Museum (*see* Tour 2, *above*).

SHOPPING

Shopping Districts

Broadway Avenue (between E. Roy and E. Pine Sts.) in the Capitol Hill neighborhood is lined with clothing stores selling new and vintage threads, high-design housewares shops, espresso bars, and restaurants. Look for the brass dance steps inlaid on the street corners.

Fremont Avenue, around its intersection with North 35th Street, north of the ship canal and the Fremont Bridge, offers products of a used and funky variety. At Armadillo & Co. (3510 Fremont Ave. N, ☎ 206/633–4241), you'll find jewelry, T-shirts, and other armadillo-theme accessories and gifts. The Daily Planet (3416 Fremont Ave. N, ☎ 206/633–0895) carries vintage everything—jewelry, furniture, clothing, rugs, and so on. Dusty Strings (3406 Fremont Ave. N, ☎ 206/634–1656) is a hammered dulcimer shop. The Frank & Dunya Gallery (3418 Fremont Ave. N, ☎ 206/547–6760) features unique art pieces, from furniture to jewelry. Guess Where (615 N. 35th St., ☎ 206/547–3793) stocks vintage men's and women's clothing and antiques.

Pike Place Market (*see* Tour 1 *in* Exploring, *above*).

University Way Northeast, called "the Ave" between Northeast 41st and Northeast 50th streets in the University District, has a few upscale shops, many bookstores, and an eclectic mixture of such student-oriented imports as ethnic jewelry and South American sweaters.

Malls and Shopping Centers

Bellevue Square, an upscale shopping center about 8 miles east of Seattle, houses more than 200 shops and includes a children's play area, the Bellevue Art Museum, and covered parking. *N.E. 8th St. and Bellevue Way,* ☎ *206/454–8096.* ☉ *Mon.–Sat. 9:30–9:30, Sun. 11–6.*

Northgate Mall, 10 miles north of downtown, encompasses 118 shops, including Nordstrom's, The Bon, Lamonts, and JCPenney. *I–5 and Northgate Way,* ☎ *206/362–4777.* ☉ *Mon.–Sat. 9:30–9:30, Sun. 11–6.*

Southcenter Mall contains 140 shops and is anchored by major department stores. *I–5 and I–405 in Tukwila,* ☎ *206/246–7400.* ☉ *Mon.–Sat. 9:30–9:30, Sun. 11–6.*

Westlake Center lies in the middle of downtown Seattle. The three-story steel-and-glass building contains 80 upscale shops, as well as covered walkways to Seattle's two major department stores, Nordstrom's and The Bon. *1601 5th Ave.,* ☎ *206/467–1600.* ☉ *Weekdays 9:30–9, Sat. 9:30–8, Sun. 11–6.*

Specialty Shops

Antiques
Antique Importers (640 Alaskan Way, ☎ 206/628–8905), a large warehouselike structure, carries mostly English oak and Victorian pine antiques.

Art Dealers
Michael Pierce Gallery (600 Pine St., ☎ 206/447–9166) specializes in limited-edition prints, oil paintings and paintings on paper.

Art Glass
The **Glass House** (311 Occidental Ave. S, ☎ 206/682–9939), Seattle's only working glass studio open for public viewing, features one of the largest displays of glass artwork in the city.

Books and Maps
The **Elliott Bay Book Company** (101 S. Main St., at 1st Ave. in Pioneer Sq., ☎ 206/624–6600), besides boasting a comprehensive selection of titles, hosts lectures and readings by authors of local and international acclaim. Most such events are free, but phone ahead to be sure.
M. Coy Books (117 Pine St., between 1st and 2nd Aves., ☎ 206/623–5354), in the heart of downtown, carries a large selection of contemporary literature and has a small espresso bar to boot.
Metsker Maps (702 1st Ave., ☎ 206/623–8747), on the edge of Pioneer Square, has a range of regional maps.
Wide World Books and Maps (1911 N. 45th St., ☎ 206/634–3453), north of downtown and west of the university in the Wallingford neighborhood, carries travel books and the city's best selection of maps.

Chocolates
Cafe Dilettante (416 Broadway Ave. E, ☎ 206/329–6463) is well-known for its mouthwatering dark chocolates. Recipes come via Julius Rudolf Franzen, who obtained them from the kitchen of the imperial

court of Russia when he was commissioned by Czar Nicholas II as master pastry chef. Franzen emigrated to the United States where he passed his recipes on to the grandfather of Cafe Dilettante's owner.

Clothing

Boutique Europa (1015 1st Ave., ☎ 206/624–5582) features sophisticated women's apparel from Europe.

Littler's (Rainier Sq., ☎ 206/223–1331) offers classic fashions for women.

Local Brilliance (1535 1st Ave., ☎ 206/343–5864) showcases fashions from local designers.

Mario's (1513 6th Ave., ☎ 206/223–1461) offers a wide selection of contemporary menswear.

Crafts

Flying Shuttle Ltd. (607 1st Ave., ☎ 206/343–9762) displays handcrafted jewelry, whimsical folk art, handknits, and handwoven garments.

Pike Place Market (*see* Tour 1 *in* Exploring, *above*).

Jewelry

Fireworks Gallery (210 1st Ave. S, ☎ 206/682–8707; 400 Pine St., ☎ 206/682–6462) features whimsical earrings and pins.

Leather and Luggage

Bergman Luggage Co. (1930 3rd Ave., ☎ 206/448–3000) carries luggage in a variety of prices and materials.

Outdoor Wear and Equipment

Eddie Bauer (5th Ave. and Union St., ☎ 206/622–2766) features sports and outdoor apparel.

Recreational Equipment, Inc. (1525 11th Ave., between E. Pike and E. Pine Sts., ☎ 206/323–8333)—which everybody calls REI—sells clothing and such outdoor equipment as water bottles, tents, bikes, and freeze-dried food in a creaky, funky building on Capitol Hill; they also rent camping and climbing gear.

Toys

Great Windup (Pike Place Market, ☎ 206/621–9370) carries all sorts of windup action toys.

Magic Mouse Toys (603 1st Ave., ☎ 206/682–8097) has two floors of toys, from small windups to giant stuffed animals.

Wine

Delaurenti Wine Shop (1435 1st Ave., ☎ 206/340–1498) has a knowledgeable staff and a large selection of Northwest Italian–style wines.

Pike & Western Wine Merchants (Pike Pl. and Virginia St., ☎ 206/441–1307 or 206/441–1308) carries a wide selection of Northwest wines from small wineries.

SPORTS AND THE OUTDOORS

Participant Sports

"The best things in life are free" is a homily that holds true, at least in part, when it comes to keeping fit in this most health-oriented of cities. Walking, bicycling, hiking, and jogging require little money; pay-as-you-go alternatives such as golf, kayak, sailboat, or sailboard rentals require only marginally more.

REI (1525 11th Ave., ☎ 206/323–8333), the largest consumer co-op in the United States and Seattle's outdoor-equipment store *ne plus ultra,* hosts free programs on travel, adventure, and outdoor activities every Thursday at 7 PM. Various suburban locations have programs on other nights; call the main branch for times and details.

Bicycling

Although much of Seattle is so hilly that recreational bicycling is strenuous, many residents nonetheless commute by bike. The trail circling **Green Lake** and the **Burke-Gilman Trail** are popular among recreational bicyclists, although at Green Lake the crowds of joggers and walkers tend to impede fast travel. The Burke-Gilman Trail is a city-maintained trail extending 12.1 miles along Seattle's waterfront from Lake Washington nearly to Salmon Bay along an abandoned railroad line; it is a much less congested path. **Myrtle Edwards Park,** north of Pier 70, has a two-lane path for jogging and bicycling. For general information about Seattle's parks and trails, call the Seattle Parks and Recreation Department (☎ 206/684–4075).

A number of shops around Seattle rent mountain bikes as well as standard touring or racing bikes and equipment. Among them are **Greg's Greenlake Cycle** (7007 Woodlawn Ave. NE, ☎ 206/523–1822) and **Mountain Bike Specialists** (5625 University Way NE, ☎ 206/527–4310).

Boating and Sailboarding

With so much water, it stands to reason that sailboating and power-boating are popular in Seattle. **Sailboat Rentals & Yachts** (301 N. Northlake Way, ☎ 206/632–3302), on the north side of Lake Union near the Fremont area, rents sailboats, with or without skippers, 14–38 feet in length, by the hour or the day. **Seacrest Boat House** (1660 Harbor Ave. SW, ☎ 206/932–1050), in West Seattle, rents 18-foot aluminum fishing boats, with or without motors, by the hour or the day. **Wind Works Rentals** (7001 Seaview Ave. NW, ☎ 206/784–9386), on Shilshole Bay, rents sailboats ranging from 27 to 42 feet on the more challenging waters of Puget Sound, with or without skippers and by the half day, day, or week. Lake Union and Green Lake are Seattle's prime sailboarding spots. Sailboards can be rented year-round at **Urban Surf** (2100 N. Northlake Way, ☎ 206/545–9463) on Lake Union. Lessons are available.

Fishing

There are plenty of good spots for fishing on Lake Washington, Green Lake, and Lake Union, and there are several fishing piers along the Elliott Bay waterfront. A number of companies operating from Shilshole Bay also offer charter trips for catching salmon, rock cod, flounder, and sea bass. A couple of the many Seattle-based charter companies are **Ballard Salmon Charter** (☎ 206/789–6202) and **Argosy** (☎ 206/623–4253). A two-day fishing license costs $3.50, and some charter companies include it in their charges.

Golf

There are almost 50 public golf courses in the Seattle area. Among the most popular municipally run courses are **Jackson Park** (1000 N.E. 135th St., ☎ 206/363–4747) and **Jefferson Park** (4101 Beacon Ave. S, ☎ 206/762–4513). For more information, contact the **Seattle Parks and Recreation Department** (☎ 206/684–4075).

Jogging, Skating, and Walking

Green Lake is far and away Seattle's most popular spot for jogging, and the 3-mile circumference of this picturesque lake is custom-made for it. Walking, bicycling, roller-skating, fishing, and lounging on the grass and feeding the plentiful waterfowl are also popular pastimes here. In summer, a large children's wading pool on the northeast side of the lake is a popular gathering spot. Several outlets clustered along the east side of the lake offer skate and cycle rentals.

Other good jogging locales are along the **Burke-Gilman Trail,** around the reservoir at **Volunteer Park,** and at **Myrtle Edwards Park,** north of the waterfront.

Kayaking

Kayaking—around both the inner waterways (Lake Union, Lake Washington, the Ship Canal) and open water (Elliott Bay)—is a terrific and easy way to get an unusual view of Seattle's busy waterfront. The **Northwest Outdoor Center** (2100 Westlake Ave. N, ☎ 206/281–9694), on the west side of Lake Union, rents one-or two-person kayaks and equipment by the hour or week and provides both basic and advanced instruction. Canoes and rowing shells are also available.

Skiing

Snoqualmie Pass in the Cascade Mountains, about an hour's drive east of Seattle on I–90, has a number of fine resorts offering both day and night downhill skiing. Among them: **Alpental, Ski Acres, Snoqualmie Summit** (for all areas: 3010 77th St. SE, Mercer Island 98040, ☎ 206/232–8182). All these areas rent equipment and have full restaurant and lodge facilities.

For ski reports for these areas and the more distant White Pass, Crystal Mountain, and Stevens Pass, call ☎ 206/634–0200 or ☎ 206/634–2754. For recorded messages about road conditions in the passes, call ☎ 206/455–7900.

Tennis

There are public tennis courts in many parks around the Seattle area. For information, contact the **King County Parks and Recreation Department** (☎ 206/296–4258).

Spectator Sports

Baseball

The **Seattle Mariners,** an American-league team, play April through early October at the Kingdome (201 S. King St., ☎ 206/628–3555).

Basketball

The NBA's **Seattle SuperSonics** play October through April at the Seattle Center Coliseum (1st Ave. N, ☎ 206/281–5850).

Boat Racing

The **unlimited hydroplane** (☎ 206/628–0888) races cap Seattle's Seafair festivities from mid-July through the first Sunday in August. The races are held on Lake Washington near Seward Park, and tickets cost $10–$20. Weekly **sailing regattas** are held in the summer on Lakes Union and Washington. Call the Seattle Yacht Club (☎ 206/325–1000) for schedules.

Football

Seattle's NFL team, the **Seahawks,** play August through December in the Kingdome (201 S. King St., ☎ 206/827–9777).

DINING

The abundance of fresh seafood and produce available in the Seattle area, as well as the wines and beers produced by local vineyards and microbreweries, has created a city with a deep appreciation of good food and drink. Additionally, Seattle's Pacific Rim location has resulted in a strong Asian influence on the city's cuisine—traditionally in the many Chinese and Japanese restaurants to be found in the International District and, more recently, in the innovative use of Asian ingredients and cooking techniques in kitchens throughout the city.

CATEGORY	COST*
$$$$	over $35
$$$	$25–$35
$$	$15–$25
$	under $15

per person for a three-course meal, excluding drinks, service, and sales tax (about 7.9%, varies slightly by community)

American/Continental

$$$$ **Canlis.** This sumptuous restaurant is a Seattle institution, dating as it
★ does from a time when steak served by kimono-clad waitresses was the pinnacle of high living in the city by the sound. Little has changed here since the '50s. The restaurant is still very expensive, very good at what it does, and very popular. The view across Lake Union is as good as ever (though curtained off by a forest of recently built high-rises on the far shore). Besides the famous steaks, there are equally famous oysters from Quilcene Bay and fresh fish in season, cooked to a turn. ✕ *2576 Aurora Ave. N, ☎ 206/283–3313. Reservations advised. Jacket required. AE, DC, MC, V. Closed Sun. No lunch.*

$$ **Metropolitan Grill.** This favorite lunch spot of the white-collar crowd serves custom-aged, mesquite-broiled steaks in a classic steak-house atmosphere. Meals here are not for timid eaters: The steaks—the best in Seattle—are huge and come with baked potatoes or pasta, and even the veal chop is extra thick. You will also find lamb, veal, chicken, and seafood entrées. Among the accompaniments, the onion rings and sautéed mushrooms are tops. ✕ *818 2nd Ave., ☎ 206/624–3287. Reservations advised. AE, DC, MC, V. No lunch weekends.*

Asian

$$ **Wild Ginger.** This restaurant near the Pike Place Market specializes in
★ seafood and Southeast Asian fare, ranging from mild Cantonese to spicier Vietnamese, Thai, and Korean dishes. House specialties include *satay* (chunks of beef, chicken, or vegetables skewered and grilled, and usually served with a spicy peanut sauce), live crab, sweetly flavored duck, and a variety of wonderful soups. A number of vegetarian dishes are also offered. The satay bar, where you can sip local brews and eat tangy, elegantly seasoned skewered tidbits until 2 AM, has quickly become a favorite local hangout. The clubby, old-fashioned dining room has high ceilings and is decorated with lots of mahogany and Asian art. ✕ *1400 Western Ave., ☎ 206/623–4450. Reservations advised. AE, DC, MC, V. No lunch Sun.*

Chinese

$$ **Linyen.** This comfortable restaurant comes into its own late at night, when Seattle celebrities come to mingle with chefs from Chinatown restaurants. The standard fare is light-style Cantonese, but you're best off sticking with the blackboard specials: clams in black-bean sauce, spicy chicken, geoduck (a large local clam), and fish dishes. The dart games in the bar are a popular—and heated—diversion. ✕ *424 7th Ave. S, ☎ 206/622–8181. Reservations advised. AE, DC, MC, V.*

$ Chau's Chinese Restaurant. This small, very plain place on the outer limits of Seattle's International District serves great seafood, such as steamed oysters in garlic sauce, Dungeness crab with ginger and onion, and geoduck. Avoid the standard Cantonese dishes, and stick to the seafood and specials. ✕ *310 4th Ave. S,* ☎ *206/621–0006. Reservations advised. MC, V. No lunch weekends.*

Deli

$ A. Jay's. Breakfast is the big draw here—on weekend mornings, people come in droves for the eggs Benedict, blintzes, whitefish, and bagels piled high with cream cheese and lox. At lunch there are large sandwiches (try the pastrami), pasta, burgers, and soup. Service is friendly, and you can sit and chat without being rushed. ✕ *2619 1st Ave.,* ☎ *206/441–1511. Reservations advised. AE, MC, V. No dinner.*

$ Three Girls Bakery. This 13-seat glassed-in lunch counter tucked behind a bakery outlet serves sandwiches, soups, and pastries to hungry folks in a hurry. Go for the chili and a hunk of Sicilian sourdough, or buy a loaf at the take-out counter, get smoked salmon at the fish place next door, and head for a picnic table in Waterfront Park. ✕ *Pike Place Market, 1514 Pike Pl.,* ☎ *206/622–1045. No reservations. No credit cards. Closed Sun. No dinner.*

Eclectic

$$ Marco's Supper Club. Multiregional cuisine is the specialty of this one-time tavern, now a casual, fun place with shrimp-color walls and mismatched flatware. Start with the fried sage-leaf appetizer with garlic aioli and salsa, than move on to Moroccan lamb, Jamaican jerk chicken, or a drunken pork loin marinated in juniper berries and served with sautéed greens and mashed potatoes. ✕ *2510 1st Ave.,* ☎ *206/441–7801. Reservations advised. AE, MC, V. No lunch Sat.*

French

$$$ Campagne. Overlooking Pike Place Market and Elliott Bay, Cam-
★ pagne is intimate and urbane. White walls, picture windows, snowy linens, candles, and fresh flowers evoke Provence, as does the menu—French cuisine here means the robust flavors of the Midi, not the more polished tastes of Paris. Dishes traditionally flavored with cream and butter are instead sauced with vegetable essences, oils, or light stocks. To start, try Campagne's own seafood sausage or the calamari fillets with ground almonds. Main plates include such flavorful treats as pan-fried scallops with a green-peppercorn and tarragon sauce, cinnamon-roasted quail served with carrot and orange essence, and Oregon rabbit accompanied by an apricot-cider and green-peppercorn sauce. The wine list includes French country varietals not readily available at other Seattle restaurants. Campagne is open only for dinner, but the nearby Cafe Campagne serves breakfast and lunch daily. ✕ *Inn at the Market, 86 Pine St.,* ☎ *206/728–2800. Reservations advised. Jacket required. AE, MC, V. No lunch.*

$$ Rover's. This is French cooking at its best, with a daily menu based on ingredients that are fresh and locally available. Specialties include salmon, pheasant, quail, venison, and rabbit in elegant yet surprisingly light sauces. The enormous pasta dishes are among Seattle's best. Each of the dishes carries chef-owner Thierry Rautureau's Northwest-French stylings. The setting is highly romantic, in a small house with a garden and herbs and flowers growing in beds just outside the windows. Service is excellent—friendly but unobtrusive. ✕ *2808 E. Madison St.,*

30

☎ *206/325–7442. Reservations advised. AE, MC, V. Closed Sun.–Mon. No lunch.*

Georgian

$$–$$$ **Pirosmani.** Named for folk painter Niko Pirosmani, this restaurant resides in a 1906 house on Queen Anne Hill. The Georgian offerings are notable for their innovative use of herbs and lack of heavy sauces: Duck is seared, then braised with coriander and savory. Lamb is skewered; grilled with basil, garlic, and cilantro; and served with a plum sauce. Other entrées have their origins on the shores of the Mediterranean—North Africa, the south of France. The signature dessert is a walnut-date rosewater tart, but you wouldn't go wrong with the baklava-ricotta cheesecake either. ✕ *2220 Queen Anne Ave. N, ☎ 206/285–3360. Reservations advised. AE, MC, V. Closed Sun.–Mon. No lunch.*

Indian

$$ **Raga.** The aromas of cardamon, cumin, and jasmine wafting through the air may make you feel like you've been transported to another continent entirely, but along with a sister restaurant, Dawat, in Vancouver, Raga offers some of the best East Indian cuisine in the Northwest. Mouthwatering dishes include *shahee panner* (cheese in a mildly spiced cream sauce) and *matar panner* (green peas with a homemade cottage cheese). Be sure to order a selection of various breads—nan, roti, *paratha, kulcha*—to accompany your meal. ✕ *555 108th Ave. NE, Bellevue, ☎ 206/450–0336. Reservations advised. MC, V. No lunch Sun.*

Italian

$$$ **Il Terrazo Carmine.** On the ground floor of a Pioneer Square office building, this restaurant owes its comfortable but refined atmosphere to ceiling-to-floor draperies, genteel service, and quiet music. Chef-owner Carmine Smeraldo prepares flavorful chicken dishes with prosciutto and fontina, and his veal baked with spinach and scallops is simply excellent. The pasta dishes, too, are superb. In the summer, you can choose to eat outdoors on the patio that faces a large fountain. ✕ *411 1st Ave. S, ☎ 206/467–7797. Reservations advised. AE, D, DC, MC, V. Closed Sun. No lunch Sat.*

$$$ **Saleh Al Lago.** Some of the best Italian fare in the city can be found north of downtown. The well-lit dining room here is done in soft colors and, with its view of Green Lake and the park, invites simple, slow-paced evening dining. The antipasti, fresh pasta, and veal dishes are always excellent. Be sure to try the ravioli *al mondo mio,* the chef's special ravioli (filling and sauce vary), or the tagliatelle (flat, ribboned egg pasta) with champagne and caviar. Even deceptively plain fare, like grilled breast of chicken with olive oil and fresh herbs, is superb. ✕ *6804 E. Greenlake Way N, ☎ 206/522–7943. Reservations advised. Jacket required. AE, MC, V. Closed Sun. No lunch Sat.*

$$ **Cafe Juanita.** This comfortable, casual place with wonderful views is more than just a restaurant: There's a winery in the basement, and the vintages made there—bottled under owner–wine maker Peter Dow's Cavatappi label—are available upstairs. The country Italian menu is best represented by the mustard-marinated rabbit served with wild mushrooms. The veal scaloppine and chicken dishes can be a bit on the rich and buttery side, but there's plenty of inexpensive Italian wine on the lengthy list to dilute the cream. ✕ *9702 N.E. 120th Pl., Kirkland, ☎ 206/823–1505. Reservations advised. MC, V. No lunch.*

$$ **Trattoria Mitchelli.** This archetypal Seattle storefront café has a bohemian atmosphere that's fast-paced and friendly, even during the wee hours of the morning—closing time isn't until 4 AM on weekends—when it can get noisy and crowded. The pasta, sandwiches, and antipasti aren't haute cuisine, but they're tasty, moderately priced, and come in generous portions. ✗ *84 Yesler Way,* ☎ *206/623–3885. No reservations. AE, DC, MC, V.*

Japanese

$$–$$$ **Nikko.** Given that the sushi bar is the architectural centerpiece of this restaurant's sophisticated low-light and black-lacquer decor, it's not surprising that Nikko serves some of the best sushi and sashimi in Seattle. The Kasuzuke cod and teriyaki salmon are also both highly recommended. ✗ *Westin Hotel, 1900 5th Ave.,* ☎ *206/322–4641. Reservations advised. AE, D, DC, MC, V. Closed Sun. No lunch.*

$$ **Takara.** In full action, the sushi chef here can look like a character from a Japanese wood-block print, perhaps a master swordsman preparing to fight heaven and earth. His real calling, however, seems to be serving up only the freshest seafood for sushi and sashimi. No wonder Japanese businessmen flock to the sushi bar for lunch. The dining room serves classic Japanese dishes using Northwest ingredients. The salmon teriyaki is superb, as is the steamed black cod. ✗ *Pike Place Market Hillclimb, 1501 Western Ave.,* ☎ *206/682–8609. Reservations advised for dining room, no reservations for sushi bar. AE, MC, V. Closed Sun. in winter.*

Mediterranean

$$–$$$ **Adriatica.** This place gathered a loyal local following, became a virtual Seattle institution, and was then discovered by visitors who spread the word. Located in a hillside Craftsman-style house, the dining room and upstairs bar offer views of Lake Union. Over several years, the fare here has evolved into a unique Pacific Northwest–influenced Greek and Italian cuisine. Regular offerings include daily fresh fish, a pasta, a risotto, and seafood souvlaki. Phyllo pastries with honey and nuts are among the tasty and interesting dessert choices. ✗ *1107 Dexter Ave. N,* ☎ *206/285–5000. Reservations advised. AE, DC, MC, V.*

Mexican

$$ **Casa-U-Betcha.** Colorful neon signs and faux granite sculptures standing in for room dividers create a fittingly lively atmosphere for the upscale crowd and cuisine at this trendy spot. Familiar Mexican dishes are served using less grease, less cheese, and black beans rather than refried. The menu isn't too strict, though, so you'll find Caribbean and Latin American influences (south of the border here seems to mean anywhere between Texas and the equator) in such inventive offerings as Coyote Moon Carnitas—lean pork seasoned with herbs and marinated in lime juice, then grilled. ✗ *2212 1st Ave.,* ☎ *206/441–1989. Reservations advised. AE, DC, MC, V.*

Northwest

$$$ **Fuller's.** The works of northwest artists hang over the booths in this
★ dining room favored by locals for special occasions. Start with a sesame-crust tuna pizza, vegetable strudel with sun-dried tomatoes and goat cheese, or spinach salad with smoked duck and honey-mustard dressing. Move on to pork loin with an apple-brandy blue-cheese sauce or monkfish with a wild-mushroom and tomato ragout. All the

dishes are enhanced by the elegant china and crystal settings atop linen tablecloths. Chef Monique Andree Barbeau specializes in low-fat sauces made from vegetable purees and natural reductions, but you'll forget all about that when you see the wonderfully decadent desserts. ✕ *1400 6th Ave. (in the Seattle Sheraton, at Pike St.), ☎ 206/447–5544 or 800/325–3535. Reservations advised. Jacket required. AE, D, DC, MC, V. Closed Sun. No lunch Sat.*

\$\$\$ **Hunt Club.** A combination of dark wood and plush seating provides a comfortable if surprisingly traditional setting for Chef Eric Leonard's innovative interpretations of Pacific Northwest meat and seafood. Potato pancakes with caviar or the squash ravioli are excellent starters. Entrées on the seasonal menu include swordfish with an almond-herb crust, pork chops stuffed with artichokes and sun-dried tomatoes, and roast venison sauced with a peppercorn and cranberry game-based demi-glace and served with candied yams. ✕ *Sorrento Hotel, 900 Madison St., ☎ 206/622–6400. Reservations advised. Jacket required. AE, DC, MC, V.*

\$\$\$ **Lampreia.** The subtle beige-and-gold interior of this Belltown restaurant is the perfect backdrop for owner and chef Scott Carsberg's sophisticated cuisine. After an appetizer of cream of polenta with shiitake mushrooms, try one of the seasonal menu's intermezzo or light main courses (how about squid and cannelloni filled with salmon) or a full entrée such as pheasant with apple-champagne sauerkraut or lamb with pesto and whipped potatoes. The clear flavors of the desserts, such as lemon mousse with strawberry sauce, bring a soothing conclusion to an exciting food experience. ✕ *2400 1st Ave., ☎ 206/443–3301. Reservations advised. AE, DC, MC, V. No lunch.*

\$\$–\$\$\$ **Painted Table.** The sand-color walls and warm mahogany paneling in
★ this sophisticated dining room at the Alexis Hotel provide an elegant backdrop for the room's displays of works by local artists. Meals are equally appealing: Chef Tim Kelly selects from the freshest regional produce available from nearby small vendors, farms, and the Pike Place Market. The resulting vegetable and seafood dishes are attractively presented, framed by hand-painted plates. The seasonal menu features such entrées as herbed prawns with linguine and shiitake mushrooms or herb-crusted lamb with grilled Japanese eggplant, fennel, and polenta. Desserts include a frozen banana soufflé and a jasmine-rice custard made with coconut milk. ✕ *Alexis Hotel, 1007 1st Ave., ☎ 206/624–3646. Reservations advised. AE, D, DC, MC, V. No lunch weekends.*

\$\$ **Dahlia Lounge.** This place feels cozy and romantic at night with low light on the dark red walls. Owner Tom Douglas is credited with introducing Seattle to crab cakes, and his reputation for fine food has only taken off from there. In addition to the famed crab concoctions, served as an entrée or appetizer, the ever-changing menu offers the best of the Northwest's bounty. Vegetarians and other lovers of produce shouldn't miss the apple-onion tart or the corn tamale served with green rice and grilled vegetables. Desserts, such as coconut cream pie and fresh cobblers, are scrumptious. At press time, Douglas had just opened Etta's Seafood Restaurant in the Pike Place Market. ✕ *1404 4th Ave., ☎ 206/682–4142. Reservations advised. MC, V. No lunch weekends.*

\$\$ **Place Pigalle.** Large windows look out over Elliott Bay from this intimate restaurant tucked behind a meat market in the Pike Place Market's main arcade; in nice weather, they're left ajar to admit the fresh salt breeze. Bright flower bouquets lighten up the café tables, and the friendly staff makes you feel right at home. Despite its French name, this is a very American restaurant and a popular place with locals. Seasonal meals feature seafood and regional ingredients. Go for the rich oyster stew, the fresh Dungeness crab (available only when it is truly fresh), or the fish of the day baked in hazelnuts. ✕ *Pike Place Market,* ☎ *206/624–1756. Reservations advised. MC, V. Closed Sun.*

Seafood

$$ **Ray's Boathouse.** The view of Puget Sound may be the drawing card
★ here, but the seafood is impeccably fresh and well prepared. Perennial favorites include broiled salmon, *kasu sake* cod, teriyaki salmon fillets, blackened cod, and oysters prepared almost any way you could want them. Ray's has a split personality: There's a fancy dining room downstairs and a casual café and bar upstairs. Go for the café; the prices are lower and the food is just as good. In warm weather, sit on the deck outside the café and watch a continuous parade of fishing and pilot boats, tugs, and pleasure yachts floating past, almost right below your table. ✕ *6049 Seaview Ave. NE,* ☎ *206/789–3770. Reservations advised for window seats in dining room; no reservations for café. AE, DC, MC, V.*

$ **Emmet Watson's Oyster Bar.** This unpretentious spot can be a bit hard to find—it's in the back of the Pike Place Market's Soames-Dunn Building, facing a small flower-bedecked courtyard—but for Seattleites (and discerning visitors) who know their oysters, it's worth the special effort. Not only are the oysters very fresh and the beer icy cold, but both are inexpensive and available in any number of varieties. If you don't like oysters, try the salmon soup or the fish-and-chips (large flaky pieces of fish with very little grease). ✕ *Pike Place Market, 1916 Pike Pl.,* ☎ *206/448–7721. No reservations. No credit cards. Closed Sun.*

Southwest

$$ **Santa Fe Cafe.** Visitors from New Mexico say that this is about as au-
★ thentic as southwestern fare gets—maybe because that's where the restaurant buys the red and green chilies for its sauces. Interesting brews on tap help mitigate the heat of such delicious dishes as spicy green-chili burritos made with blue-corn tortillas. Other choices are less *picante,* but still flavorful. Try the red or green enchiladas or house specialties like the artichoke ramekin, chili-relleno torte, and roasted-garlic appetizer. Of the two locations, the 65th Street restaurant offers a cozier, homey appeal, with its woven rugs and dried flowers, and is popular with graduate students and professors. The Phinney Avenue location is slicker and more chic; skylights fill the place with light that brightens the soft pink-and-mauve color scheme. ✕ *2255 N.E. 65th St.,* ☎ *206/524–7736; no lunch Sat.–Mon. 5910 Phinney Ave. N,* ☎ *206/783– 9755; lunch Sat. only. Reservations advised at both. MC, V.*

Thai

$ **Bahn Thai.** Thai cooking is ubiquitous in Seattle—it can almost be considered a mainstream cuisine. Because of the variety of dishes and the quality of the preparations, the Bahn Thai, one of the pioneers of local Thai food, is still one of the best and most popular. Start your meal with a skewer of tangy chicken or pork satay, or with the *tod mun goong* (spicy fish cake), and continue with hot-and-sour soup and one of the many prawn or fish dishes. The deep-fried fish with garlic sauce is particularly good—and you can order it very hot. This restaurant promises a relaxed, romantic atmosphere in the evenings. ✕ *409 Roy St.,* ☎ *206/ 283–0444. Reservations advised. AE, DC, MC, V. No lunch weekends.*

Vegetarian

$–$$ **Cafe Flora.** This lovely place in Madison Valley is attracting vegetarians and meat eaters alike for artistically presented, full-flavored meals. The menu includes a portobella mushroom Wellington, a Mediterranean plate, and a four-onion pizza, as well as great salads. ✗ *2901 E. Madison St.,* ☎ *206/325–9100. Reservations advised. MC, V. Closed Mon. No dinner Sun.*

Vietnamese

$ **Saigon Gourmet.** This small café in the International District is about
★ as plain as it gets, but the food is superb. Aficionados make special trips for the Cambodian soup and the shrimp rolls. The peanut dipping sauce is more flavorful than usual. Do try the papaya with beef jerky—it's unusual but enjoyable. The prices are incredibly low, just one reason why this is one of the best lunch places in town. Parking, however, can be a problem. ✗ *502 S. King St.,* ☎ *206/624–2611. No reservations. MC, V. Closed Mon.*

LODGING

There is no shortage of lodging in Seattle. The variety ranges from the elegant deluxe hotels of downtown to the smaller, less expensive hotels in the University District; from a number of budget motels along Aurora Avenue North (Highway 99), many of which are legacies of the 1962 World's Fair, to the large, standard hotels strung along Pacific Highway South (also Highway 99) that accommodate travelers near Seattle-Tacoma International Airport. Always inquire about special rates based on occupancy, weekend stays, or special packages.

A number of bed-and-breakfast accommodations are also available. For more information, contact the **Washington State Bed-and-Breakfast Guild** (2442 N.W. Market St., Seattle 98107, ☎ 800/647–2918) or the **Pacific Bed & Breakfast Agency** (701 N.W. 60th St., Seattle 98107, ☎ 206/784–0539).

CATEGORY	COST*
$$$$	over $170
$$$	$110–$170
$$	$60–$110
$	under $60

All prices are for a standard double room, excluding 14.1% combined hotel and state sales tax.

Downtown Seattle

$$$$ **Alexis.** The Alexis is an intimate four-story, European-style hotel in an
★ artfully restored historic 1901 building on 1st Avenue near the waterfront, the Public Market, and the Seattle Art Museum. Guests are greeted with complimentary sherry at this understated and elegant hotel. The rooms are decorated in subdued colors, with at least one piece of antique furniture in each. Some suites feature hot tubs and wood-burning fireplaces, and some have marble fixtures. Unfortunately, none of the rooms have any kind of view, and those facing the avenue can be noisy. Amenities include complimentary Continental breakfast, shoe shines, morning newspaper, and access to workout facilities and a private steam room. The Painted Table restaurant is on the hotel's ground floor (*see* Dining, *above*). ☎ *1007 1st Ave., 98104,* ☎ *206/624–4844*

36

or 800/426–7033, ☒ *206/621–9009. 54 rooms. Restaurant, bar, café.
AE, MC, V.*

$$$$ Four Seasons Olympic Hotel. The Olympic is Seattle's most elegant
★ hotel. In 1982, Four Seasons restored it to its 1920s Renaissance Revival–style grandeur, with the public rooms appointed with marble,
wood paneling, potted plants, and thick rugs, and furnished with plush
armchairs. Palms and skylights in the Garden Court provide a relaxing background for lunch, afternoon tea, or dancing to a live swing
band on the weekends. The Georgian Room, the hotel's premier dining room, exudes Italian Renaissance elegance, while Shuckers oyster bar is more casual. Guest rooms are less luxurious than the public
rooms and have a homey feel. They are furnished with sofas, comfortable reading chairs, and desks and decorated with period reproductions and floral print fabrics. Amenities include valet parking,
stocked bar, chocolates on your pillow, complimentary shoe shines,
and a bathrobe in the room for each guest. Locals drop in occasionally to pamper themselves with a massage and swim at the health club.
☒ *411 University St., 98101,* ☎ *206/621–1700 or 800/223–8772,*
☒ *206/682–9633. 450 rooms. 3 restaurants, room service, indoor
pool, health club. AE, DC, MC, V.*

$$$$ Hotel Vintage Park. As a tribute to the state's growing wine industry,
each guest room in this small hotel is named for a Washington winery
or vineyard. The theme is extended to complimentary servings of local
wines each evening in the elegant lobby, where guests can relax on richly
upholstered sofas and chairs arranged around the ornate marble fireplace. The rooms, which are decorated in rich color schemes of dark
green, plum, deep reds, taupe and gold, are furnished with custom-made
cherry-wood pieces. Each room also contains original works by San Francisco artist Chris Kidd. For literary-minded guests, hotel staff will check
out and deliver your choice of books from the nearby Seattle Public Library. ☒ *1100 5th Ave., 98101,* ☎ *206/624–8000 or 800/624–4433,*
☒ *206/623–0568. 129 rooms. Restaurant, no-smoking floors, room
service, health club access, business services. AE, DC, MC, V.*

$$$$ Westin Hotel. This large high-rise hotel in the heart of downtown, the
flagship of the Westin chain, is the preferred accommodation of such
visiting dignitaries as the President. Located just north and east of the
Pike Place Market, it is easily recognizable by its twin cylindrical towers. With this design, all rooms have terrific views over the waterfront
and Lake Union. The rooms themselves are airy and bright, and furnished in a plain but high-quality style. A number have been turned
into environmentally friendly, "green" accommodations; the children's
programs, which include an interactive, kids-only radio network, are
equally innovative. The informal Market Cafe, the more formal Palm
Court, and Nikko, a stylish Japanese restaurant (*see* Dining, *above*),
as well as three lounges, are located in-house. ☒ *1900 5th Ave., 98101,*
☎ *206/728–1000 or 800/228–3000,* ☒ *206/728–2259. 829 rooms,
48 suites. 3 restaurants, 3 bars, no-smoking floors, room service, indoor pool, hot tub, beauty salon, massage, sauna, exercise room, children's programs, laundry service, concierge, business services, convention
center, car rental. AE, D, DC, MC, V.*

$$$ Edgewater. The only hotel on Elliott Bay, the Edgewater is an institu-
tion, known for the now-defunct tradition of guests' fishing from their
waterside windows. In 1988 the new owners banned hotel fishing but
remodeled the 238 rooms, the results of which are magnificent. The
lobby features oak furnishings and comfortable chairs and sofas, with
a fireplace and a panoramic bay window from which you can some-
times see sea lions frolicking. Spacious rooms on the water provide views

of ferries, barges, and the Olympic Mountains, and are decorated in rustic Northwest plaids and unfinished wood furnishings. ☎ *Pier 67, 2411 Alaskan Way, 98121,* ☎ *206/728–7000 or 800/624–0670,* FAX *206/441–4119. 238 rooms. Restaurant, bar. AE, DC, MC, V.*

$$$ **Seattle Hilton.** This Hilton is a favorite for conventions and meetings, especially because of its central location. Rooms are furnished in the same nondescript but tasteful style characteristic of Hiltons worldwide, and have soothing color schemes. One of its two restaurants, the Top of the Hilton, serves well-prepared variations of salmon steak and other local specialties, and has excellent views of the city. An underground passage connects the Hilton with a shopping concourse, Rainier Square, as well as with the 5th Avenue Theater and the Washington State Convention Center. ☎ *1301 University St., 98101,* ☎ *206/624–0500, 800/542–7700, or 800/426–0535,* FAX *206/682–9029. 237 rooms, 6 suites. 2 restaurants, piano bar, no-smoking floors. AE, D, DC, MC, V.*

$$$ **Seattle Sheraton Hotel and Towers.** The Sheraton is a modern, 840-room hotel (renovated in 1991) catering largely to conventioneers, as it is conveniently located near the Washington State Convention & Trade Center. The lobby features an art-glass collection by Dale Chihuly, a Northwest artist of international repute. The Towers (top five floors) feature larger, more elegant rooms with concierge service, and complimentary Continental breakfast. Within the complex is a diverse selection of restaurant and entertainment options, including Banners, which offers an authentic Japanese breakfast, buffet luncheon, and Continental menu; Fuller's (*see* Dining, *above*), one of the best restaurants in Seattle, serving nouvelle cuisine using local ingredients; and Gooey's (named after the geoduck, a large, sausagelike northwestern clam that is the subject of many jokes), the bar-disco nighttime hot spot. ☎ *1400 6th Ave., 98101,* ☎ *206/621–9000 or 800/325–3535,* FAX *206/621–8441. 840 rooms. 2 restaurants, 2 bars, indoor pool, health club. AE, D, DC, MC, V.*

$$$ **Sorrento.** This deluxe European-style hotel, built in 1909 for the
★ Alaska-Yukon Exposition, was designed to look like an Italian villa. The dramatic entrance is along a circular driveway around an Italian fountain, and ringed by palm trees. Sitting high on First Hill, it has wonderful views overlooking downtown and the waterfront. The rooms are smaller than those in a more modern hotel, but are quiet and very comfortable; they're decorated in understated, elegant earth tones. The largest rooms are the corner suites, which have some antiques and spacious baths. The stylish Hunt Club (*see* Dining, *above*) restaurant features exquisite Northwest-Asian dishes, while the dark-paneled Fireside Lounge in the lobby is a warm and inviting spot for sipping coffee, tea, or a cocktail. Other amenities include a complimentary limousine service within the downtown area, concierge, and guest privileges at a nearby athletic club. ☎ *900 Madison St., 98104,* ☎ *206/622–6400,* FAX *206/625–1059. 76 rooms, 42 suites. Restaurant, bar. AE, DC, MC.*

$$$ **Stouffer Madison Hotel.** This high-rise hotel, located between downtown and I-5, was built in 1983. Rooms are decorated in peach and green tones, and come equipped with wood cabinets and marble countertops; those on the 10th floor and up have good views of downtown, Elliott Bay, and the Cascade Mountains. Views above the 20th floor are excellent. Club-level floors (25 and 26) feature their own concierge, complimentary Continental breakfast, and a library. Amenities on other floors include complimentary coffee, morning newspaper, and shoe shines. The health club includes a 40-foot rooftop pool and a Jacuzzi. ☎ *515 Madison St., 98104,* ☎ *206/583–0300 or 800/468–*

3571, FAX *206/622–8635. 554 rooms. 2 restaurants, bar. AE, D, DC, MC, V.*

$$$ Warwick Hotel. The Warwick manages to combine its somewhat large size with intimate European-style charm. Service is friendly and leisurely (but not slow), and the rooms are understated without being bland. All rooms have small balconies and good views of downtown. There is live entertainment in the Liaison restaurant and lounge, and 24-hour courtesy transportation within downtown. ☎ *401 Lenora St., 98121,* ☎ *206/443–4300,* FAX *206/448–1662. 230 units, 4 suites. Restaurant, bar, no-smoking rooms, pool, hot tub, sauna, exercise room. AE, D, DC, MC, V.*

$$–$$$ Inn at the Market. This sophisticated but unpretentious hotel has a great
   ★   location just up the street from the Pike Place Market. It combines the best aspects of a small, French country inn with the informality of the Pacific Northwest, offering a lively setting that's perfect for travelers who prefer originality, personality, and coziness to big-hotel amenities. The rooms are spacious and tastefully decorated with comfortable modern furniture and small touches such as fresh flowers and ceramic sculptures. Ask for a room with views of the Market and Elliott Bay. An added plus is a 2,000-square-foot deck, furnished with Adirondack chairs and overlooking the water and the market. Guests also have access to a health club and spa. Three restaurants share the building: Campagne (*see* Dining, *above*); the Gravity Bar, an ultratrendy hangout with a variety of juices and coffees; and Cafe Dilettante (*see* Dining, *above*) for light meals, fine chocolates, and coffees. ☎ *86 Pine St., 98109,* ☎ *206/443–3600,* FAX *206/448–0631. 65 rooms. 3 restaurants, no-smoking rooms, room service. AE, D, DC, MC, V.*

$$–$$$ Mayflower Park Hotel. This pleasant older hotel, built in 1927, is conveniently connected with Westlake Center and the Monorail terminal to Seattle Center. Brass fixtures and antiques give both the public and private spaces a muted Oriental feel, and the service is similarly unobtrusive and smooth. The rooms are somewhat smallish, but the Mayflower Park is so sturdily constructed that it is much quieter than many modern downtown hotels. Guests can use a nearby health club. ☎ *405 Olive Way, 98101,* ☎ *206/623–8700,* FAX *206/382–6997. 168 rooms, 14 suites. Restaurant, bar, no-smoking rooms. AE, DC, MC, V.*

$$ Camlin Hotel. This 1926 Seattle apartment-hotel has a gracious lobby featuring Oriental carpets, large mirrors, and lots of marble. Located on the edge of the downtown office area, but close to the convention center, this reasonably priced hotel is popular with business travelers. Rooms ending with 10 are best because they feature windows on three sides, and all have working spaces with a chair and a table, along with cushioned chairs for relaxing. One drawback here, though, is the noisy heating, air-conditioning, and ventilation system. ☎ *1619 9th Ave., 98101,* ☎ *206/682–0100 or 800/426–0670,* FAX *206/682–7415. Restaurant, bar, pool. AE, D, DC, MC, V.*

$$ Pacific Plaza. Built in 1929 and refurbished in 1992, this hotel reflects its original character. The rooms and furnishings, reminiscent of the '20s and '30s, are appropriate for singles or couples but are too small to comfortably accommodate a family. Because of its downtown location and modest rates (which include a Continental breakfast), the Plaza is a good choice for anyone who is not seeking contemporary luxury. ☎ *400 Spring St., 98104,* ☎ *206/623–3900 or 800/426–1165,* FAX *206/623–2059. 160 rooms. 2 restaurants. AE, DC, MC, V.*

$ Seattle YMCA. This accommodation has 198 units and is a member of the American Youth Hostels Association. Rooms are clean and plainly furnished with a bed, phone, desk, and lamp. Rooms cost about $40;

bunk units, designed to accommodate four people each, are about $20. ☎ 909 4th Ave., 98104, ☎ 206/382–5000. 198 units. Pool, health club. No credit cards.

$ **Youth Hostel: Seattle International.** Situated near the Pike Place Market is a bright, clean youth hostel with 128 dormitory-style beds for about $20 a night. Guests can use the kitchen or eat in the dining room. ☎ 84 Union St., 98101, ☎ 206/622–5443. 128 units. Bar, library. No credit cards.

Seattle Center

$$ **Meany Tower Hotel.** This pleasant hotel is just a few blocks from the
★ University of Washington's campus. Built in 1931 and remodeled many times since, it has managed to retain much of its old-fashioned charm, with a muted-peach color scheme throughout, brass fixtures, and careful, attentive service. The rooms, especially those on the higher floors, have good views of the college grounds with glimpses of Green Lake and Lake Union. The Meany Grill on the ground floor serves breakfast, lunch, and dinner; there is a large street-level lounge as well. ☎ 4507 Brooklyn Ave. NE, 98105, ☎ 206/634–2000, FAX 206/634–2000. 55 rooms. Restaurant, bar, no-smoking rooms, room service. AE, DC, MC, V.

$$ **Sixth Avenue Inn.** Families and business travelers patronize this small but comfortable motor hotel a few blocks north of downtown; it's also the hotel of choice for musicians playing at Dimitriou's Jazz Alley, the highly regarded club across the street. Rooms are pleasant, with wicker furnishings and standard-issue but well-maintained decor and color schemes; the service is cheerful. ☎ 2000 6th Ave., 98121, ☎ 206/441–8300, FAX 206/441–9903. 166 rooms. Restaurant, bar, no-smoking rooms. AE, DC, MC, V.

$$ **University Plaza Hotel.** This is a full-service motor hotel, just across I–5 from the University of Washington's campus, making it popular with families and others who have business in the area. The mock-Tudor decor gives its lobby and other public areas a slightly outdated feel, but the service is cheerful and the rooms are spacious and pleasantly decorated in teak furniture, with pale pinks and grays being the predominant colors. The rooms on the freeway side, however, can be noisy. ☎ 400 N.E. 45th St., 98105, ☎ 206/634–0100, FAX 206/633–2743. 135 rooms. Restaurant, bar, no-smoking rooms, pool, beauty salon, exercise room. AE, D, DC, MC, V.

Seattle-Tacoma Airport

$$$ **Red Lion/Sea-Tac.** The Red Lion is a popular, hospitable 850-room, full-service convention hotel. Rooms are spacious and bright, with large panoramic balconies and decor in shades of mauve, teal, and gray. The corner "King Rooms" feature wraparound balconies and have the best views. Furnishings include chests of drawers, comfortable chairs, a dining table, and a desk. ☎ 18740 Pacific Hwy. S, 98168, ☎ 206/246–8600, FAX 206/242–9727. 850 rooms. 2 restaurants, 2 bars, coffee shop, pool, health club. AE, D, DC, MC, V.

$$$ **Seattle Airport Hilton.** This relatively small hotel (for a Hilton) has an intimate, original feel accentuated by the lobby's oak furnishings, cozy fireplace, and paintings of Northwest scenery. The large rooms are bright and decorated in pastel colors. It is also conveniently located only a half-hour drive from downtown and a 10-minute drive from Southcenter shopping mall. ☎ 17620 Pacific Hwy. S, 98188, ☎ 206/244–4800, FAX 206/439–7439. 173 rooms. Restaurant, bar, pool, health club, airport shuttle. AE, D, DC, MC, V.

$$–$$$ **Doubletree Inn** and **Doubletree Suites.** These two hotels, situated across the street from each other, are adjacent to Southcenter shopping mall and convenient to the myriad business-park offices there. The inn is a classic Pacific Northwest–style lodge. Rooms are smaller and less lavish than those at the Suites, but are otherwise perfectly nice and cost at least $25 less. Suites, decorated in neutrals, mauves, and pinks, feature a sofa, table and chairs, and a wet bar in the living room. The vanity area includes a full-size closet with mirrored doors. ⊞ *Doubletree Inn, 205 Strander Blvd., Tukwila 98188,* ☎ *206/246–8220,* ℻ *206/575–4743. 198 rooms. Bar, coffee shop, dining room, pool. Doubletree Suites, 16500 Southcenter Pkwy., Tukwila 98188,* ☎ *206/575–8220,* ℻ *206/575–4743. 221 suites. Restaurant, bar, pool, hot tub, sauna, health club, racquetball. AE, D, DC, MC, V (for both).*

$$–$$$ **Seattle Marriott.** A surprisingly luxurious and substantial hotel con-
★ sidering its nondowntown location, this Marriott features a five-story-high, 20,000-square-foot tropical atrium that's complete with waterfall, dining area, indoor pool, and lounge. The rooms are decorated in greens and mauve with dark wood and brass furnishings. Special rates are available to AAA and AARP members. ⊞ *3201 S. 176th St., 98188,* ☎ *206/241–2000, international reservations* ☎ *800/228–9290,* ℻ *206/248–0789. 459 rooms. Restaurant, no-smoking rooms, 2 hot tubs, health club, concierge, airport shuttle. AE, D, DC, MC, V.*

$$ **Holiday Inn Sea-Tac.** The atrium lobby of this hotel, built in 1970, has an attractive garden room that's convenient for meeting people. Most of the spacious guest rooms have been redecorated in a color scheme of mauve and peach with maroon and green accents. The Top of the Inn revolving-view restaurant features singing waiters. ⊞ *17338 Pacific Hwy. S, 98188,* ☎ *206/248–1000 or 800/465–4329,* ℻ *206/242–7089. 260 rooms. Restaurant, bar, coffee shop, indoor pool, hot tub, health club. AE, DC, MC, V.*

Bellevue/Kirkland

$$$ **Hyatt Regency Bellevue.** This deluxe high-rise complex is in the heart of downtown Bellevue, within a few blocks of Bellevue Square and other fine shopping locales. The exterior looks pretty much like any other sleek high-rise, but the interior has such Asian touches as antique Japanese *tansu* (wood chests of drawers) and huge displays of fresh flowers. The rooms are decorated in similarly understated ways, with floor-to-ceiling windows and dark wood and earth tones predominating the color scheme. The service is impeccable. Some rooms have been specially designed for Japanese travelers. Deluxe suites include two bedrooms, bar facilities, and meeting rooms with desks and full-length tables. Guests have access to a health club and pool. The Eques restaurant serves excellent and reasonably priced breakfast, lunch, and dinner; an English-style pub serves a variety of drinks as well as lunch and dinner. ⊞ *900 Bellevue Way NE, 98004,* ☎ *206/462–2626,* ℻ *206/646–7567. 352 rooms, 30 suites. Restaurant, pub, no-smoking rooms, room service. AE, D, DC, MC, V.*

$$$ **Red Lion Bellevue.** This 10-story hotel has a large, airy atrium filled with trees, shrubs, and flowering plants. The property also has a formal dining room, a lounge with two dance floors, and oversize guest rooms decorated in mauve and sea-foam green. Rooms have either king- or queen-size beds, and two-room suites feature wet bars and hot tubs. A new Italian restaurant, Velato's, opened here in 1993. ⊞ *300 112th Ave. SE, Bellevue 98004,* ☎ *206/455–1300 or 800/274–1415,* ℻ *206/454–0466. 353 rooms. 2 restaurants, bar, pool, health club. AE, D, DC, MC, V.*

$$$ **Woodmark Hotel.** Only steps away from downtown Kirkland, this hotel
★ is the only one on the shores of Lake Washington. Its contemporary-
style rooms face the water, courtyard, or street and are tastefully dec-
orated in earth tones, with heavy comforters and numerous amenities
such as terry-cloth bathrobes and fragrant soaps. Guests can use a nearby
health club. Comfortable chairs surround the fireplace in the large, open
lobby, and a circular staircase descends to the lounge, passing a huge
bay window and vast view of Lake Washington. The Carillon Room
restaurant offers pasta and fresh fish dishes and excellent water views.
⌕ *1200 Carillon Point, Kirkland 98033,* ☎ *206/822–3700 or 800/822–
3700,* ⅂⅄ *206/822–3699. 100 rooms. Restaurant, bar. AE, MC, V.*

$ **West Coast Bellevue Hotel.** This hotel–motor inn features a number
of town-house suites, suitable for two to four people, with sleeping lofts
and wood-burning fireplaces. Rooms are clean; those in the corporate
wing face the courtyard and are larger and quieter than the others. The
hotel is about eight blocks or a 20-minute walk from Bellevue Square.
A complimentary appetizer buffet, offered in the lounge weekdays be-
tween 5 and 7 PM, is substantial and includes seafood and roast beef.
⌕ *625 116th Ave. NE, Bellevue 98004,* ☎ *206/455–9444,* ⅂⅄ *206/455–
2154. 160 rooms, 16 suites. Restaurant, bar, coffee shop, pool. AE,
D, DC, MC, V.*

THE ARTS

Seattle has gained a world-class reputation as a theater town, and it
also has a strong music and dance scene for local, national, and in-
ternational artists. A good handle on what's happening in town can
be found in any of several periodicals. Both the *Seattle Times* and *Post-
Intelligencer* have pullout sections on Friday detailing most of the
coming week's events. The *Seattle Weekly,* which hits most newsstands
on Wednesday, has even more detailed coverage and arts reviews. *The
Rocket,* a lively free monthly, covers music news, reviews, and concert
information, with an emphasis on rock and roll.

The Arts for Free
Seattle's summer concerts, the **Out to Lunch Series** (☎ 206/623–
0340), runs from mid-June to early September every weekday at noon
in various parks, plazas, and atriums in downtown. Concerts feature
local and national musicians and dancers. Call ahead for schedules
and locations.

Gallery Walk (begin at any gallery in Pioneer Square, ☎ 206/587–0260),
an open house hosted by Seattle's art galleries, explores new local ex-
hibits the first Thursday of every month, starting at 5.

Ticket Services
Ticketmaster (☎ 206/628–0888) provides tickets to most productions
in the Seattle area; you can charge by phone. The two locations of
Ticket/Ticket (Broadway Market, 401 Broadway E, 2nd Floor, ☎
206/324–2744; Pike Place Market Information Booth, 1st Ave. and
Pike St., ☎ 206/682–7453, ext. 26) sell half-price tickets for many events
on the day of the performance (or the day before for matinees). Sales
are cash only and in-person only.

Dance

Allegro Dance Company (Broadway Performance Hall, 1625 Broad-
way, ☎ 206/323–2623) presents the best in local and regional chore-
ography, with some productions that include other elements of the

performing arts. It schedules about 10 concerts a year between September and June.

Meany Hall for the Performing Arts (University of Washington campus, ☎ 206/543–4880) presents important national and international companies, September–May, with an emphasis on modern and jazz dance.

On the Boards (Washington Performance Hall, 153 14th Ave., ☎ 206/325–7901) presents and produces a wide variety of contemporary performances, including not only dance but also theater, music, and multimedia events by local, national, and international artists. Although the main subscription series runs October–May, OTB events happen nearly every weekend year-round.

Pacific Northwest Ballet (Opera House at Seattle Center, ☎ 206/441–2424) is a resident company and school that presents 60–70 performances annually. Its Christmastime production of *The Nutcracker,* with choreography by Kent Stowell and sets by Maurice Sendak, has become a beloved Seattle tradition.

Orchestras and Opera

Civic Light Opera (11051 34th Ave. NE, ☎ 206/363–2809) is a non-Equity, semipro company that offers three or four high-quality productions of large-scale American musical theater per season. The season runs roughly October–May.

Northwest Chamber Orchestra (☎ 206/343–0445) is the Northwest's only professional chamber-music orchestra. At the Moore Theater, the Nippon Kan, and other venues, it presents a full spectrum of music, from Baroque to modern. The season, generally September–May, includes a Bach festival every fall, a spring subscription series, and special holiday performances in December.

Seattle Opera (Opera House at Seattle Center, Mercer St. at 3rd Ave., ☎ 206/389–7600) is a world-class company, generally considered to be one of the top operas in the United States. During the August–May season, it presents six performances of six productions.

Seattle Symphony (Opera House at Seattle Center and other locations, ☎ 206/443–4747) presents some 120 concerts from September to June and—under the musical direction of Gerard Schwartz—continues its long tradition of excellence. A new $99 million Symphony Hall at 2nd Avenue and University Street is set to open in 1997.

Performance Spaces

Part of the legacy left by the 1962 World's Fair is a series of performance halls at **Seattle Center** (305 Harrison St., ☎ 206/684–8582). Seattle also boasts two fine classic early 20th-century music halls—the **Fifth Avenue** (1308 5th Ave., ☎ 206/625–1900) and the 3,000-seat **Paramount** (907 Pine St., ☎ 206/682–1414), which reopened in 1995 after a $37 million renovation.

The **Cornish College of the Arts** (710 E. Roy St., ☎ 206/323–1400) is an internationally recognized school that also serves as home to a number of distinguished professional groups, including jazz and dance, performing September–May.

Other prominent venues are the **Moore Theater** (1932 2nd Ave., ☎ 206/443–1744), the small but acoustically outstanding **Broadway Performance Hall** (1625 Broadway, ☎ 206/323–2623) at Seattle Central Community College, and **Kane** and **Meany halls** on the University of Washington campus (☎ 206/543–4880).

Theater Companies

Annex Theatre (1916 4th Ave., ☎ 206/728–0933) is a cabaret-style, avant-garde theater that performs new works and is run by a collective of artists.

A Contemporary Theater (100 W. Roy St., ☎ 206/285–5110) specializes in developing works by emerging playwrights, including at least one world premiere every year. The season runs May–November, and every December ACT mounts a popular production of Dickens's *A Christmas Carol.* ACT will move to the Eagle's Auditorium (7th Ave. and Union St.), near the Convention Center, in mid-1996.

Bathhouse Theater (7312 W. Greenlake Dr. N, ☎ 206/524–9108) produces six productions on a year-round schedule, specializing in innovative updates on classics. In addition, it mounts numerous free public shows in various Seattle parks.

Crêpe de Paris (1333 5th Ave., ☎ 206/623–4111), a restaurant in the Rainier Tower building downtown, offers some sidesplitting cabaret theater and musical revues, such as The Bouffants, an all-girl group complete with tall beehive hairdos and cat's-eye glasses.

Empty Space Theater (3509 Fremont Ave., ☎ 206/547–7500) has a reputation for introducing Seattle to new playwrights. The season generally runs November–June, with five or six main-stage productions and several smaller shows throughout the season.

Fifth Avenue Musical Theater Company (Fifth Avenue Theater, 1308 5th Ave., ☎ 206/625–1900) is a resident professional troupe that mounts four lavish musicals between October and May each year, with each run lasting about two weeks. (During the rest of the year, this chinoiserie-style historical landmark, carefully restored to its original 1926 condition, hosts a variety of other traveling musical as well as theatrical performances.)

Group Theater (305 Harrison St., on the fountain level of the Center House in Seattle Center, ☎ 206/441–1299) is a multicultural troupe that prides itself on presenting socially provocative works—old and new—by artists of varied cultures and colors. The season runs September–June, and the Group also mounts a special summertime playwrights' festival. Of the regular season's six productions, one is always the popular *Voices of Christmas,* a study of the holidays with consideration to cultural differences and ethnic and emotional barriers.

Intiman Theater (Playhouse at Seattle Center, 2nd and Mercer Sts., ☎ 206/626–0782) presents classics of the world stage in an intimate, high-quality setting. The season generally runs May–November.

New City Theater and Arts Center (1634 11th Ave., ☎ 206/323–6800) is home to a wide range of experimental performances produced by a resident company as well as in conjunction with major national and international artists. Its yearly output includes six plays, a director's festival and a playwright's festival, three dance concerts, a monthly film showing, and a lively, late-night monthly cabaret.

Seattle Repertory Theater (Bagley Wright Theater at Seattle Center, 155 Mercer St., ☎ 206/443–2222) presents a variety of high-quality programming, from classics to new plays. During its October–May season, six main stage productions and three smaller shows (in the adjoining PONCHO Forum) are presented.

Village Theater (303 and 120 Front St. N, Issaquah, ☎ 206/392–2202) produces high-quality family musicals, comedies, and dramas September–May in Issaquah, a town east of Seattle. The main stage is at the 303 Front Street location; the theater's original venue, at 120 Front, is now known as First Stage.

NIGHTLIFE

For a city its size, Seattle has a remarkably strong and diverse nightlife scene. On any given night, you can hear high-quality live sounds—from traditional jazz and ethnic folk music to garage bands—at a variety of venues. Jazz, blues, and R&B have long been Seattle favorites, and each year are showcased on major stages at the Labor Day Bumbershoot Festival at the Seattle Center. Seattle has also gained a certain notoriety as the birthplace of grunge rock; some of the better-known Seattle bands to spring from this scene include Nirvana, Pearl Jam, Screaming Trees, and Alice in Chains. Beyond music, there are plenty of spots to see a comedian, catch a movie, dance, or just have a drink while watching the lights on the water.

Bars and Lounges

Areas with high concentrations of clubs and taverns include Ballard, Pioneer Square, and Capitol Hill, and Belltown, also known as the Denny Regrade, just north of the Pike Place Market. Many of these clubs feature a wide variety of live bands (*see* Music, *below*).

Given Seattle's setting, bars with waterfront views are plentiful—you just have to pick your body of water. **Anthony's Home Port** (6135 Seaview Ave. NW, ☎ 206/783–0780) has great views of Shilshole Bay. **Arnie's Northshore** (1900 N. Northlake Way, ☎ 206/547–3242) overlooks Lake Union. **Ernie's Bar & Grill** (2411 Alaskan Way, Pier 67, ☎ 206/728–7000), in the Edgewater Hotel, has great views of Elliott Bay and the Olympic Mountains. **Kayak Grill** (1200 Westlake Ave. N, ☎ 206/284–2535) is set on Lake Union. **Pescatore** (5300 34th Ave. NW, ☎ 206/784–1733) has a view of the Ship Canal. **Ray's Boathouse** (6049 Seaview Ave. NW, ☎ 206/789–3770) is on Shilshole Bay.

Other options include **F. X. McRory's** (419 Occidental Ave. S, ☎ 206/623–4800), near the Kingdome, which is famous for its huge selection of single-malt whiskies and fresh oysters. Also downtown, the **Garden Court** (411 University St., ☎ 206/621–1700) at the Four Seasons Olympic is a rather formal and elegant locale. **Salty's** (1396 Harbor Ave. SW, ☎ 206/937–1600), a noisy, sprawling restaurant and lounge in West Seattle, has unparalleled views of downtown.

Comedy

Comedy Underground (222 S. Main St., ☎ 206/628–0303), a Pioneer Square club that's literally underground, beneath Swannie's, presents stand-up comedy nightly, with Monday and Tuesday reserved as open-mike nights.

Giggles (5220 Roosevelt Way NE, ☎ 206/526–5653), in the University District, presents the best local and nationally known comedians five nights a week (Tuesday–Saturday), with late shows on weekend nights.

Dancing

Ballroom Dancing

The local chapter of the **U.S. Amateur Ballroom Dancing Association** (☎ 206/822–6686) holds regular classes and dances throughout the year at the **Avalon Ballroom** (1017 Stewart St.). The **Washington Dance Club** (1017 Stewart St., ☎ 206/628–8939) sponsors nightly workshops and dances on various styles.

Dance Clubs

There are several popular clubs in Pioneer Square that feature recorded dance music; **Fenix** (315 2nd Ave., ☎ 206/467–1111) and **Fenix Underground** (323 2nd Ave. S, ☎ 206/467–1111) are connected by an underground passageway and play very danceable music. In the downtown area, **Fitzgerald's on Fifth** (1900 5th Ave., ☎ 206/728–1000) in the Westin Hotel and **Pier 70 Bay Cafe** (2815 Alaskan Way at Broad St., ☎ 206/728–7071) are dance clubs that feature Top-40 music. A number of Seattle's rock clubs (*see* Music, *below*) also offer dancing.

Movies

Seattle is a movie-loving town, as best exemplified by the popularity of the **Seattle International Film Festival** (☎ 206/324–9996), held each May. For show times and theater locations of current releases, call the **Seattle Times InfoLine** (☎ 206/464–2000, ext. 3456).

Egyptian Theater (801 E. Pine St., at Broadway, ☎ 206/323–4978), an Art Deco movie palace that was formerly a Masonic temple, screens art films and is the prime venue of the film festival.

Gran Illusion Cinema (1403 N.E. 50th St., at University Way, ☎ 206/523–3935), in the U district, seats less than 100 and shows mainly independent and art films.

Neptune Theater (1303 N.E. 45th St., at Brooklyn, ☎ 206/633–5545), located near the university, often shows double features of classic films.

U.A. Seattle Center Theaters (2131 6th Ave., at Blanchard St., ☎ 206/443–9591) shows second-run films for the bargain price of $2.

Music

For $8 you can purchase the Pioneer Square joint cover charge, which will admit you to up to 10 area clubs; contact the Central Saloon (*see* Rock, *below*) for details.

Blues and R&B

Ballard Firehouse (5429 Russell St. NW, ☎ 206/784–3516) is the music mecca in the heart of Ballard, with an emphasis on local and national blues acts.

Chicago's (315 1st Ave. N, ☎ 206/282–7791), a reasonably priced Italian restaurant just west of the Seattle Center, has live blues on the weekend.

Larry's (209 1st Ave. S, ☎ 206/624–7665) features live R&B and blues nightly in an unpretentious, friendly, and usually jam-packed tavern-restaurant in Pioneer Square.

Old Timer's Cafe (620 1st Ave., ☎ 206/623–9800) is a popular Pioneer Square restaurant and bar with live music—mostly R&B—nightly.

Scarlet Tree (6521 Roosevelt Way NE, ☎ 206/523–7153), a neighborhood institution just north of the University District, offers great burgers and live R&B most nights.

Folk

Backstage (2208 N.W. Market St., ☎ 206/781–2805) is an often-packed basement venue in Ballard that hosts a lively mix of national and local acts with the emphasis on world music, offbeat rock, and new folk.

Kells (1916 Post Alley, ☎ 206/728–1916), a snug Irish-style pub, is located near the Pike Place Market and presents live Celtic music Wednesday–Saturday starting at 9 PM.

Murphy's Pub (2110 45th St. NE, ☎ 206/634–2110) is a cozy neighborhood bar that has open-mike Wednesdays, with Irish and other folk music on Friday and Saturday.

Jazz

Dimitriou's Jazz Alley (2037 6th Ave., ☎ 206/441–9729) is a downtown club with nationally known, consistently high-quality performers every night but Sunday. Excellent dinners are served before the first shows.

Latona Tavern (6423 Latona Ave. NE, ☎ 206/525–2238) is a funky, friendly, often jazz-oriented, neighborhood bar at the south end of Green Lake that features a variety of local musicians playing folk, blues, and jazz nightly.

New Orleans Restaurant (114 1st Ave. S, ☎ 206/622–2563) is a popular Pioneer Square restaurant with good food and live jazz nightly—mostly top local performers but occasionally national acts as well.

Rock

The **Moore Theater** (1932 2nd Ave., ☎ 206/443–1744) and the **Paramount** (907 Pine St., ☎ 682–1414, or Ticketmaster, ☎ 206/628–0888) are elegant former movie-music halls that now host visiting big-name acts.

Central Saloon (207 1st Ave. S, ☎ 206/622–0209) is a crowded Pioneer Square tavern with an ever-changing roster of local and national rock acts.

Crocodile Café (2200 2nd Ave., ☎ 206/448–2114) is one of Seattle's most successful rock clubs, featuring a variety of folk-rock, acoustic-rock, hard-rock, and new-wave groups every night but Monday.

Doc Maynard's (610 1st Ave., ☎ 206/682–4649) is a classic rock-and-roll-oriented tavern with a small and always jam-packed dance floor.

Off-Ramp Music Cafe (109 Eastlake E, ☎ 206/628–0232) features a rock band nightly, often the loud and alternative kind.

O.K. Hotel Cafe (212 Alaskan Way S, ☎ 206/621–7903) offers rock, folk, and jazz nightly in a small venue near Pioneer Square.

Re-Bar (1114 Howell St., ☎ 206/233–9873) presents an eclectic mix of music nightly, including acid-jazz, rock, and soul.

Vogue (2018 1st Ave., ☎ 206/443–0673), a club in Belltown, the artists' community just north of the Public Market, hosts au courant local and national rock acts, as well as industrial, reggae, and gothic music.

EXCURSIONS

Bainbridge Island

The best short excursion from Seattle may be a ride on the Bainbridge Island ferry to take in great views of the city skyline and the surrounding hills. The ferry leaves from Seattle's busy downtown terminal at Colman Dock on Pier 52, south of the Pike Place Market and just north of Pioneer Square; the trip takes about a half hour each way (*see* Getting Around *in* Seattle Essentials, *below*).

While the ferry trip draws most of the island's visitors, Bainbridge itself has a pleasant small-town atmosphere and plenty of scenic countryside. Once you reach the Bainbridge Island terminal, continue north up a short hill on Olympic Drive to Winslow Way. If you turn west, you'll find yourself in **Winslow,** where there are several square blocks of interesting antiques shops, clothing boutiques, gift stores, galleries, bookstores, restaurants, and other services.

If you pass the Winslow Way turn off and go about a ¼-mile farther north on Olympic you'll find the **Bainbridge Island Vineyard and Winery** (682 S.R. 305, ☎ 206/842–9463), which is open for tastings and tours Wednesday–Sunday noon–5.

Bloedel Reserve, the 150-acre estate of Vancouver, B.C., lumber baron Prentice Bloedel, was opened to the public in 1988. The grounds were designed to recapture the natural, untamed look of the island. Within the park are ponds with ducks and trumpeter swans, Bloedel's grand mansion, and 2 miles of trails. In spring the displays of blooming rhododendrons and azaleas are dazzling, and in fall the leaves of the Japanese maples and other trees colorfully signal the change of seasons. *7571 N.E. Dolphin Dr., Bainbridge Island 98110,* ☎ *206/842–7631.* ☛ *$6, $4 senior citizens, children under 5 free. Reservations necessary.* ◷ *Wed.–Sun. 10–4.*

Bainbridge Island Essentials
VISITOR INFORMATION
The **Bainbridge Island Chamber of Commerce** (590 Winslow Way, Bainbridge Island, ☎ 206/842–3700), two blocks from the ferry dock, has maps and information on restaurants, shops, and sights.

Whidbey Island

On a nice day, there's no better excursion from Seattle than a ferry trip across Puget Sound to Whidbey Island. It's a great way to watch seagulls, sailboats, and massive container vessels in the sound—not to mention the surrounding scenery, which takes in the Kitsap Peninsula and Olympic Mountains, Mt. Rainier, the Cascade Mountains, and the Seattle skyline. Even when the weather isn't all that terrific, travelers can stay snug inside the ferry, have a snack, and listen to the folk musicians who entertain the cross-sound commuters.

The island, 30 miles northwest of Seattle, is one of the nearest "escapes" from the city. In fact, some folks escape to it from Seattle every night— they live on Whidbey and commute to work. The island is a blend of bucolic rolling hills, forests, meadows, sandy beaches, and dramatic, high cliffs. It's a great place for country drives, bicycle touring, exploring the shoreline by boat or kayak, and viewing sunsets. On the west side of the island, visitors can watch container ships ply the waters of Puget Sound between Asia and ports in Seattle and Tacoma.

Whidbey is easily accessible via the Washington State Ferry system from Mukilteo (pronounced muck-ill-*tee*-oh) to Clinton on the southern part of the island or a drive across Deception Pass on the northern end of the island on Highway 20.

Exploring
Numbers in the margin correspond to points of interest on the Puget Sound map.

At 60 miles long and 8 miles wide, Whidbey Island is the second-longest in the contiguous United States—Long Island in New York takes the honors as the longest. This tour begins at the southern tip of the island, which has a mostly rural landscape of undulating hills, gentle beaches, and little coves. Wildlife is plentiful, and it's not unusual to see eagles, great blue herons, and oystercatchers, as well as orcas, gray whales, dolphins, and otters.

 Perhaps the best view of the sea creatures can be had from **Langley,** the quaint town that sits atop a 50-foot-high bluff overlooking the southeastern shore. In the heart of town, along 1st Street and 2nd Street, there are boutiques that sell art, glass, antiques, jewelry, and clothing.

② About halfway up this long, skinny island is the town of **Greenbank,** home to the historically recognized **Loganberry Farm.** The 125-acre site is now the place of production for the state's unique spirit, Whidbey's Liqueur. *657 Wonn Rd., ☎ 360/678–7700. ☛ Free. Self-guided tours offered daily 10–4.*

While in Greenbank, you may want to see the 53-acre **Meerkerk Rhododendron Gardens,** with 1,500 native and hybrid species of rhododendrons, numerous walking trails, and ponds. The flowers are in full bloom in April and May. *Resort Rd., Greenbank, ☎ 360/678–1912. ☛ $2. ☉ Daily 9–4.*

③ Farther north you'll come to **Keystone,** notable because it is the port of call for the ferry bound for Port Townsend on the Olympic Peninsula.

④ **Ft. Casey State Park** (☎ 360/678–4519), just north of Keystone, is one of three forts built in 1890 to protect Puget Sound. Today it offers a small interpretive center, camping, picnic sites, fishing, and a boat launch.

⑤ About two-thirds the way up the island is **Coupeville,** home of many restored Victorian houses and one of the largest National Historic Districts in the state. The town was founded in 1852 by Captain Thomas Coupe; his house, built in 1853, is one of the state's oldest. The town is also the site of the **Island County Historical Museum** (908 N.W. Alexander St., ☎ 360/678–3310), which has exhibits on the history of the island's fishing, timber, and agriculture industries. The museum also offers historical tours and walks.

⑥ **Ebey's Landing National Historic Reserve** (☎ 360/678–4636), a 22-acre area west of Coupeville, was established by Congress in 1980 and is the first and largest reserve of its kind. It is dotted with some 91 nationally registered historical structures, farmland, parks, and trails.

⑦ About 11 miles farther north is **Oak Harbor,** which derived its name from the Garry oaks that grow in the area. It was settled by Dutch and Irish immigrants in the mid-1800s, and several Dutch windmills are still in existence. Unfortunately, the island's largest city has not maintained the sleepy fishing-village pace that much of the rest of the island follows. Instead, Oak Harbor has the look of suburban sprawl, with strips of fast-food restaurants and service stations. Just north of Oak Harbor is **Whidbey Island Naval Air Station** (☎ 360/257–2286), at which group tours can be arranged. At **Deception Pass State Park,** 3 miles from the naval base, take some time to notice the spectacular view and stroll among the madrona trees with their reddish-brown peeling bark. While walking across the bridge, you won't be able to miss seeing the dramatic gorge below, well-known for its tidal currents.

⑧ From the northern side of the island, the Deception Pass bridge links Whidbey to Fidalgo Island. From here it's just a short distance to **Anacortes,** Fidalgo's main town and the terminus for ferries going to the San Juan Islands.

Shopping

Langley's 1st Street and 2nd Street offer a number of unique items. **Annie Steffen's** (101 1st St., ☎ 360/221–6535) specializes in wearables—hand-painted, handwoven, and hand-knit apparel and jewelry. You can meet artist and shop owner Gwenn Knight at the **Glass Knit** (214 1st St., Langley, ☎ 360/221–6283), where her glass art and jewelry are for

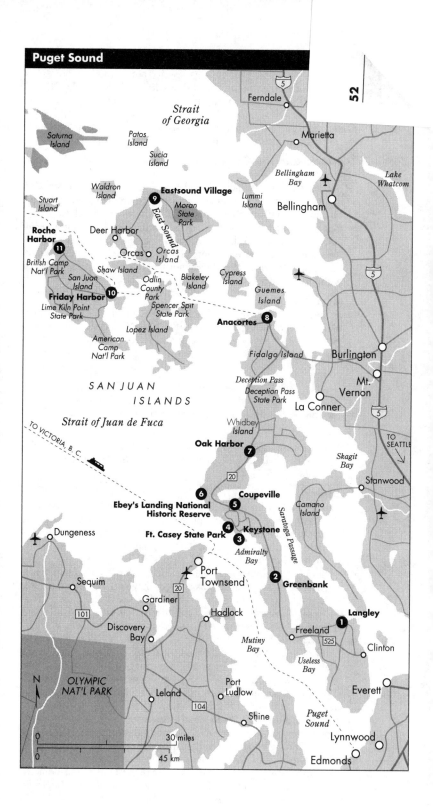

Strait of Georgia

Saturna Island

Patos Island

Sucia Island

Ferndale

Marietta

Bellingham Bay

Lake Whatcom

Waldron Island

Eastsound Village

⑨

Moran State Park

Lummi Island

Bellingham

Stuart Island

Roche Harbor

⑪

Deer Harbor

Orcas ○

Orcas Island

British Camp Nat'l Park

Shaw Island

San Juan Island

Friday Harbor

⑩

Lime Kiln Point State Park

Odlin County Park

Spencer Spit State Park

Blakeley Island

Cypress Island

Guemes Island

Anacortes

⑧

American Camp Nat'l Park

Lopez Island

S A N   J U A N

I S L A N D S

Fidalgo Island

Burlington

Mt. Vernon

La Conner

Strait of Juan de Fuca

Deception Pass

Deception Pass State Park

Whidbey Island

TO VICTORIA, B. C.

Oak Harbor

⑦

Skagit Bay

Stanwood

20

Coupeville

⑥

⑤

Camano Island

Saratoga Passage

Ebey's Landing National Historic Reserve

④

Keystone

③

Ft. Casey State Park

Admiralty Bay

Dungeness

②

Greenbank

Sequim

Port Townsend

Langley

①

Gardiner

101

Hadlock

Freeland

525

Clinton

Discovery Bay

20

Mutiny Bay

Useless Bay

Everett

N

OLYMPIC NAT'L PARK

Leland

Port Ludlow

Puget Sound

Lynnwood

104

Shine

Edmonds

0   30 miles

0   45 km

TO SEATTLE

sale. The **Childers/Proctor Gallery** (302 1st St., Langley, ☎ 360/221–2978) exhibits and sells paintings, jewelry, pottery, and sculpture. Just outside of Langley is the **Blackfish Studio** (5075 S. Langley Rd., ☎ 360/221–1274), where you can see works in progress as well as finished pieces by artist Kathleen Miller, who produces enamel jewelry and hand-painted clothing and accessories, and photographer Donald Miller's depictions of the land and people of the Northwest.

Sports and the Outdoors

BEACHES

Beaches are best on Whidbey Island's west side, where the sand stretches out to the sea and you have a view of the shipping lanes and the Olympic Mountains. **Maxwelton Beach** (Maxwelton Beach Rd.), popular with the locals, is on the west side of the island. **Possession Point** (west on Coltas Bay Rd.) includes a park, a beach, and a boat launch. **Forts Casey** and **Ebey** offer more hiking trails and bluff outlooks than wide, sandy beaches. **West Beach,** north of the forts, is a stormy beach with lots of driftwood.

BICYCLING

In the Bayview area of Whidbey Island, just off Highway 20, **The Pedaler** (5603½ S. Bayview Rd., ☎ 360/221–5040) bicycle sales and service shop also has around 25 mountain bikes and hybrids for rent year-round.

BOATING

Langley's **small boat harbor** (☎ 360/221–6765) offers moorage for 35 boats, utilities, and a 160-foot fishing pier, all protected by a 400-foot timber-pile breakwater. No reservations are accepted.

FISHING

You can catch salmon, perch, cod, and bottomfish from the Langley dock. Supplies are available from the **Langley Marina** (202 Wharf St., ☎ 360/221–1771).

Dining

$$$ Country Kitchen. Entering the restaurant at the Inn at Langley (*see* Lodging, *below*), you first see a fireplace and what looks like a living room, until you notice the tables for two unobtrusively lining the walls. On the other side of the fireplace is the "great table," which seats 10. Dinner may include locally gathered mussels in a black-bean sauce, breast of duck in a loganberry sauce, or rich Columbia River salmon. Appetizers, side dishes, salad greens so fresh they've never seen the inside of a refrigerator, and desserts such as a bowl of island-grown strawberries with cream complement the entrées. ✕ *400 1st St., Langley,* ☎ *360/221–3033. Reservations required. Jacket and tie. MC, V.*

$$ Christopher's. Tucked away at the back of Mariner's Court in Coupeville is this small, eclectically furnished restaurant with a warm yet casual ambience. High ceilings bring a light and airy quality to the main dining room, where the tables are laid with linens, fresh flowers, and candles. Chef and owner Christopher Panek favors regional seafood, vegetarian fare, and fresh local produce. Start with local oysters broiled with prosciutto and provolone and served with sun-dried tomatoes and pickled peppers. Try pork medallions dressed in a cream sauce flavored with Whidbey's loganberry liqueur or have one of the vegetarian dishes—lentil *dahl* tossed with roasted vegetables and served on a bed of couscous is recommended. More than 50 French and domestic wines are also available. ✕ *23 Front St., at Alexander St., Coupeville,* ☎ *360/678–5480. Reservations advised. AE, D, MC, V. Closed Mon., Tues. No lunch Sat.–Thurs.*

$$ **Garibyan Brothers Café Langley.** Terra-cotta tile floors, antique oak tables, Italian music, and the aromas of garlic, basil, and oregano set the tone for your lunch or dinner. Greek salads, vegetarian eggplant, fresh mussels, lamb loin chops, moussaka, and lamb shish kebabs are just a few of the offerings. ✕ *113 1st St., Langley,* ☎ *360/221–3090. Reservations advised. MC, V.*

$$ **Star Bistro.** This black, white, and red bistro, atop the Star Store, serves up Caesar salads, shrimp-and-scallop linguine, and gourmet burgers. ✕ *201½ 1st St., Langley,* ☎ *360/221–2627. No reservations. AE, MC, V.*

$ **Dog House Backdoor Restaurant.** This extremely casual waterfront tavern and restaurant serves large, juicy burgers and has a pool table, as well as a great view of Saratoga Passage. ✕ *230 1st St., Langley,* ☎ *360/221–9996. No reservations. No credit cards.*

Lodging

$$$$ **Cliff House.** This luxury house, situated near Freeland, sleeps one to two couples in a secluded setting overlooking Admiralty inlet. The three-story house, one side nearly all glass, affords romantic views to the guests enjoying the elegant bedroom loft. Rain and occasionally snow whisk through the open-air atrium in the middle of the house. Guests are pampered with fresh flowers, a huge stone fireplace, and miles of driftwood beach. ☷ *5440 Windmill Rd., Freeland 98249,* ☎ *360/221–1566. 1 room. No credit cards.*

$$$ **Guest House Cottages.** This B&B, just outside Greenbank, includes a luxurious log lodge for one couple, four private cottages, and a three-room suite in a farmhouse located on 25 acres of forest and pastureland. The accommodations are cozy, with fireplaces, stained-glass pieces, and country antique furnishings; some have kitchens and all have microwaves. ☷ *835 E. Christianson Rd., Greenbank 98253,* ☎ *360/678–3115. 6 units. Pool, exercise room. No credit cards.*

$$$ **Inn at Langley.** This concrete-and-wood Frank Lloyd Wright–inspired
★ structure perches on the side of a bluff that descends to the beach. Guest rooms feature Asian-style decor in neutral colors and spectacular views of Saratoga Passage and the Cascade Mountains. Meals are served in the inn's acclaimed restaurant, the Country Kitchen (*see* Dining, *above*). Continental breakfast (for guests) is available Monday–Wednesday, 8–10. Dinner starts promptly at 7, with a glass of sherry and a tour of the wine cellar. ☷ *400 1st St., Langley,* ☎ *360/221–3033. 24 rooms. Restaurant. MC, V.*

$$ **Captain Whidbey Inn.** This inn offers a wide variety of accommodations, including the original madrona log inn (listed on the National Register of Historic Places), cottages, a duplex, and houses with views of Penn Cove. Inn rooms are rustic and have shared baths, though they do feature a few antiques and feather beds. Lagoon rooms are large and have private baths. Cottages and the duplex have one or two bedrooms, sitting rooms, and some have kitchens, fireplaces, and private baths. The dining room, serving breakfast, lunch, and dinner, is cozy, with dark paneling, soft lighting, and several tables overlooking Penn Cove. ☷ *2072 W. Captain Whidbey Inn Rd., Coupeville 98239,* ☎ *360/678–4097. 33 units. Boating, bicycles. MC, V.*

$$ **Fort Casey Inn.** These restored, two-story, Georgian Revival officers' quarters were built in 1909. Each has a fireplace, two bedrooms, a living room, and a full country kitchen (with breakfast fixings on hand). Owners Gordon and Victoria Hoenig have restored the tin ceilings and decorated the units with rag rugs, old quilts, hand-painted furniture, and sundry Colonial touches. ☷ *1124 S. Engle Rd., Coupeville 98239,* ☎ *360/678-8792. 9 units. Bicycles. AE, MC, V.*

$$ **Twickenham House.** The weekend-in-the-country ambience of this new cedar-sided inn takes hold as soon as you catch sight of the sheep grazing and ducks wandering in the surrounding pasture. The rooms are decorated simply with trunks, pine armoires, and matching duvets and pillow shams. One of the highlights of a stay here is the gourmet breakfast, made from fresh, local ingredients and reflecting the English and French Canadian heritage of the inn's owners. ⬚ *5023 Langley Rd., Langley 98260,* ☎ *800/874–5009. 4 rooms, 2 suites. MC, V.*

Whidbey Island Essentials

GETTING AROUND

By Car: Whidbey Island can be reached by going north from Seattle along I–5, then heading west on Highway 20; cross the dramatic Deception Pass via the bridge at the north end of the island.

By Ferry: For complete information on the **Washington State Ferry System** (☎ 206/464–6400), *see* Getting Around *in* The San Juan Islands, *below.*

By Plane: Harbor Airlines (☎ 800/359–3220) flies to Whidbey Island from Friday Harbor and Sea-Tac Airport. **Kenmore Air** (☎ 206/486–1257 or 800/543–9595) can arrange charter float plane flights to Whidbey Island.

The San Juan Islands

The San Juan Islands are the jewels of the Northwest. Because the islands are reachable only by ferry or airplane, they beckon to souls longing for a quiet change of pace, whether it be kayaking in a cove, walking a deserted beach, or nestling by the fire in an old farmhouse. Unfortunately, solitude becomes a precious commodity in the summer when the San Juans are overrun by tourists. Island residents enjoy their peace and quiet, and many would just as soon not have their country roads and villages jammed with "summer people." Not surprisingly, tourism and development are hotly contested issues on the islands.

On weekends and even some weekdays, expect to wait at least three hours in line once you arrive at the ferry terminal. You will face the same challenge or worse if you return on Sunday afternoon or evening. One way to avoid crowds and the possibility of a cantankerous island resident is to plan a trip in the spring, fall, or winter. Reservations are a must anytime in the summer and are advised for weekends in the off-season, too.

Exploring

Numbers in the margin correspond to points of interest on the Puget Sound map.

There are 172 named islands in the San Juan archipelago, although at low tide the islands total 743 and at high tide, 428. Sixty are populated and 10 are state marine parks. Ferries stop at Lopez, Shaw, Orcas, and San Juan; other islands, many privately owned, must be reached by private plane or boat. In any case, the San Juan Islands are a gold mine for naturalists, because they are home to more than 94 orcas, a few minke whales, seals, dolphins, otters, and more than 100 active pairs of breeding bald eagles.

LOPEZ AND SHAW ISLANDS

The first ferry stop is Lopez Island, with old orchards, weathered barns, and pastures of sheep and cows. Because of the relatively flat terrain, this island is a favorite for bicyclists. Two popular parks to note are **Odlin County Park** and **Spencer Spit State Park.**

At the next stop, Shaw Island, a local order of nuns wear their traditional habits while running the ferry dock. You may notice that few people get off here; the island is mostly residential, and tourists rarely stop.

ORCAS ISLAND

Orcas Island, the next in line, is a large, mountainous, horseshoe-shape island. Roads sweep down through wide valleys and rise to marvelous hilltop views. A number of little shops featuring the island's cottage industries—jewelry, weaving, pottery—are in **Eastsound Village,** the island's business and social center, which is situated in the middle of the horseshoe. Walk along Prune Alley, where you'll find a handful of small shops and restaurants.

On the other side of the horseshoe from the ferry landing, following aptly named Horseshoe Highway, is **Moran State Park** (Star Rte., Box 22, Eastsound 98245, ☎ 360/376–2326). The ranger station will supply information, but applications for camping permits within the park for Memorial Day through Labor Day must be received by mail at least two weeks prior to the requested date. From the summit of the 2,400-foot-tall **Mt. Constitution** are panoramic views of the San Juan Islands, the Cascades, the Olympics, and Vancouver Island.

SAN JUAN ISLAND

The last ferry stop in the San Juan Islands is at **Friday Harbor** on San Juan Island, with a colorful, active waterfront that always conveys a holiday feeling. Friday Harbor—the islands' county seat and the only incorporated town on San Juan Island—is also the most convenient destination in the San Juans for visitors traveling on foot. The shops here cater to tourists, offering clever crafts, gifts, and whimsical toys.

Standing at the ferry dock facing the bluff and downtown, you'll recognize the **Whale Museum** by the mural of the whale painted on the wall. To reach the entrance, walk up Spring Street and turn right on 1st Street. This modest museum doesn't attempt to woo you with expensive exhibits; models of whales, whale skeletons, baleen, recordings of whale sounds, and videos of whales are the attractions. There are also workshops on marine mammals and San Juan ecology. *62 1st St. N,* ☎ *360/378–4710.* ☛ *$3 adults, $2.50 senior citizens, $1.50 children 3–12.* ☉ *June–Sept., daily 10–5; Oct.–May, daily 11–4.*

For an opportunity to see whales cavorting in the Strait of San Juan de Fuca, go to **Lime Kiln Point State Park,** on San Juan's west side, just 6 miles from Friday Harbor. This viewpoint is America's first official whale-watching park. The best seasons to visit are late spring, summer, and fall. *6158 Lighthouse Rd.,* ☎ *360/378–2044.* ☛ *Free.* ☉ *Daily 6:30 AM–10 PM. Day use only; no camping facilities.*

The **San Juan Island National Historic Park** is a remnant of the "Pig War," a prolonged scuffle between American and British troops who were brought in after a Yank killed a Brit's pig in 1859, setting off tempers on both sides. The mere presence of the soldiers was pretty much the extent of the hostilities (no gunfire was ever exchanged), although troops from both countries remained on the island until 1872. The park encompasses two separate areas: a British camp on the west side of the island, containing a blockhouse, commissary, and barracks; and an American camp with a laundry, fortifications, and a visitor's center. From June through August the park offers hikes and historic reenactments of 1860s-era military life. For information contact the **San Juan Island Visitor Information Service** (☎ 360/468–3663).

⑪ Roche Harbor, at the northern end of San Juan, is an elegant little town of well-manicured lawns, rose gardens, cobblestone waterfront, hanging flower baskets on the docks, and the Hotel de Haro, with its restaurant and lounge.

Shopping

LOPEZ ISLAND

The **Chimera Gallery** (Lopez Village, ☎ 360/468–3265) is a local artists' cooperative exhibiting crafts, jewelry, and fine art. **Grayling Gallery** (3630 Hummel Lake Rd., ☎ 360/468–2779) features the paintings, prints, sculptures, and pottery of about 10 artists from Lopez Island, some of whom live and work on the gallery's premises. The gallery is open Friday–Sunday 10–5.

ORCAS ISLAND

Darvill's Rare Print Shop (Eastsound, ☎ 360/376–2351) specializes in antique and contemporary prints.

SAN JUAN ISLAND

Boardwalk Bookstore (5 Spring St., Friday Harbor, ☎ 360/378–2787) is strong in classics and has a collection of good, popular literature selected by a most literate owner, Dorthea Augusztiny. **Cabezon Gallery** (60 1st St. W, ☎ 360/378–3116) features the works of local artists. **Island Wools, Weaving, and Quilting** (30 1st St. S, Friday Harbor, ☎ 360/378–2148) carries wonderful yarns, some hand-spun and hand-dyed; imaginative buttons; quilting supplies; and some hand-knit items. **Waterworks Gallery** (315 Argyle St., Friday Harbor, ☎ 360/378–3060) emphasizes marine art.

Sports and the Outdoors

BEACHES

The best beaches on Lopez Island include the low-bank beach at **Odlin County Park** (Rte. 2, Box 3216, ☎ 360/468–2496) and a mile of waterfront at **Spencer Spit State Park** (Rte. 2, Box 3600, ☎ 360/468–2251). On San Juan Island, you'll find 10 acres of beachfront at the **San Juan County Park** (380 Westside Rd. N, Friday Harbor, ☎ 360/378–2992) and 6 miles of public beach at American Camp.

BICYCLING

Lopez Island: The **Bike Shop** (Rte. 1, Box 1162, Lopez 98261, ☎ 360/468–3497) provides bikes for rent year-round. **Cycle San Juans Tours and Rentals** (Rte. 1, Box 1744, Lopez 98261, ☎ 360/468–3251) provides free bicycle delivery all year.

Orcas Island: Key Moped Rental (Box 279, Eastsound, ☎ 360/376–2474) rents mopeds during the summer. **Wildlife Cycles** (Box 1048, Eastsound, ☎ 360/376–4708) has bikes for rent in Eastsound.

San Juan Island: San Juan Island Bicycles (380 Argyle St., Friday Harbor, ☎ 360/378–4941) has a reputation for good service as well as equipment. **Susie's Mopeds** (Box 1972, Friday Harbor, ☎ 360/378–5244 or 800/532–0087) rents mopeds.

BOATING AND KAYAKING

Marine State Parks (☎ 360/753–2027) are accessible by private boat only. No moorage or camping reservations are available, and fees are charged at some parks from May through Labor Day. Fresh water, where available, is limited. Island parks are Blind, Clark, Doe, James, Jones, Matia, Patos, Posey, Stuart, Sucia, and Turn. All have a few campsites; there are no docks at Blind, Clark, Patos, Posey, or Turn islands.

Skippered sailing charters are available through **Amante Sail Tours** (☎ 360/376–4231), **Custom Designed Charters** (☎ 360/376–5105), **Harmony Sailing Charters** (☎ 360/468–3310), **Kismet Sailing Charters** (☎ 360/468–2435), **Nor'wester Sailing Charters** (☎ 360/378–5478), and **Wind N' Sails** (☎ 360/378–5343).

If you are kayaking on your own, beware of ever-changing conditions, ferry and shipping landings, and strong tides and currents. Go ashore only on known public property. Day trips and longer expeditions are available from **Shearwater Sea Kayak Tours** (☎ 360/376–4699), **Doe Bay Resort** (☎ 360/376–2291), **San Juan Kayak Expeditions** (☎ 360/378–4436), and **Seaquest** (☎ 360/378–5767).

Marinas: On Lopez Island, **Islands Marine Center** (☎ 360/468–3377) has most standard marina amenities, repair facilities, and transient moorage. On Orcas Island, **Deer Harbor Resort & Marina** (☎ 360/376–4420), **Lieber Haven Marina Resort** (☎ 360/376–4420), and **West Sound Marina** (☎ 360/376–2314) offer standard marina facilities and more. **Russell's Landing/Orcas Store** (☎ 360/376–4389) has gas, diesel, tackle, and groceries at the ferry landing. On San Juan Island, **Port of Friday Harbor** (☎ 360/378–2688), **San Juan Marina** (☎ 360/378–2841), and **Roche Harbor Resort** (☎ 360/378–2155) have standard marina facilities; Port of Friday and Roche harbors are also U.S. Customs ports of entry.

FISHING

You can fish year-round for bass and trout at Hummel Lake on Lopez Island, and at Egg and Sportsman lakes on San Juan Island. On Orcas, there are three lakes at Moran State Park that are open to fishing from late April through October. You can go saltwater fishing through **Buffalo Works** (☎ 360/378–4612) and **King Salmon Charters** (☎ 360/468–2314).

Dining

LOPEZ ISLAND

$$ Bay Café. Fine entrées served with an international flair, plus an excellent wine list, attract everyone from locals and vacationers to movie stars filming on the island to this modest-looking restaurant near the water in Lopez Village. Highlights of the seasonal menu include grilled pork tenderloin with a honey-mustard glaze, smoked ham aioli, and garlic mashed potatoes. ✕ *Lopez Village,* ☎ *360/468–3700. Reservations advised. MC, V. No lunch.*

ORCAS ISLAND

$$–$$$ Christina's. The emphasis at this elegant restaurant is on fresh, local seafood. Order the steamed lemongrass and ginger rockfish served with rice noodles, leeks, and carrots, and then relax on the enclosed porch or the rooftop terrace with views of East Sound. Other specialties include a stuffed breast of chicken served with an eggplant relish and grilled vegetables. Desserts include the likes of pumpkin flan with cookies or a Chocolate Blackout Torte. ✕ *N. Beach Rd. and Horseshoe Hwy.,* ☎ *360/376–4904. Reservations advised. AE, DC, MC, V. Closed Tues. Oct.–mid June. No lunch.*

$–$$ Bilbo's Festivo. Stucco walls, Mexican tiles, wood benches, and weavings from New Mexico betray the culinary theme of this restaurant with a courtyard. The menu features burritos, enchiladas, and other Mexican favorites like orange-marinated chicken grilled over mesquite and served with fresh asparagus, potatoes, and salad. ✕ *N. Beach Rd. and A St., Eastsound,* ☎ *360/376–4728. No reservations. AE, MC, V. No lunch Oct.–May.*

$$$ **Duck Soup Inn.** Everything the Duck Soup Inn serves is made from scratch daily, including the fresh bread, Mediterranean-inspired entrées, vegetarian dishes, and delicious ice cream. Start with apple-wood-smoked Westcott Bay oysters, followed with pan-seared sea scallops served in a red-curry coconut sauce on a bed of cashews and greens. There is also a good list of Northwest, California, and European wines. ✕ *3090 Roche Harbor Rd.,* ☎ *360/378–4878. Reservations advised. MC, V. Closed Mon.–Tues. Apr.–Oct.; closed entirely Nov.–Mar. No lunch.*

$$ **Springtree Café.** This bistro-style café in downtown Friday Harbor has an innovative daily menu built around fresh seafood and vegetarian entrées. The kitchen uses fresh, Waldron Island organic produce to create such dishes as ginger shrimp with mango and dark rum or steamed San Juan Island mussels. The restaurant also offers a good wine list. ✕ *Spring St.,* ☎ *360/378–4848. Reservations advised. MC, V. Closed Sun.–Mon. Oct. 11–May 1.*

$ **Front Street Ale House.** This English-style pub serves sandwiches and salads, as well as such traditional pub fare as lamb stew, meat pastries, steak-and-kidney pie, and trifle. For vegetarians, there's a vegetable patty lightly sautéed, then stacked with cheese, mushrooms, lettuce, tomato, and onions. On-tap brews from the San Juan Brewing Company carry such locally inspired names as Pig War Stout. ✕ *1 Front St., Friday Harbor,* ☎ *360/378–2337. No reservations. MC, V.*

Lodging

$$$–$$$$ **Majestic Hotel.** An old mercantile has been turned into one of the finest small hotels in the Northwest. From the elegant, Victorian-style, two-story lobby, guests can enter the Rose & Crown pub and the banquet rooms or ascend the sweeping stairway to the guest rooms and the dark, English-style library. The top-floor gazebo has views of the marina, Mt. Baker, and the Cascades. Rooms are individually decorated with European antiques and down comforters; several contain whirlpool tubs. A complimentary Continental breakfast is served in the dining room, and the full-service restaurant, the Courtyard Bistro, turns out excellent meals. 🏨 *419 Commercial Ave., Anacortes, Fidalgo Island 98221,* ☎ *360/293–3355,* 🖷 *360/293–5214. 23 rooms. Restaurant, pub, library. MC, V.*

$$$ **Edenwild.** The imposing gray Victorian-style farmhouse, surrounded by rose gardens, looks as if it's a restored island building, but dates only from 1990, not 1890. Rooms feature whitewashed oak floors, a muted gray interior, and white painted woodwork, along with botanical prints, lace curtains from Scotland, leaded-glass windows, and some antiques. In summer a three-course breakfast is served in the dining room. 🏨 *Box 271, Lopez Island 98261,* ☎ *360/468–3238. 7 rooms. MC, V.*

$$–$$$ **Inn at Swifts Bay.** Robert Herrman and Chris Brandmeir invite guests into their sumptuously comfortable Tudor-style home as if they were welcoming old friends. The English-country ambience is enhanced by eclectic furnishings and well-stocked book and video libraries. Bay windows in the living and dining areas overlook well-kept gardens, and a crackling fire warms the living room on winter evenings. Robes, thongs, and flashlights are available for your walk through the garden to a hot tub under the stars. Guest rooms and suites are all decorated tastefully. In the morning, Chris treats you to a gourmet breakfast, such as eggs Dungeness (poached eggs with hollandaise and fresh crab). 🏨 *Rte. 2,*

Box 3402, Lopez Island 98261, ☎ 360/468–3636. *2 rooms, 3 suites, waterfront cabin. Hot tub, beach. AE, D, MC, V.*

$$ Mackaye Harbor Inn. At the south end of Lopez Island, across the road from MacKaye Harbor, is this two-story inn, a frame 1920s sea captain's house with a half mile of beach. Rooms feature golden oak and brass details and wicker furniture; three have views of the harbor. Owners Robin, who is Swedish, and Mike Bergstrom take turns cooking breakfast, which often includes Scandinavian specialties such as *aebleskiver* (apple pancake) and *panukakku* (Finnish pancake). ☎ *Box 1940, Lopez Island 98261, ☎ 360/468–2253. 5 rooms. Kayaking, boating, bicycles. MC, V.*

ORCAS ISLAND

$$$ Rosario Spa & Resort. This 1905 Mediterranean-style mansion, which supports a six-ton copper roof, has finally received its due: The interior of the building, done in teak and mahogany and featuring original Mission-style furniture, has been renovated. Shipbuilding magnate Robert Moran, who commissioned the structure, was told he had six months to live so he went all-out—to the tune of $1.5 million—on this, his last extravagance. As it happened, Moran lived another 30 years, and now the mansion is on the National Register of Historic Places. The villas and hotel units, added after Rosario was converted into a resort in 1960, now have modern bathrooms, soundproofing, and fresh color schemes; many have great views of the water. Avoid long ferry lines in the summer by leaving your car in Anacortes; the resort shuttle meets every ferry and offers transportation into Eastsound. The resort also is accessible from Seattle by floatplane and Victoria clipper boats. ☎ *Horseshoe Hwy., Eastsound 98245, ☎ 360/376–2222 or 800/562–8820. 179 rooms. Dining room, indoor pool, 2 outdoor pools, hot tub, sauna, spa, 2 tennis courts, hiking, dock, boating, fishing. AE, DC, MC, V.*

$$–$$$ Orcas Hotel. On the hill overlooking the Orcas Island ferry landing is this three-story, red-roof Victorian hotel, complete with a wraparound porch and white picket fence. Construction first began in 1900, and the building is on the National Register of Historic Places. Guest rooms feature wicker, brass, antique furnishings, and feather beds, and some units have small sundecks. The dining room (open to nonguests as well) overlooks the ferry landing and gardens; an on-site bakery offers espresso drinks. A complimentary breakfast is served in the dining room, where guests order from the restaurant's regular menu of French toast, omelets, and other egg dishes. ☎ *Box 155, Orcas 98280, ☎ 360/376–4300, ℻ 360/376–4399. 12 rooms. Restaurant, bar. AE, DC, MC, V.*

$$–$$$ Turtleback Farm Inn. Just 15 minutes from the ferry landing is this forest green inn, trimmed in white, set on 80 acres of meadow, forest, and farmland in the shadow of Turtleback Mountain. The interior is spacious and airy, without frills. Guest rooms have easy chairs, good beds with woolen comforters made from the fleece of resident sheep, some antiques, cream-color muslin curtains, and views of meadows and forest. Breakfast, cooked by Susan Fletcher and served by her husband, Bill, can be taken in the dining room or on the deck overlooking the valley. ☎ *R.R. 1, Box 650, Eastsound 98245, ☎ 360/376–3914. 7 rooms. MC, V.*

$$ Deer Harbor Inn. The original 1915 log lodge—situated on a knoll overlooking Deer Harbor—was the first resort built on the island and is now the dining room of the inn. A newer log cabin features eight spacious, airy rooms with peeled-log furniture, lovely views from balconies, and breakfast delivered to the door in a picnic basket. The dining room, which specializes in fresh seafood, is large but cozy, with its natural wood and floral prints, and has an adjoining deck for outdoor dining. ⌧ *Box 142, Eastsound 98243,* ☏ *360/376–4110. 8 units. Restaurant. AE, MC, V.*

$–$$ Doe Bay Village Resort. This is a rustic place that is a personal-growth center and retreat. The resort feels faintly countercultural, a holdover from its earlier days as an artists' colony. Units vary from dormitory rooms to cottages, some with sleeping quarters only and access to shower house and community kitchen; other units feature kitchens and baths. A natural-food café and general store are also on-site. The peaceful, scenic grounds are great for walks or for sitting and reading. ⌧ *S.R. 86, Olga 98279,* ☏ *360/376–2291. 100 units. Café, hot tub, massage, kayaking. AE, MC, V.*

SAN JUAN ISLAND

$$$ Friday Harbor House. On a bluff overlooking the marina, ferry landing, and San Juan Channel, this contemporary villa hotel opened in late 1994. Each of the 20 guest rooms has a fireplace, view, oversize whirlpool tub, and refrigerator; complimentary continental breakfast is included. ⌧ *130 West St., Box 1385, Friday Harbor 98250,* ☏ *360/ 378–8455. 20 rooms. Restaurant. MC, V.*

$$–$$$ Roche Harbor Resort. Here you've got a choice between rather nondescript cottages and condominiums, or rooms in the 1886 restored Hotel de Haro. The old hotel building is better to look at than to stay in; its guest rooms are fairly shabby or, at best, very rustic. On the other hand, the resort has extensive facilities, including boat slips for 200 yachts, full marina facilities, and a 4,000-foot airstrip. ⌧ *Box 1, Friday Harbor 98250,* ☏ *360/378–2155. 60 rooms. Restaurant, pool, tennis court. MC, V.*

$$ Blair House. This B&B sits on more than an acre of landscaped grounds just four blocks uphill from the ferry landing in Friday Harbor. The two-story gray Victorian house with dormer windows and a wide wraparound porch, now furnished with wicker chairs and table, was built in 1909 and has since been enlarged several times. The rooms are decorated with sophisticated wallpapers, color-coordinated linens, and ivory comforters on the beds. Guests can eat breakfast in the large dining room, on the front porch, or alongside the outdoor pool. ⌧ *345 Blair Ave., Friday Harbor 98250,* ☏ *360/378–5907. 7 rooms, 1 cottage. Dining room, pool, hot tub. AE, MC, V.*

$$ Fridays. Since it was built in 1891, this house near the ferry terminal has been a hotel, restaurant, private home, and a youth hostel. Debbie and Steve Demarest have converted it into a downtown bed-and-breakfast hideaway with Arts and Crafts–style furniture in the sitting room and several guest rooms that open onto decks flanked by roses, geraniums, and other flowers. All rooms are upstairs and are decorated with antiques, colorful floral-print comforters on the beds, and art on the walls. Continental breakfast features fresh orange juice, scones baked daily, and gourmet coffee. ⌧ *35 1st St., Friday Harbor 98250,* ☏ *360/ 378–5848 or 800/352–2632. 4 rooms with bath, 4 rooms share 2 baths, 2 suites. MC, V.*

$$ Hillside House. Less than a mile outside Friday Harbor, this contemporary house sits on a hill, providing stunning views of the harbor and Mt. Baker from a large deck. The Eagle's Nest suite features several windows with expansive views, a king-size bed, sitting area, and spacious bathroom, where guests can luxuriate in the whirlpool tub while gazing up at the moon through large, high windows. Queen-size beds, oak chests, and one- or two-person window seats are in all the rooms. Some feature sophisticated decor while others are more whimsical. Oth-

ers overlook the 10,000-square-foot full-fligh
who own the inn, encourage guests to use t
hallway—take one or leave one. Breakfast ir
resident hens' eggs, island jams, and fresh be
Friday Harbor 98250, ☎ *360/378–4730 o*
1 suite. AE, MC, V.

$$ **San Juan Inn.** This restored 1873 inn is comfortably furnisheᴅ aᴅᴅ
walking distance of the ferry terminal. Rooms, which are all on the
second floor, are small but have brass, iron, or wicker beds, a few an-
tiques, and decorative wallpaper. Some rooms have views of a lovely
courtyard garden. A breakfast of muffins, coffee, and juice is served
each morning in a parlor overlooking the harbor. ⊠ *50 Spring St., Box
776, Friday Harbor 98250,* ☎ *360/378–2070 or 800/742–8210. 10
rooms. Car rental. MC, V.*

San Juan Islands Essentials

GETTING AROUND

By Car: To reach the San Juan Islands from Seattle, drive north on I–5
to Mt. Vernon, Exit 230, go west and follow signs to Anacortes; pick
up the Washington State Ferry (*see below*). It is convenient to have a
car in the San Juan Islands, but taking your car with you may mean
waiting in long lines at the ferry terminals. With prior arrangement,
most bed-and-breakfast owners can pick up walk-on guests at the
ferry terminals.

By Ferry: The **Washington State Ferry System** (☎ 206/464–6400), the
biggest in the United States, includes vessels ranging from the 40-car
Hiyu to jumbo ferries capable of carrying more than 200 cars and 2,000
passengers each. They connect points all around Puget Sound and the
San Juan Islands.

Car and passenger ferries leave from Fauntleroy, in West Seattle, to
Vashon Island and Southworth; from Edmonds, north of Seattle, to
Kingston; from Port Townsend to Keystone (Whidbey Island); from
Mukilteo, farther north, to Clinton on Whidbey Island; and from Ana-
cortes, about 90 miles north of Seattle, to the San Juan Islands.

Sunny weekends are heavy traffic times all around the San Juan Islands,
and weekday commuting hours for ferries headed into or out of Seat-
tle are also crowded. Peak times on the Seattle runs are sunny week-
ends, eastbound in the morning and Sunday nights, as well as westbound
Saturday morning and weekday afternoons. Since no reservations are
accepted on Washington State Ferries (except for the Sidney–Ana-
cortes run during summer), arriving at least a half hour before a sched-
uled departure is always advised.

The advantages of walking on board are obvious; it's cheaper than tak-
ing your car and hassle-free (no long waits in lines of frustrated drivers
during peak commute hours or on weekends). If you do take your car,
there are several points to note: Passengers and bicycles always load
first unless otherwise instructed. Prior to boarding, lower antennas. Only
parking lights should be used at night, and it is considered bad form
to start your engine before the ferry docks. Also, no smoking is allowed
in public areas.

You don't have to rely solely on the state ferries: **San Juan Islands Shut-
tle Express** (Alaska Ferry Terminal, 355 Harris Ave., No. 105, Belling-
ham 98225, ☎ 360/671–1137) takes passengers from Bellingham to
Orcas Island and Friday Harbor.

By Plane: West Isle Air (☎ 800/874–4434) flies to Friday Harbor on San Juan Island from Sea-Tac and Bellingham airports. **Kenmore Air** (☎ 206/486–8400 or 800/543–9595) flies floatplanes from Lake Union in Seattle to the San Juan Islands.

GUIDED TOURS

San Juan Islands Shuttle Express (Alaska Ferry Terminal, 355 Harris Ave., No. 105, Bellingham 98225, ☎ 360/671–1137) offers whale-watching trips.

Victoria San Juan Cruises (355 Harris Ave., Bellingham 98225, ☎ 800/443–4552) operates 3½-hour nature cruises through the San Juan Islands to Victoria. ►

Western Prince Cruises (Box 418, Friday Harbor 98250, ☎ 360/378–5315) in the San Juan Islands charters boats for half-day whale-watching cruises during the summer; in the spring and fall, bird-watching and scuba-diving tours are offered. Cruises depart from Friday Harbor on San Juan Island.

VISITOR INFORMATION

San Juan Islands Visitor Information Service (Box 65, Lopez 98261, ☎ 360/468–3663).

Snoqualmie Falls

Driving east out of Seattle on I–90, you'll travel through bucolic farmland with snowcapped mountains in the background. Nestled in the foothills is Snoqualmie Falls, one of the area's most popular attractions. Small mining towns dot the mountains, and to the north of the main I–90 route, you'll find Leavenworth, an alpine-style village with excellent sporting opportunities. Crossing over the mountains, you'll emerge in eastern Washington—seemingly a different state, in both attitude and climate.

★ Spring and summer snowmelt turns the Snoqualmie River into the thundering torrent known as **Snoqualmie Falls** as it cascades through a 268-foot rock gorge (100 feet higher than Niagara Falls) to a 65-foot-deep pool below. These falls are the biggest attraction of Snoqualmie, which is about 30 miles east of Seattle at Exit 27 off I–90, although a sizable contingent of visitors come to see where David Lynch filmed his short-lived—but deeply loved—TV series *Twin Peaks.*

A 2-acre park, including an observation platform 300 feet above the Snoqualmie River, offers a view of the falls and surrounding area. Hike the **River Trail,** a 3-mile round-trip route through trees and open slopes, ending with a view from the base of the falls. (Note: Be prepared for an uphill workout on the return to the trailhead.)

Steam locomotives power vintage trains on **Puget Sound** and **Snoqualmie Valley Railway.** The 75-minute trip travels through woods and farmland. Railroad artifacts and memorabilia are displayed at both the Snoqualmie Depot (Hwy. 202, in downtown Snoqualmie) and Railroad Park Depot in downtown Northbend. For children, a special Santa train runs the first two weekends in December and a spook train runs the last two weekends in October; tickets for all special trips must be prepurchased. *Box 459, Snoqualmie,* ☎ *206/746–4025 in Seattle or 206/888–0373.* ► *$6 adults, $5 senior citizens, $4 children. Trains* *operate Sept., May, and June, weekends; Oct. and Apr., Sun.; July–Aug., Fri.–Sun. Call for departure times.*

Skiing

Snoqualmie Pass is the site of three ski areas—**Alpental, Ski Acres,** and **Snoqualmie Summit** (for all areas: 3010 77th St. SE, Mercer Island 98040, ☎ 206/232–8182). Both downhill and cross-country skiing are available in winter and spring, and there's hiking in the summer. Each area rents equipment and has full restaurant and lodge facilities.

Dining

$$$ **The Herbfarm.** If there is such a thing as Northwest cuisine, then The
★ Herbfarm must rank as its temple. But the attraction here is more than the fine, fresh food: This restaurant offers intimate, elegant dining among wildflower bouquets, Victorian-style prints, and a friendly staff. Try such delicacies as goat's milk cheese and parsley biscuits, green pickled walnuts in the husk, fresh salmon with a sauce of fresh garden herbs, and sorbet of rose geranium and lemon verbena. There's only one drawback: The Herbfarm is commonly booked up months ahead of time, which means you should plan a meal long before you're getting to Seattle. Is all that effort worth it? Yes. Wine is the only alcohol served. ✕ *From I–90, Exit 22, go 3 mi. to 32804 Issaquah-Fall City Rd., Fall City,* ☎ *206/784–2222. 75% of the 24 seats for each lunch or special dinner are reserved in early Apr. The other 6 seats can be reserved by phoning at 1 PM the Fri. before you wish to go. Allow 2 hrs for lunch ($60 per person) and the garden tour. Dinners, including 9 courses and 5 fine wines, are scheduled in the summer ($115 per person). MC, V. Closed Mon.–Thurs. No dinner Jan.–early Apr.*

$$$ **Salish.** The restaurant at the Salish lodge (*see below*) serves three meals daily, but gained its widespread reputation for its Saturday and Sunday brunch. Five- or eight-course brunches are available, including such items as eggs, bacon, fish, fresh fruit, pancakes, and the Salish's renowned oatmeal. ✕ *37807 Snoqualmie-Fall City Rd., Fall City 37807,* ☎ *206/888–2556. Reservations required. Jacket and tie (for dinner). AE, DC, MC, V.*

Lodging

$$$ **Salish.** This lodge at the top of the falls has been rebuilt and is operated by the Oregon-based Salishan Lodge. Eight of the 91 rooms look out over the falls, and others have a view upriver. All the rooms have an airy feeling, wood furniture, and window seats or balconies. You can sit in the whirlpool bath and open a window to view the fire in the flagstone fireplace. ☎ *37807 Snoqualmie-Fall City Rd., Fall City 37807,* ☎ *206/888–2556. 91 rooms. 2 restaurants, bar, health club. AE, DC, MC, V.*

Arts and Nightlife

Snoqualmie Falls Forest Theater produces three plays a summer (the Passion Play, a melodrama, and a well-known classic performed by acting students and community theater performers) in the 250-seat outdoor amphitheater near Fall City, usually on Friday and Saturday nights and Sunday afternoons. *From I–90 take Exit 22 and go 4 mi; take a right on David Powell Rd., follow signs, continue through gate to parking area. 36800 S.E. David Powell Rd.,* ☎ *206/222–7044.* ☛ *$8.50; for another $9 per person, you can enjoy a salmon or steak barbecue after the matinee and before the evening performances. Reservations required for dinner.*

Snoqualmie Falls Essentials

VISITOR INFORMATION
Upper Snoqualmie Valley Chamber of Commerce (Box 356, North Bend 98045, ☎ 206/888–4440).

Leavenworth

Some of the best skiing, hiking, rock climbing, rafting, canoeing, and snowshoeing in the Northwest (*see* Sports and the Outdoors, *below*) are accessible from Leavenworth, a cute pseudo-Bavarian resort town about 50 miles north of I–90. Take Rte. 970 from Cle Elum to Rte. 97 and continue north 40 miles, or catch Rte. 97 at its junction with I–90 just 4 miles west of Ellensburg. (You can also reach Leavenworth by traveling northeast from Seattle along I–5 and U.S. 2.)

Although it was once a center for mining and railroading, by the early 1960s Leavenworth had become a moribund village. Civic leaders seeking ways to revitalize the area decided to capitalize on the town's spectacular alpine setting; the result is a charming (and only sometimes *too* cute) center for both winter and summer sports. Shopkeepers and hostelers, maintaining the town's buildings in gingerbread Tyrolean style and sponsoring events modeled after those found in a typical Bavarian village, keep a European spirit of simple elegance alive in a setting that is never short of spectacular.

Virtually all the many specialty shops, restaurants, and hotels subscribe to the Bavarian theme. There are restaurants specializing in Bavarian food; candy shops with gourmet Swiss-style chocolate; shops featuring music boxes, nutcrackers, and other Bavarian specialties; and charming European-style pension hotels. (There's even a laundromat called Die Washerie.) Throughout the year the village engages in festivities that reflect the alpine theme.

Sports and the Outdoors

GOLF

Those hankering for placid, or at least warmer-weather, sports can try the **Leavenworth Golf Club** (Box 247, 98826, ☎ 509/548–7267), an 18-hole, par-71 course with a pro shop and clubhouse.

HIKING AND ROCK CLIMBING

Leavenworth also offers hiking trails that take in some of the most breathtaking vistas in the entire Cascades. There are more than 320 miles of scenic trails in the Leavenworth Ranger District alone, including **Hatchery Creek, Icicle Ridge,** the **Enchantments, Tumwater Canyon, Fourth of July Creek, Snow Lake, Stuart Lake,** and **Chatter Creek.** Contact the **Leavenworth Ranger District** (600 Sherburne St., 98826, ☎ 509/782–1413) for more details, or consult one of the many fine books detailing backcountry hikes in the Northwest. Rock climbing is also popular because of the solid granite cliffs in the area.

HORSEBACK RIDING

Hourly and daily horseback rides and pack trips are available at **Eagle Creek Ranch** (7951 Eagle Creek Rd., Leavenworth 98826, ☎ 509/548–7798).

SKIING

Beginning and advanced skiers will find more than 20 miles of maintained cross-country ski trails in the Leavenworth area. Meanwhile, Stevens Pass has downhill slopes and lifts for skiers of every level. Several shops in Leavenworth rent and sell ski equipment. For more information, contact the **Leavenworth Winter Sports Club** (Box 573, 98826, ☎ 509/548–5115).

WHITE-WATER RAFTING

Rafting is a popular sport March–July, with the prime high-country runoff in May and June. The **Wenatchee River,** which runs through Leavenworth, is generally considered the best white-water river in the state—a Class 3 (out of six on a scale of difficulty) on the International Canoeing Association scale. Depending on the season and location, anything from a relatively calm scenic float to an invigorating white-water shoot is possible on the Wenatchee or on one of several other nearby rivers. Some rafting outfitters and guides in the Leavenworth area are **Northern Wilderness River Riders** (10645 Hwy. 209, Leavenworth 98826, ☎ 509/548–4583), **All Rivers Adventures/Wenatchee White-water** (Box 12, Cashmere 98815, ☎ 509/782–2254), and **Leavenworth Outfitters** (21588 S.R. 207, Leavenworth 98826, ☎ 509/763–3733).

Dining

$$–$$$ **Edelhaus.** From its prime spot in downtown Leavenworth, the Edelhaus exudes quiet, European country–style ambience with white stucco walls, old wooden tables, and crisp white linens. The sophisticated menu is closer to that of the Asian-accented Northwest cuisine found in Seattle restaurants than it is to the German-theme restaurants hereabouts. ✕ *320 9th St., Leavenworth,* ☎ *206/548–4412. MC, V.*

$$ **Cougar Inn.** This stylish family restaurant is on the shores of Lake Wenatchee, about 25 miles outside Leavenworth. Locals often come by boat and tie up at the restaurant's dock for the good country food. The atmosphere is pleasant, with lots of natural wood, airy rooms, great views of the lake and, in summer, a big outdoor deck. Breakfast, lunch, and dinner are served daily, and the hearty American-style Sunday brunch is especially popular. The menu, featuring burgers, steaks, and prime rib, is not particularly adventurous, but the food is well prepared and the service friendly. ✕ *23379 S.R. 207, Lake Wenatchee,* ☎ *509/763–3354. Reservations advised, especially for Sun. brunch. AE, MC, V.*

$$ **Pewter Pot.** This intimate restaurant with lace curtains and fresh flowers in downtown Cashmere is some 10 miles from Leavenworth, but worth the drive. Owner Kristi Bjornstad focuses on comfort food and very personal service. Start with one of her great soups. Entrées include a stuffed breast of chicken with an apple-cider sauce, turkey and dressing, and sour-cream beef potpie. The deep-dish marionberry pie is memorable. Ms. Bjornstad serves lunch and afternoon tea, but stops serving dinner at 8 PM. ✕ *124 ½ Cottage Ave., Cashmere 98815,* ☎ *509/782–2036. Reservations advised. MC, V.*

$$ **Reiner's Gasthaus.** Authentic central European cuisine with a Hungarian-Austrian accent is presented in this small, cheerful restaurant. The decor is heavy on the pine furnishings and thick drapes, with lots of vintage photographs and knickknacks on the walls, and the service is bustling and friendly. Music is performed on weekend evenings: Usually a jolly accordion player is featured. Specialties include pork schnitzel and Hungarian goulash; these two dishes, as well as all the reasonably priced and well-prepared dinners, come with hearty soups and salads. ✕ *829 Front St. (upstairs), Leavenworth,* ☎ *509/548–5111. No reservations. MC, V.*

$ **Baren Haus.** Hearty, unpretentious food is served in this spacious, noisy, and often crowded high-ceiling beer-hall-style room. The cuisine may not be haute, or even particularly interesting, but the generous servings and low prices will appeal to families and those traveling on a tight budget. Seating is at large booths with blue tablecloths. House specialties include German-style sandwiches (such as bratwurst on grilled whole-wheat bread with sauerkraut and hearty mustards) and pizzas. ✗ *208 9th St.,* ☏ *509/548–4535. Reservations accepted, except during festival time (Aug. and late Sept.–early Oct.). MC, V.*

$ **Danish Bakery.** Tasty homemade pastries, good strong espresso drinks, and a self-serve coffee bar are the attractions in this small, pleasant shop. The decor is tastefully done with dark woods and mural paintings, and the service is fast and friendly. This is a perfect place to escape the crowds on the sidewalks. ✗ *731 Front St.,* ☏ *509/548–7514. No reservations. No credit cards.*

$ **Homefires Bakery.** Locals come to this bakery when they want hearty, chewy bread baked in an old brick oven. Try the German sourdough black rye bread—it's great for sandwiches or eaten simply with unsalted butter. The cinnamon rolls and cookies will make a hit with your sweet tooth. ✗ *13013 Bayne Rd., Leavenworth,* ☏ *509/548–7362. No reservations. No credit cards.*

Lodging

The number of hotels, motels, B&Bs, and long-term-rental cabins in Leavenworth has increased as the area has become more popular. **Bavarian Bedfinders** (309 8th St., Suite 1, Leavenworth 98826, ☏ 509/ 548–4410 or 800/323–2920 in WA) matches travelers with more than 100 facilities such as condominiums, private cabins, small lodges, and B&Bs, in Leavenworth and around the state.

$$–$$$ **Pension Anna.** This small, family-run Austrian-style pension in the middle of the village has a farmhouse atmosphere. Rooms and suites are decorated with sturdy, antique pine furniture, with such added touches as fresh flowers and comforters on the beds. Two of the suites have whirlpool baths, and all except the ground-level rooms have small balconies. The two largest suites have fireplaces and handsome four-poster beds. A hearty European-style breakfast (cold cuts, meats, cheeses, soft-boiled eggs), included in the room price, is served in a breakfast room decorated in traditional European style with crisp linens, pine decor, dark green curtains, and (of course) a cuckoo clock. The staircases to the upper floors are quite steep. Two suites are in a 1913 onion-dome steepled church building that has been relocated on the property. ☷ *926 Commercial St., 98826,* ☏ *509/548–6273. 14 units. AE, D, MC, V.*

$$ **Evergreen Motel.** Popular with hikers and skiers, the Evergreen was built in the 1930s and still has a lot of the charm of the old-fashioned roadside inn it once was. Some of its two-bedroom suites have fireplaces and/or kitchens (though no utensils), while some have multiple beds and can sleep up to six comfortably. Thus, although there are only 26 units, the motel's capacity is about 80 guests. Complimentary Continental breakfast is offered by a very friendly staff, and the motel is one block from downtown. ☷ *1117 Front St., 98826,* ☏ *509/548– 5515 or 800/327–7212. 26 rooms. AE, D, DC, MC, V.*

$$ **Haus Rohrbach.** This alpine-style B&B sits on the side of a hill overlooking its own pool and hot tub, the village of Leavenworth, and the valley beyond. The center of activity here is a large lodgelike room with a wood stove, a kitchen area, and tables for dining, playing games, socializing, or just taking in the view. Guest rooms have double or queen-size beds (some have a sofa bed or daybed, as well), down comforters, and pine furniture. The suites offer king-size beds, whirlpool tubs, a gas fireplace, easy chairs, and small but fully equipped kitchens. The full breakfast served here typically features Dutch babies or sourdough pancakes and sausage. ☷ *12882 Ranger Rd., 98826,* ☏ *509/548–7024. 9 rooms with bath, 4 rooms share 2 baths, 3 suites. Pool, hot tub. AE, D, MC, V.*

$$ Linderhoff Motor Inn. This small place at the west end of Leavenworth is one of the nicest in town for the money. It offers a variety of options: standard rooms, honeymoon suites with whirlpool tubs and fireplaces, and town-house units that sleep up to eight and have fully equipped kitchens and two bathrooms. In contrast to the Bavarian-style exterior, with its overflowing flower boxes, guest rooms are decorated in a contemporary style of soft colors and feature locally crafted pine furnishings. The complimentary Continental breakfast choices of fresh fruit juice and locally baked muffins and Danishes can be taken back to the rooms or eaten outside on the inn's balcony. ☎ *690 Hwy. 2, 98826,* ☎ *509/548–5283. 26 units. Pool, hot tub. AE, MC, V.*

$ Edelweiss Hotel. This is an unpretentious hotel above the restaurant of the same name. Small rooms, plainly furnished and with either shared or private baths, are available. This is not the place to go for a romantic weekend, but if you're on a budget and simply need a place to lay your head, the Edelweiss's price ($15 for a single room, no windows or TV) is hard to beat in this hotel-hungry town. The service is genial if sometimes harried, and the staircase is steep. ☎ *843 Front St., 98826,* ☎ *509/548–7015. 14 units. MC, V.*

Leavenworth Essentials

VISITOR INFORMATION

Leavenworth Chamber of Commerce (894 Hwy. 2, Box 327, 98826, ☎ 509/548–5807).

SEATTLE ESSENTIALS

Arriving and Departing

By Bus

Seattle is served by **Greyhound** (8th Ave. and Stewart St., ☎ 800/231–2222), a nationwide bus line.

By Car

I–5 enters Seattle from the north and south, I–90 from the east. Washington law requires all passengers to be buckled into seat belts. Children under age five should use car seats. Cars are allowed to turn right at a red light after stopping to check for oncoming traffic.

By Plane

Seattle-Tacoma International Airport (Sea-Tac) is 20 miles from downtown Seattle and is served by Air BC (☎ 206/467–7928 or 800/663–8868), Air Canada (☎ 206/467–7928), Alaska (☎ 206/433–3100), American (☎ 800/433–7300), America West (☎ 800/247–5692), British Airways (☎ 206/433–6714), Continental (☎ 206/624–1740 or 800/525–0280), Delta (☎ 206/433–4711), EVA Airways (☎ 206/687–2833 or 800/695–2833), Hawaiian (☎ 800/367–5320), Horizon (☎ 800/547–9308), Japan (☎ 206/624–4737 or 800/225–2525), Northwest (☎ 206/433–3500 or 800/221–2000), Thai Airways (☎ 800/426–5204), TWA (☎ 206/447–9400), United (☎ 206/441–3700 or 800/241–6522), United Express (☎ 206/441–3700), and USAir (☎ 206/587–6229 or 800/428–4322).

BETWEEN THE AIRPORT AND THE CITY

Taxis to the airport take 30–45 minutes; the fare is about $25.

Gray Line Airport Express (☎ 206/626–6088) operates buses from major downtown hotels from 6:10 AM to 11:45, with departures every 20–30 minutes, depending on the hotel. The fare is $7.50 one-way, $13 round-trip.

Shuttle Express (☏ 206/622–1424) offers service to and from the air-port. Fares are $18 for singles one-way or $24 for two one-way tick-ets from downtown.

By Train

Amtrak (303 S. Jackson St., ☏ 800/872–7245) provides rail trans-portation into Seattle. After a 14-year hiatus, rail service between Seat-tle and Vancouver was reinstated in 1995; at press time, the trip took about four hours, but Amtrak was hoping to bring that down.

Getting Around

By Bus

Metropolitan Transit (821 2nd Ave., ☏ 206/553–3000) provides a free-ride service in the downtown waterfront area until 7 PM. Fares to other destinations range from 85¢ to $1.60, depending on the zone and time of day.

By Car

Many downtown streets are one-way, so a map with arrows is especially helpful. Main thoroughfares into downtown are Aurora Avenue (the part through downtown is called the Alaskan Way Viaduct) and I–5.

By Ferry

The **Washington State Ferry System** (☏ 206/464–6400; 206/464–2000, ext. 5500; or 800/843–3779) is the largest in the United States. Ferries leave from downtown Seattle for Bainbridge Island and Bremerton (Kit-sap Peninsula) several times daily. Ferries for pedestrians travel to Vashon Island and Southworth (Kitsap Peninsula). Car and passenger ferries leave from Fauntleroy, in West Seattle, to Vashon Island and Southworth; from Edmonds, north of Seattle, to Kingston; and from Mukilteo, farther north, to Clinton (Whidbey Island). In Anacortes, about 90 minutes north of Seattle, ferries depart for the San Juan Islands and Vancouver Island, British Columbia. Fares range from as low as $1.15 for senior citizens and chil-dren 5–11 traveling the Mukilteo-to-Clinton route, to $33.50 for a car and driver going one-way from Anacortes to Sydney.

Clipper Navigation, Inc.'s (☏ 206/448–5000) passenger catamarans leave from Pier 69. They make the trip to Victoria in under three hours and depart four times daily in the summer, two times daily in the spring and fall, and once daily in winter. The fares are $89 round-trip. The ships offer summer sunset cruises. Clipper Navigation also makes runs to Port Townsend and Friday Harbor on San Juan Island in the summer. Reservations are necessary.

By Monorail

The **Monorail** (☏ 206/684–7200), built for the 1962 World's Fair, shut-tles between its terminals in Westlake Center and the Seattle Center every 15 minutes; the trip takes under three minutes. Hours are Sun-day to Thursday 9–9 and Friday and Saturday 9 AM–midnight. The fare is 90¢ each way, free for children under 6.

By Taxi

Taxis can be hailed on the street; the fare is $1.80 at the flag drop and $1.80 per mile. Major companies are **Farwest** (☏ 206/622–1717) and **Yellow Cab** (☏ 206/622–6500).

By Trolley

Waterfront trolleys (☏ 206/553–3000) run from Pier 70 into Pioneer Square. The fares (85¢ nonpeak and $1.60 for travel during peak hours) are the same as bus fares.

Guided Tours

Art and Cultural

Seattle's International District is one of the largest Asian-American enclaves in North America. **Chinatown Discovery Tours** offers a program and information on Asian history and cultural traditions, as well as a walk through the area. Tours end with a traditional dim-sum brunch, afternoon tea, or dinner banquet. *Box 3406, 98114, ☎ 206/236–0657.* ☛ *$29.95 for tour and meal. Tours offered several times during the day and evening.*

You'll find unusual, self-guided tours in **"A Directory of Seattle's Public Art,"** an illustrated brochure published by the Seattle Arts Commission. It describes walks and drives to see more than 256 innovative works of art in public places. Among these treasures are brass dance steps inlaid on the sidewalks of Broadway, whirligigs festooning a neighborhood electric power substation, an "ark" of animals at Woodland Park Zoo, murals on downtown high-rises, and a "sound garden" of acoustical sculptures in a lakeside park. To receive the brochure, send a SASE with $1 in postage to the Seattle Arts Commission. *221 1st Ave. W, Suite 100, 98109, ☎ 206/684–7171.*

Tillicum Village Tours sails across Puget Sound to Blake Island, south of Bainbridge Island, for a four-hour examination of traditional Native American life. A dinner including steamed clams and salmon is served, and Native American dancers perform a production, *Dance on the Wind. Pier 56, ☎ 206/443–1244. Tour schedule varies during the year, with up to 3 tours leaving daily during peak months.* ☛ *$46.50 adults, $43 senior citizens, $30 youths 13–18, $18.50 children 6–12, $9.50 children 4–5.*

Ballooning

Balloon Depot (16138 N.E. 87th St., Redmond 98052, ☎ 206/881–9699) offers 60- to 90-minute balloon flights for $99–$145 per person, depending on the length of flight and whether it's a weekday or weekend. **Lighter Than Air Adventures** (21808 N.E. 175th St., Woodinville 98072, ☎ 206/488–4135) has one-hour evening flights for $110 per person, as well as sunset flights for $120 per person.

Boat

Argosy Cruises offers a variety of one-hour tours exploring Elliott Bay and the Port of Seattle. Some seven vessels take visitors on trips through the Hiram Chittenden Locks and Lake Washington. Sailings vary according to season. *Pier 55, Suite 201, 98101, ☎ 206/623–1445.* ☛ *$12.50 adults, $10.50 senior citizens, $5.75 children 5–12.*

Emerald City Charters offers a unique look at Seattle's waterfront from beneath the sails of a refurbished 64-foot 1939 yawl. There are 90-minute harbor sails and a 2½-hour sunset sail. *Pier 56, ☎ 206/624–3931. May–Oct.* ☛ *Harbor sail: $20, sunset sail: $37.*

Gray Line (*see* Orientation, *below*).

The *Spirit of Puget Sound* runs dinner and lunch cruises in Elliott Bay on a sleek, 175-foot yacht. Besides the beef, salmon, and chicken buffet offered on all sailings, the dinner cruise includes a 30-minute Broadway-style revue and one hour of dancing to a five-piece band. Summer moonlight cocktail cruises, which have a nightclub atmosphere, set sail at about 11:30 and return at 2 AM. *2819 Elliot Ave., Suite 204, Seattle 98121, ☎ 206/443–1439.* ☛ *Dinner cruise is about $50, depend-*

*ing on day of wk; call for schedules and details for lunch and moon-
light cruises.*

The **Victoria Clipper** offers two-hour sunset cruises in the summer. The
itinerary includes Elliott Bay, Agate Passage, and Vashon Island. *Pier
69, ☎ 206/448–5000. ☛ $16 adults, $8.50 children.*

Orientation

Gray Line offers some 20 guided bus tours of the city and environs ranging in scope from a daily 2½-hour spin to a six-hour "Grand City Tour."
The company also offers specialized tours of, among others, the Boeing 747–767 plants, Mt. Rainier, and Seattle's waterways by boat. From
May to October, Gray Line has tours via Seattle Trolleys through
downtown. Tours depart from the Seattle/Kings County Convention
and Visitors Bureau (800 Convention Pl., ☎ 206/461–5840), at the
I–5 end of Pike Street; the only exceptions are the Seattle Trolley tours
and the *Victoria Star* service between Bellingham and Victoria, which
operates June 1–Oct. 15. ☎ 206/626–5208. *Free transfers from major
downtown hotels. Reservations required.*

Train

The **Spirit of Washington** is a diesel-powered dinner train that takes
passengers along the eastern shore of Lake Washington from the depot
in Renton to the Columbia winery in Woodenville. Passengers on this
3½-hour, 45-mile round-trip excursion ride in regular or domed dining cars and are served dinner on the first leg of the trip, then disem-
bark for a tour and wine tasting. Dessert and coffee are served on the
return trip. The route offers views of Lake Washington, the Bellevue
skyline, and Mt. Rainier. The menu includes entrées such as prime rib,
baked cherry-smoked salmon with pineapple chutney, and Dungeness
crab cakes. Desserts are flavorful and usually decadent, and bar offerings
include Washington wines, beers and ales. There are also Saturday lunch
and Sunday brunch trips. *Renton Depot, ☎ 800/876–7245. Reservations required. No runs Mon. mid-Sept.–mid-May. ☛ $57; $69 for dome-
car seating.*

Walking

One of the most beloved of Seattle's tours is the **Underground Tour,**
begun in 1965 by feisty entrepreneur-historian Bill Speidel as an effort
to help preserve the then-derelict Pioneer Square area. This 90-minute
walking tour explores (with tongue-in-cheek narration) the rough-
and-tumble history of early Seattle; the Great Fire of 1889, which destroyed most of downtown; and the fascinating below-ground sections
of Pioneer Square that have been abandoned (and built on top of) since
1907. This tour, however, is not wheelchair- or stroller-accessible, as
six flights of stairs are involved. *Departure from Doc Maynard's Public House, 610 1st Ave., reservations ☎ 206/682–4646, schedules ☎
206/682–1511. ☛ $5.95 adults, $4.87 senior citizens, $4.33 youths
13–17 or with valid student ID, $2.71 children 6–12. Reservations
advised. Tours run daily except major holidays; schedule varies sea-
sonally, with up to 8 tours daily in summer.*

Important Addresses and Numbers

Radio Stations

KBSG-AM (1210)/FM (97.3), '50s, '60s, and '70s music; **KING-FM
(98.1)**, classical; **KIRO-AM (710)**, news, sports, and features; **KMPS-AM
(1300)/FM (94.1)**, country music; **KUOW-FM (94.9)**, National Public
Radio—news, classical music, and features; and **KUBE-FM (93.3)**, contemporary rock.

Emergencies

For **police, ambulance,** or **other emergencies,** dial 911.

HOSPITALS

Area hospitals with emergency rooms include **Harborview Medical Center** (325 9th Ave., ☎ 206/223–3074) and **Virginia Mason Hospital** (925 Seneca St., ☎ 206/583–6433).

PHARMACY

Fred Meyer (417 Broadway Ave. E, ☎ 206/323–6586) is open until 10 PM.

Visitor Information

Drop by the **Seattle/King County Convention and Visitors Bureau** (800 Convention Pl., at the I–5 end of Pike St., 98101, ☎ 206/461–5840) or the information booth at Westlake Center (400 Pine St., street level, ☎ 206/467–1600) for maps and information about lodging, restaurants, and attractions throughout the city. You can receive the same through the mail by writing to the **Visitor Information Center** (520 Pike St., Suite 1300, 98101, ☎ 206/461–5840).

3 Vancouver

Cosmopolitan Vancouver, Canada's answer to San Francisco, enjoys a spectacular setting. Tall fir trees stand practically downtown, rock spires tower close by, the ocean is at your doorstep, and people from every corner of the earth create a young and vibrant atmosphere.

Updated by
Melissa Rivers

VANCOUVER IS A YOUNG CITY, even by North American standards. While 300–400 years of settlement may make cities like Québec and Halifax historically interesting to travelers, Vancouver's youthful vigor attracts visitors to its powerful elements that have not yet been ground down by time. Vancouver is just over a hundred years old; it was not yet a town in 1870, when British Columbia became part of the Canadian confederation. The city's history, such as it is, remains visible to the naked eye: Eras are stacked east to west along the waterfront like some century-old archaeological dig—from cobbled, late-Victorian Gastown to shiny postmodern glass cathedrals of commerce grazing the sunset.

The Chinese were among the first to recognize the possibilities of Vancouver's setting. They came to British Columbia during the 1850s seeking the gold that inspired them to name the province Gum-shan, or Gold Mountain. They built the Canadian Pacific Railway that gave Vancouver's original townsite a purpose—one beyond the natural splendor that Royal Navy captain George Vancouver admired during his lunchtime cruise around its harbor on June 13, 1792. The transcontinental railway, along with the city's Great White Fleet of clipper ships, gave Vancouver a full week's edge over the California ports in shipping tea and silk to New York at the dawn of the 20th century.

Vancouver's natural charms are less scattered than in other cities. On clear days, the mountains appear close enough to touch. Two 1,000-acre wilderness parks lie within the city limits. The salt water of the Pacific and fresh water direct from the Rocky Mountain Trench form the city's northern and southern boundaries.

Bring a healthy sense of reverence when you visit: Vancouver is a spiritual place. For its original inhabitants, the Coast Salish peoples, it was the sacred spot where the mythical Thunderbird and Killer Whale flung wind and rain all about the heavens during their epic battles—how else to explain the coast's occasional fits of climatic temper? Devotees of a later religious tradition might worship in the sepulchre of Stanley Park or in the polished, incense-filled quiet of St. James Anglican Church, designed by English architect Sir Adrian Gilbert Scott and perhaps Vancouver's finest building.

Vancouver has a level of nightlife possible only in a place where the finer things in life have never been driven out to the suburbs and where sidewalks have never rolled up at 5 PM. There is no shortage of excellent hotels and restaurants here either. But you can find good theater, accommodations, and dining almost anywhere these days. Vancouver's real culture consists of its tall fir trees practically downtown and its towering rock spires close by, the ocean at your doorstep, and people from every corner of the earth all around you.

EXPLORING

The heart of Vancouver—which includes the downtown area, Stanley Park, and the West End high-rise residential neighborhood—sits on a peninsula bordered by English Bay and the Pacific Ocean to the west; by False Creek, the inlet home to Granville Island, to the south; and to the north by Burrard Inlet, the working port of the city, past which loom the North Shore mountains. The oldest part of the city—Gastown and Chinatown—lies at the edge of Burrard Inlet, around Main Street, which runs north–south and is roughly the dividing line between

Tour 2

Lions Gate Br.

1A
99A

STANLEY PARK

Burrard Inlet

Denman St.

English Bay

Thurl

Planetarium
Ogden Ave.

Burrard Br.

Kitsilano Beach Park

Burrard St.

Granville

Jericho Beach Park

Point Grey Rd.

Gran Isla

4th Ave.

4th Ave.

To

Alma St.

8th Ave.

Balsam St.

Broadway

Granville St.

Hemlock St.

10th Ave.

Connaught Park

12th Ave.

Macdonald St.

16th Ave.

Shaughne Park

Discovery St.

Wallace St.

Dunbar St.

Blenheim St.

Carnarvon Park

Trafalgar St.

Valley Dr.

Arbutus St.

Cypress St.

Ave.

Matthews

99

Chaldercott Park

King Edward Ave.

27th Ave.

McKenzie St.

Eddington Dr.

Quilchena Park

Memorial Park West

Balaclava Park

NORTH VANCOUVER

Burrard Inlet

N

0   1 mile

0   1 km

Pender St.

Georgia St.

Robson St.

Haro St.

ow St.

Burrard St.

Howe St.

Hastings St.

Dunsmuir St.

Granville St.

Seymour St.

Davie St.

Richards St.

Pacific St.

Br.

Centennial

Powell St.

Cordova St.

7A

Hastings St.

Dunlevy Ave.

Powell St.

Clark

Victoria

Tour 1

B.C. Place Stadium ■

Strathcona Park

Terminal Ave.

Cambie Br.

False Creek

2nd Ave.

Quebec St.

Commercial Dr.

anville
and

ur 3

Broadway

7

Cedar Cottage Park

Oak St.

Heather St.

12th Ave.

16th Ave.

Cambie St.

Manitoba St.

Main St.

Fraser St.

Windsor St.

Knight St.

Clarke Park

Victoria Dr.

essy

28th Ave.

King Edward

1A

99A

Queen Elizabeth Park

the east side and the west side. All the avenues, which are numbered, have east and west designations.

Numbers in the margin correspond to points of interest on the Tour 1: Downtown Vancouver map.

❶ You can logically begin your downtown tour in either of two ways. If you're in for a day of shopping, amble down **Robson Street** (*see* Shopping, *below*), where you'll find any item from souvenirs to high fashions, from espresso to sushi.

❷ If you opt otherwise, start at **Robson Square,** built in 1975 and designed by architect Arthur Erickson to be the gathering place of downtown Vancouver. The complex, which functions from the outside as a park, encompasses the Vancouver Art Gallery, government offices and law courts that have been built under landscaped walkways, a block-long glass canopy, and a waterfall that helps mask traffic noise. An ice-skating rink and restaurants occupy the below-street level.

❸ The **Vancouver Art Gallery,** which heads the square, was a classical-style 1912 courthouse until Erickson converted it in 1980. Notice the detail: lions that guard the majestic front steps and the use of columns and domes—features borrowed from ancient Roman architecture. In back of the old courthouse, a more modest staircase now serves as a speakers' corner. *750 Hornby St.,* ☎ *604/682–5621.* ☛ *$5 adults, $2.50 students and senior citizens; free Thurs. eve.* ☉ *Mon., Wed., Fri., and Sat. 10–5; Thurs. 10–9; Sun. and holidays noon–5.*

❹ Directly across Hornby Street is the **Hotel Vancouver** (1939), one of the last of the railway-built hotels. (The last one built was the Chateau Whistler, in 1989.) Reminiscent of a medieval French castle, this château style has been incorporated into hotels in almost every major Canadian city. With the onset of the Depression, construction was halted here, and the hotel was finished only in time for the visit of King George VI in 1939. It has been renovated twice: During the 1960s it was unfortunately modernized, but the more recent refurbishment is more in keeping with the spirit of what is the most recognizable roof on Vancouver's skyline. The exterior of the building has carvings of malevolent-looking gargoyles at the corners, an ornate chimney, Indian chiefs on the Hornby Street side, and an assortment of grotesque mythological figures.

TIME OUT   If you're in the vicinity of the Hotel Vancouver between 2 PM and 4:30 PM, stop in for afternoon tea in the lobby lounge. Tea sandwiches, fruit, scones with Devonshire cream, and a large selection of pastries are served in regal style as classical musicians perform in the background.

❺ The tiny **Christ Church Cathedral** (1895), across the street from the Hotel Vancouver, is the oldest church in Vancouver. Built in Gothic style with buttresses and pointed-arch windows, it looks like the parish church of an English village. By contrast, the cathedral's rough-hewn interior is that of a frontier town, with Douglas-fir beams and ornate woodwork that offers excellent acoustics for the vespers, carol services, and Gregorian chants frequently presented here. *690 Burrard St.,* ☎ *604/ 682–3848.* ☉ *Weekdays 10–4.*

❻ **Cathedral Place,** on the corner of Hornby and Georgia streets, is a spectacular office tower adjacent to Christ Church Cathedral. Three large sculptures of nurses at the corners of the building are replicas of the statues that ornamented the art deco Georgia Medical-Dental Building, the site's previous structure.

Tour 1: Downtown Vancouver

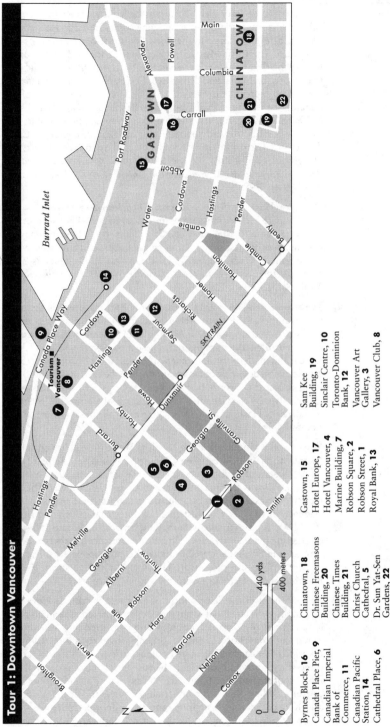

Byrnes Block, **16**
Canada Place Pier, **9**
Canadian Imperial Bank of Commerce, **11**
Canadian Pacific Station, **14**
Cathedral Place, **6**

Chinatown, **18**
Chinese Freemasons Building, **20**
Chinese Times Building, **21**
Christ Church Cathedral, **5**
Dr. Sun Yat-Sen Gardens, **22**

Gastown, **15**
Hotel Europe, **17**
Hotel Vancouver, **4**
Marine Building, **7**
Robson Square, **2**
Robson Street, **1**
Royal Bank, **13**

Sam Kee Building, **19**
Sinclair Centre, **10**
Toronto-Dominion Bank, **12**
Vancouver Art Gallery, **3**
Vancouver Club, **8**

A restored terra-cotta arch—formerly the front entrance to the medical building—and frieze panels showing scenes of individuals administering care now decorate the **Canadian Craft Museum,** across the courtyard. The Craft Museum, which opened in 1992, is one of the first national cultural facilities dedicated to crafts—historical and contemporary, functional and decorative. Craft embodies the human need for artistic expression in everyday life, and examples here range from elegantly carved utensils with decorative handles to colorful hand-spun and hand-woven garments. The two-level museum offers exhibits, lectures, and the Museum Shop, which specializes, of course, in Canadian crafts. The restful courtyard is a quiet place to take a break. *639 Hornby St.,* ☎ *604/687–8266.* ☛ *$4 adults, $2 senior citizens and students, children under 12 free.* ☉ *Mon. and Wed.–Sat. 10–5, Sun. and holidays noon–5.*

Cathedral Place also is the site of the **Sri Lankan Gem Museum,** which opened in 1993. The museum, with a floor of 9,000 polished Brazilian agates set in pyrite, has some $5 million worth of gemstones, including moonstones, rubies, lapis, garnets, jade, and emeralds. Many of the gems are from Sri Lanka. *925 W. Georgia St.,* ☎ *604/688–8528.* ☛ *$3.50 (proceeds go to the Vancouver Symphony Orchestra).* ☉ *Mon.–Sat. 10:30–5:30.*

❼ The **Marine Building** (1931), at the foot of Burrard Street, is Canada's best example of Art Deco architecture. Terra-cotta bas-reliefs depict the history of transportation: Airships, biplanes, steamships, locomotives, and submarines are figured. These motifs were once considered radical and modernistic adornments, because most buildings were still using classical or Gothic ornamentation. From the east, the Marine Building is reflected in bronze by 999 West Hastings, and from the southeast in silver by the Canadian Imperial Bank of Commerce. Stand on the corner of Hastings and Hornby streets for the best view of the Marine Building.

You can take a nice walk along Hastings Street—the old financial district. Until the period between 1966 and 1972, when the first of the bank towers and underground malls on West Georgia Street were developed, this was Canada's westernmost business terminus. The temple-style banks, businessmen's clubs, and investment houses survive as evidence of the city's sophisticated architectural advances prior to **❽** World War I. The **Vancouver Club,** built between 1912 and 1914, was a gathering place for the city's elite. Its architecture evokes that of private clubs in England inspired by Italian Renaissance palaces. The Vancouver Club is still the private haunt of city businessmen. *915 W. Hastings St.,* ☎ *604/685–9321.*

❾ At the foot of Howe Street, north of Hastings, is **Canada Place Pier.** Originally built on an old cargo pier to be the off-site Canadian pavilion in Expo '86, Canada Place was later converted into Vancouver's Trade and Convention Center. It is dominated at the shore end by the luxurious Pan Pacific Hotel (*see* Lodging, *below*), with its spectacular three-story lobby and waterfall. The convention space is covered by a fabric roof shaped like 10 sails, which has become a landmark of Vancouver's skyline. Below is a cruise-ship facility, and at the north end are an Imax theater, a restaurant, and an outdoor performance space. A promenade runs along the pier's west side with views of the Burrard Inlet harbor and Stanley Park. *999 Canada Pl.,* ☎ *604/775–8687.*

Just across the street (next door to the Waterfront Centre Hotel) is the **Tourism Vancouver Infocentre** (200 Burrard St., ☎ 604/683-2000), with brochures and personnel to answer questions, as well as an attractive Northwest Coast native art collection.

⑩ Walk back up to Hastings and Howe streets to the **Sinclair Centre.** Outstanding Vancouver architect Richard Henriquez has knitted four government office buildings (built 1905–1939) into an office-retail complex. The two Hastings Street buildings—the 1905 post office with the elegant clock tower and the 1913 Winch Building—are linked with the Post Office Extension and Customs Examining Warehouse to the north. Painstaking and very costly restoration involved finding master masons—the original terrazzo suppliers in Europe—and uncovering and refurbishing the pressed-metal ceilings.

⑪ A bit farther up Hastings, at Granville Street, you'll find one of Vancouver's oldest and most impressive charter banks, the former **Canadian Imperial Bank of Commerce (CIBC)** headquarters (1906–1908); the columns, arches, and details are of typically Roman influence. The **⑫** **Toronto–Dominion Bank,** one block east, is of the same style but was built in 1920.

⑬ Backtrack directly across from the CIBC on Hastings Street to the more Gothic **Royal Bank.** It was intended to be half of a symmetrical building that was never completed, due to the Depression. Striking, though, is the magnificent hall, reminiscent of a European cathedral.

⑭ At the foot of Seymour Street is the **Canadian Pacific Station,** the third and most pretentious of three Canadian Pacific Railway passenger terminals. Constructed in 1912–1914, this terminal replaced the other two as the western terminus for Canada's transcontinental railway. After Canada's railways merged, the station became obsolete until a 1978 renovation turned it into an office-retail complex and SeaBus terminal. Murals in the waiting rooms show passengers what kind of scenery to expect on their journeys across Canada.

★ ⑮ From Seymour Street, pick up Water Street, on your way to **Gastown.** Named for the original townsite saloon keeper, "Gassy" Jack Deighton, Gastown is where Vancouver originated. Deighton arrived at Burrard Inlet in 1867 with his Indian wife, a barrel of whiskey, and few amenities. A statue of Gassy Jack stands on the north side of Maple Tree Square, the intersection of five streets, where he built his first saloon.

When the transcontinental train arrived in 1887, Gastown became the transfer point for trade with the Orient and was soon crowded with hotels and warehouses. The Klondike gold rush encouraged further development until 1912, when the "Golden Years" ended. The 1930s–1950s saw hotels being converted into rooming houses and the warehouse district shifting elsewhere. The area gradually became unattended and run-down. However, both Gastown and Chinatown were declared historic areas and have been revitalized.

⑯ The **Byrnes Block** building was constructed on the corner of Water and Carrall streets (the site of Gassy Jack's second saloon) after the 1886 Great Fire. The date is just visible at the top of the building above the door where it says "Herman Block," which was its name for a short time.

Tucked behind 2 Water Street are **Blood Alley** and **Gaoler's Mews.** Once the site of the city's first civic buildings—the constable's cabin and courthouse, and a two-cell log jail—today the cobblestone street with antique street lighting is the home of architectural offices.

⑰ The **Hotel Europe** (1908–1909), a flatiron building at Powell and Alexander streets, once billed as the best hotel in the city, was Vancouver's first reinforced concrete structure. Designed as a functional commercial building, the hotel lacks ornamentation and fine detail, a style unusually utilitarian for the time.

★ ⑱ From Maple Tree Square, walk three blocks up Carrall Street to Pender Street, where Chinatown begins. There was already a sizable Chinese community in British Columbia because of the 1858 Cariboo gold rush in central British Columbia, but the greatest influx from China came in the 1880s, during construction of the Canadian Pacific Railway, when 15,000 laborers were imported. The Chinese were among the first inhabitants of Vancouver, and some of the oldest buildings in the city are in Chinatown.

Even while doing the hazardous work of blasting the rail bed through the Rocky Mountains, the Chinese were discriminated against. The Anti-Asiatic Riots of 1907 stopped growth in Chinatown for 50 years, and immigration from China was discouraged by more and more restrictive policies, climaxing in a $500 head tax during the 1920s.

In the 1960s the city council planned bulldozer urban renewal for Strathcona, the residential part of Chinatown, as well as freeway connections through the most historic blocks of Chinatown. Fortunately, the project was halted, and today Chinatown is an expanding, vital district fueled by investment from Vancouver's most notable newcomers—immigrants from Hong Kong. It is best to view the buildings in Chinatown from the south side of Pender Street, where the Chinese Cultural Center stands. From here you'll get a view of important details that adorn the upper stories. The style of architecture in Vancouver's Chinatown is patterned on that of Canton and won't be seen in any other Canadian cities.

The corner of Carrall and East Pender streets, now the western boundary of Chinatown, is one of the neighborhood's most historic spots. Stand-
⑲ ing at 8 West Pender Street is the **Sam Kee Building,** recognized by *Ripley's Believe It or Not!* as the narrowest building in the world, at just 6 feet wide. The 1913 structure still exists; its bay windows overhang the street and the basement burrows under the sidewalk.

⑳ The **Chinese Freemasons Building** (1901) at 1 West Pender Street has two completely different styles of facade: The side facing Chinatown presents a fine example of Cantonese-imported recessed balconies; on the Carrall Street side, the standard Victorian style common throughout the British Empire is displayed. It was in this building that Dr. Sun Yat-sen hid for months from the agents of the Manchu dynasty while he raised funds for its overthrow, which he accomplished in 1911.

㉑ Directly across Carrall Street is the **Chinese Times Building,** constructed in 1902. Police officers could hear the clicking sounds of clandestine mah-jongg games played after sunset on the building's hidden mezzanine floor. Attempts by vice squads to enforce restrictive policies against the Chinese gamblers proved fruitless, because police were unable to find the players.

㉒ Planning for the **Chinese Cultural Center** and **Dr. Sun Yat-sen Gardens** (1980–1987) began in the late 1960s; the first phase was designed by James Cheng, a former associate of Arthur Erickson. The cultural center has exhibition space, classrooms, and meeting rooms. The Dr. Sun Yat-sen Gardens, located behind the cultural center, were built by 52 artisans from Suzhou, the Garden City of the People's Republic. The gardens incorporate design elements and traditional materials from several of that city's centuries-old private gardens and are the first living classical Chinese gardens built outside China. As you walk through the gardens, remember that no power tools, screws, or nails were used in the construction. Free guided tours are offered throughout the day; telephone for times. Dr. Sun Yat-sen Gardens. *578 Carrall St.,* ☎ *604/689–7133.* ☛ *$5 adults, $3 senior citizens and students, $10 families.* ☉ *Daily 10–4:30.*

Tour 2: Stanley Park

Numbers in the margin correspond to points of interest on the Tour 2: Stanley Park map.

A 1,000-acre wilderness park just blocks from the downtown section of a major city is a rarity. In the 1860s, due to a threat of American ★ invasion, the area that is now **Stanley Park** was designated a military reserve (though it was never needed). When the city of Vancouver was incorporated in 1886, the council's first act was to request that the land be set aside for a park. In 1888 permission was granted and the grounds were named Stanley Park after Lord Stanley, then governor general of Canada.

An afternoon in Stanley Park gives you a capsule tour of Vancouver that includes beaches, the ocean, the harbor, Douglas fir and cedar forests, and a good look at the North Shore mountains. The park sits on a peninsula, and along the shore is a pathway 9 kilometers (5½ miles) long called the seawall. You can walk or bicycle all the way around or follow the shorter route suggested below.

Bicycles are for rent at the foot of Georgia Street near the park entrance. Cyclists must ride in a counterclockwise direction and stay on their side of the path. A good place for pedestrians to start is at the foot of Alberni Street beside **Lost Lagoon.** Go through the underpass and veer right to the seawall past **Malkin Bowl,** an open amphitheater where theater-under-the-stars plays during the summer (call 604/687–0174 for performance information).

The old wood structure that you pass is the **Vancouver Rowing Club,** a private athletic club (established 1903); a bit farther along is the **Royal Vancouver Yacht Club.**

About ½ kilometer (⅓ mile) away is the causeway to **Deadman's Island,** a former burial ground for the local Salish Indians and the early settlers. It is now a small naval training base called the HMCS Discovery that is not open to the public. Just ahead is the **Nine O'Clock Gun,** a cannonlike apparatus that sits by the water's edge. Originally used to alert fishermen to a curfew ending weekend fishing, it now automatically signals every night at 9.

Farther along is **Brockton Point** and its small but functional lighthouse and foghorn. The **totem poles,** which stand farther inland, make a popular photo stop for tourists. Totem poles were not carved in the Vancouver area; these were brought to the park from the north coast of British Columbia and were carved of cedar by the Kwakiutl and Haida peoples late in the last century. The carved animals, fish, birds, and mythological creatures were like family coats-of-arms or crests.

At kilometer 3 (mile 2) is **Lumberman's Arch,** a huge log archway dedicated to the workers in Vancouver's first industry. Beside the arch is an asphalt path that leads back to Lost Lagoon. This path also leads to the **Vancouver Aquarium.** The humid Amazon rain-forest gallery has piranhas, giant cockroaches, alligators, tropical birds, and jungle veg-

Tour 2: Stanley Park

etation. Other displays show the underwater life of coastal British Columbia, the Canadian arctic, and other areas of the world. *Aquarium,* ☎ *604/682–1118.* ☛ *$9.50 adults, $8.25 senior citizens and students, $6.25 children 5–12, $27 families.* ☉ *July–Labor Day, daily 9:30–8; Labor Day–June, daily 10–5:30.*

② About 1 kilometer (¾ mile) farther is the **Lions Gate Bridge**—the halfway point of the seawall. Just past the bridge is **Prospect Point,** where cormorants build their seaweed nests along the cliff's ledges. The large black diving birds are distinguished by their long necks and beaks; when not nesting, they often perch atop floating logs or boulders. Another remarkable bird found along the park's shore is the beautiful great blue heron, which reaches up to 4 feet tall and has a wing span of 6 feet. The heron preys on passing fish in the waters here; the oldest heron rookery in British Columbia is in the trees near the aquarium.

★ Continuing around the seawall you will come to the **English Bay** side and the beginning of sandy beaches. The imposing rock just offshore **③** is **Siwash Rock.** Legend tells of a young Indian who, about to become a father, bathed persistently to wash his sins away so that his son could be born pure; for his devotion he was blessed by the gods and immortalized in the shape of Siwash Rock. Two small rocks, said to be his wife and child, are up on the cliff just above the site.

TIME OUT Along the seawall is one of Vancouver's best restaurants, the **Teahouse at Ferguson Point** (*see* Dining, *below*). Set on the great lawn among Douglas fir and cedar trees, the restaurant is the perfect stopover for a summer weekend lunch or brunch. For just a snack, try the park concession stand at Ferguson Point.

34 The next attraction along the seawall is the large saltwater pool at **Second Beach.** In summer it is a children's pool with lifeguards; but in winter, when the pool is drained, skateboarders perform stunts here. You can take a shortcut from here back to Lost Lagoon by walking along the perpendicular road behind the pool, which cuts into the park. The wood footbridge that's ahead will lead you to a path along the south side of the lagoon to your starting point at the foot of Alberni or Georgia street.

If you continue along the seawall, you will emerge from the park into a high-rise residential neighborhood, the **West End.** You can walk back to Alberni Street along Denman Street, where there are plenty of places to stop for coffee, ice cream, or a drink.

Tour 3: Granville Island

Numbers in the margin correspond to points of interest on the Tour 3: Granville Island map.

★ **Granville Island** was just a sandbar until World War I, when the federal government dredged False Creek for access to the sawmills that lined the shore. The sludge from the creek was heaped up onto the sandbar to create the island to house much-needed industrial- and logging-equipment plants. By the late 1960s, however, many of the businesses that had once flourished on Granville Island had deteriorated. Buildings were rotted, rat-infested, and dangerous. In 1971, the federal government bought up leases from businesses that wanted to leave and offered an imaginative plan to refurbish the island with a public market, marine activities, and artisans' studios. The opposite shore of False Creek was the site of the 1986 World's Fair and is now part of the largest urban redevelopment plan in North America.

The small island has no residents except for a small houseboat community. Most of the former industrial buildings and tin sheds have been retained but are painted in upbeat reds, yellows, and blues. Through a committee of community representatives, the government regulates the types of businesses that settle on Granville Island; most of the businesses permitted here involve food, crafts, marine activities, and the arts.

To reach Granville Island on foot, make the 15-minute walk from downtown Vancouver to the south end of Thurlow Street. Aquabuses (☎ 604/689–5858) depart from the foot of Hornby Street downtown and deliver passengers across False Creek to Granville Island Public Market. Another option is the Granville Island Ferries (☎ 604/684–7781) which leave every five minutes from a dock behind the Vancouver Aquatic Center. These pudgy boats are a great way to see the sights on False Creek, but for a longer ferry ride, stay on until you reach the Maritime Museum (*see* Other Museums, *below*), where visitors can board a tugboat and chart the coastal waters of British Columbia.

Another way to reach the island is to take a 20-minute ride on a BC Transit (☎ 604/261–5100) bus. Take a University of British Columbia (UBC), Granville, Arbutus, Cambie, or Oak bus from downtown to Granville and Broadway, and transfer to Granville Island Bus 51 or False Creek Bus 50 from Gastown or stops on Granville Street for direct service to Granville Island.

35 The ferry to Granville Island will drop you off at the **Granville Island Public Market,** where food stalls are enclosed in the 50,000-square-foot building. As the government allows no chain stores, each outlet is unique,

Tour 3: Granville Island

and most are of good quality. You probably won't be able to leave the market without a snack, espresso, or fixings for a lunch out on the wharf. Don't miss the fish chowder or bouillabaisse from the **Stock Market,** fresh fudge at **Olde World Fudge,** or smoked salmon from the **Salmon Shop.** Year-round you'll see mounds of raspberries, strawberries, blueberries, and more exotic fruits like persimmons and litchis. You'll find plenty of outdoor seating on the water side of the market. *Public Market,* ☎ *604/666–6477.* ☽ *Daily 9–6.*

㊱ The **Granville Island Information Centre,** catercorner to the market, is a good place to get oriented. Maps are available, and a slide show depicts the evolution of Granville Island. Ask here about special-events days; perhaps there's a boat show, an outdoor concert, a dance performance, or some other happening. *1592 Johnston St.,* ☎ *604/666–5784.* ☽ *Daily 8–6.*

Walk south on Johnston Street to begin a clockwise loop tour of the island. Next is **Ocean Cement,** one of the last of the island's former industries; its lease does not expire until the year 2004.

㊲ Next door is the **Emily Carr Institute of Art and Design.** Just inside the front door, to your right, is the **Charles H. Scott Gallery,** which hosts contemporary multimedia exhibits. *1399 Johnston St.,* ☎ *604/687–2345.* ☛ *Free.* ☽ *Daily noon–5.*

Past the art school, on the left, is **Sea Village,** one of the only houseboat communities in Vancouver; others have been banned by the city because of problems with sewage and property taxes. The owners of this community appealed the ban and won special status. Take the boardwalk that starts at the houseboats and continues partway around the island.

As you circle around to Cartwright Street, stop in **Kakali** at No. 1249, where you can watch the fabrication of fine handmade paper from such materials as blue jeans, herbs, and sequins. Another unusual artisan on the island is the glassblower at the **Small Sterling Glass Studio** at 1404 Old Bridge Street, around the corner.

The next two attractions will make any child's visit to Granville Island
38 a thrill. First, on Cartwright Street, is the children's **water park,** with a wading pool, sprinklers, and a fire hydrant made for children to shower
39 one another. A bit farther down, beside Isadora's restaurant, is the **Kids Only Market,** with two floors of small shops selling toys, arts-and-crafts materials, dolls, records and tapes, chemistry sets, and other sorts of kid stuff. *Water park: 1318 Cartwright St.,* ☎ *604/665–3425;* ☛ *Free.* ☉ *June–Aug., daily 10–6. Kids Only Market: 1496 Cartwright St.,* ☎ *604/689–8447.* ☉ *Daily 10–6.*

40 At the **Granville Island Brewery,** across the street, you can take a half-hour tour every afternoon; at the end of the tour, sample the Granville Island lager that is produced here and sold locally in most restaurants. *1441 Cartwright St.,* ☎ *604/687–2739.* ☛ *Free. Tours daily at 1 and 3.*

Cross Anderson Street and walk down Duranleau Street. On your left,
41 **Rowand's Reef Scuba Shop** marks the start of the **Maritime Market,** a string of businesses all geared to the sea. The first walkway to the left, Maritime Mews, leads to marinas and dry docks. There are dozens of outfits in the Maritime Market that charter boats (with or without skippers) or run cruise-and-learn trips. Another way to take to the water is by kayak. Take a lesson or rent a kayak from **Ecomarine Ocean Kayak Centre** (1668 Duranleau St., ☎ 604/689–7575).

TIME OUT **Bridges** (1696 Duranleau St., ☎ 604/687–4400), in the bright yellow building across from the market, is a good spot to have lunch, especially on a warm summer's day. Eat on the spacious deck that looks out on the sailboats, fishing boats, and other water activities.

The last place to explore on Granville Island is the blue building next
42 to Ecomarine on Duranleau Street, the **Net Loft.** The loft is a collection of small, high-quality stores, including a bookstore, a crafts store–gallery, a kitchenware shop, a postcard shop, a custom-made hat shop, a handmade paper store, a British Columbian native Indian gallery, a do-it-yourself jewelry store, and more.

43 Behind Blackberry Books, in the Net Loft complex, is **Bill Reid's studio,** belonging to British Columbia's most respected Haida Indian carver. His *The Raven and the First Men*, which took five carvers more than three years to complete, is in the Museum of Anthropology (see *Other Museums,* below); Reid's Pacific Northwest Coast artworks are world renowned. Although you can't visit the studio, there are large windows to peer through. Sadly, Mr. Reid was very ill at press time, and there was talk that the studio might close.

Once you have come full circle, you can either take the ferry back to downtown Vancouver or stay for dinner and catch a play at the **Arts Club** (☎ 604/687–1644) or the **Waterfront Theater** (☎ 604/685–6217).

Other Museums

The **Maritime Museum** traces the history of marine activities on the West Coast. Permanent exhibits depict the port of Vancouver, the fishing industry, and early explorers; the model ships on display are a delight.

Traveling exhibits vary but always have a maritime theme. Guided tours are led through the double-masted schooner *St. Roch,* the first ship to sail in both directions through the treacherous Northwest Passage. A changing variety of restored heritage boats from different cultures is moored behind the museum, and a huge Kwakiutl totem pole stands out front. *1905 Ogden Point at north end of Cypress St., ☎ 604/257–8300. ☛ $5 adults, $2.50 children, students, and senior citizens, $10 families. ☉ Spring–fall, daily 10–5; winter, Tues.–Sun. 10–5. Access via Granville Island Ferries.*

★ The **Museum of Anthropology,** focusing on the arts of the Pacific Northwest natives and aboriginals from around the world, is Vancouver's most spectacular museum. On the campus of the University of British Columbia, it is housed in an award-winning glass-and-concrete structure designed by Arthur Erickson. In the Great Hall are large and dramatic totem poles, ceremonial archways, and dugout canoes—all adorned with carvings of frogs, eagles, ravens, bears, and salmon. Also showcased are exquisite carvings of gold, silver, and argillite (a black stone found in the Queen Charlotte Islands), as well as masks, tools, and costumes from many other cultures. The museum contains a ceramics wing, which houses about 600 pieces from 15th- to 19th-century Europe. *6393 N.W. Marine Dr., ☎ 604/822–3825. ☛ $5 adults, $2.50 students 6–18 and senior citizens, $12 families; free Tues. ☉ Tues. 11–9, Wed.–Sun. 11–5.*

Science World is in a gigantic shiny dome that was built for Expo '86 for an Omnimax Theater. The hands-on museum encourages visitors to touch and participate in the theme exhibits. A special gallery, the Search Gallery, is aimed at younger children, as are the fun-filled demonstrations given in Center Stage. *1455 Quebec St., ☎ 604/268–6363. ☛ Science World: $8 adults, $5 senior citizens and children. ☛ Omnimax: $9; discounted admission to both. ☉ Weekdays 10–5, weekends 10–6.*

Vancouver Museum displays permanent exhibits that focus on the city's early history and native art and culture. Life-size replicas of an 1897 Canadian Pacific Railway passenger car, a trading post, and a Victorian parlor, as well as a real dugout canoe are highlights. *1100 Chestnut St., ☎ 604/736–4431. ☛ $5 adults, $2.50 senior citizens and children; surcharges may apply for special exhibitions. ☉ Winter, Tues.–Sun. 10–5; summer, daily 10–9.*

Video documentaries, photographs, costumes, and an array of sporting equipment are displayed at the **B.C. Sports Hall of Fame and Museum.** There's a high-tech, hands-on participation gallery, so bring tennis shoes. *B.C. Place Stadium, 777 Pacific Blvd. S, ☎ 604/687–5523. ☛ $2. ☉ Wed.–Sun. 9–5.*

Other Parks and Gardens

The small (2½-acre) **Nitobe Memorial Garden** is considered the most authentic Japanese garden outside Japan. The circular path around the park symbolizes the cycle of life and provides a tranquil view from every direction. In April and May cherry blossoms are the highlight, and in June the irises are magnificent. *1903 West Mall, Univ. of B.C., ☎ 604/822–6038. ☛ $3 adults, $1.50 senior citizens and students. ☉ Summer, daily 10–6; winter, weekdays 10–3.*

Pacific Spirit Park (4915 W. 16th Ave., ☎ 604/224–5739), more rugged than Stanley Park, has 61 kilometers (30 miles) of trails, a few washrooms, and a couple of signboard maps. Go for a wonderful walk in the West Coast arbutus and evergreen woods—it's hard to believe you're only 15 minutes from downtown Vancouver.

Queen Elizabeth Park has lavish gardens and an abundance of grassy picnicking spots. Illuminated fountains; the Bloedel Conservatory, with tropical and desert plants and 35 species of free-flying tropical birds; and other facilities including 20 tennis courts, lawn bowling, pitch and putt, and a restaurant are on the grounds. *Cambie St. and 33rd Ave.,* ☎ *604/872–5513.* ☞ *Conservatory: $3 adults, $1.50 senior citizens and children 6–18, $6 families.* ⊙ *Apr.–Sept., weekdays 9–8, weekends 10–9; Oct.–Mar., daily 10–5.*

Van Dusen Botanical Garden was a 55-acre golf course but is now the grounds of one of the largest collections of ornamental plants in Canada. Native and exotic plant displays include a shrubbery maze and rhododendrons in May and June. For a bite to eat, stop in Sprinklers Restaurant (☎ 604/261–0011), on the grounds. *5251 Oak St. at 37th Ave.,* ☎ *604/266–7194.* ☞ *$4.50 adults, $2.25 senior citizens and children 6–18, $9 families; half-price off-season.* ⊙ *Garden: July–Aug. 10–9; Oct.–Apr. 10–4; May, June, and Sept. 10–6.*

What to See and Do with Children

Take your pint-size chef out to Sunday brunch at **Griffin's** (900 W. Georgia St., ☎ 604/662–1900), the bistro-style restaurant in the Hotel Vancouver, where the little ones don miniature chef's hats and make their own pancakes and churn ice cream.

The **miniature steam train** in Stanley Park, just five minutes northwest of the aquarium, is a big hit with children as it chugs through the forest. The **children's water park** across the road is also popular throughout the summer.

Splashdown Park (Rte. 17, just before the Tsawwassen Ferry causeway, ☎ 604/943–2251), 38 kilometers (24 miles) outside Vancouver, is a giant water-slide park with 11 slides (for toddlers to adults), heated water, picnic tables, and miniature golf.

Richmond Nature Park (No. 5 Rd. exit from Rte. 99, ☎ 604/273–7015), with its displays and games in the Nature House, is geared toward children. Guides answer questions and give tours. As the park sits on a natural bog, rubber boots are recommended if it's been wet, but a boardwalk around the duck pond makes some of the park accessible to strollers and wheelchairs.

Maplewood Farms (405 Seymour River Pl., ☎ 604/929–5610), a 20-minute drive from downtown Vancouver, is set up like a small farm, with all the barnyard animals for children to see and pet. Cows are milked every day at 1:15.

Kids Only Market (*see* Tour 3, *above*).

Science World (*see* Other Museums, *above*).

Vancouver Aquarium (*see* Tour 2, *above*).

Off the Beaten Path

On the North Shore you can get a taste of the mountains and test your mettle at the **Lynn Canyon Suspension Bridge** (off Peters Rd. in Lynn Canyon Park, North Vancouver, ☎ 604/987–5922), which hangs 170 feet above Lynn Creek. Also on the North Shore is the **Capilano Fish**

Hatchery in the Capilano Regional Park (4500 Capilano Park Rd., ☎ 604/666–1790), with exhibits about salmon.

If the sky is clear, the telescope at the **Gordon McMillan Southam Observatory** is focused on whatever stars or planets are worth watching that night. While you're there, visit the planetarium on the site. *1100 Chestnut St., Vanier Park,* ☎ *604/738–7827.* ⊘ *Fri.–Sun. and holidays.*

Rock and Roll Heaven, formerly the Beatles Museum, exhibits memorabilia from Jimi Hendrix, Jim Morrison, the Beatles, and other rock icons. *19 Water St.,* ☎ *604/685–8841.* ☛ *$4.* ⊘ *Mon.–Sat. 11–7, Sun. noon–7.*

SHOPPING

Unlike many cities where suburban malls have taken over, Vancouver has a downtown that is still lined with individual boutiques and specialty shops. Stores are usually open daily and on Thursday and Friday nights, and Sunday noon to 5.

Shopping Districts

The immense **Pacific Centre Mall** (550–750 W. Georgia St., ☎ 604/688–7236), on two levels and mostly underground, in the heart of downtown, connects Eaton's and the Bay department stores, which stand at opposite corners of Georgia and Granville streets.

A commercial center has developed around **Sinclair Centre** (757 W. Hastings St., ☎ 604/666–4483; *see* Tour 1 *in* Exploring, *above*), which caters to sophisticated and upscale tastes.

On the opposite side of Pacific Centre is **Robson Street,** stretching from Burrard to Bute streets and chockablock with small boutiques and cafés. Vancouver's liveliest street is not only for the fashion-conscious; it also provides many excellent corners for people-watching and attracts an array of street performers.

Fourth Avenue, from Burrard to Balsam streets, offers an eclectic mix of stores (from sophisticated women's clothing to surfboards).

In addition to the Pacific Centre Mall, **Oakridge Shopping Centre** (650 W. 41st Ave. at Cambie St., ☎ 604/261–2511) has chic, expensive stores that are fun to browse.

Ethnic Districts
Chinatown (*see* Tour 1 *in* Exploring, *above*)—centered on Pender and Main streets—is an exciting and animated place for restaurants, exotic foods, and distinctive architecture.

Commercial Drive (around East 1st Avenue) is the heart of the Italian community, here called **Little Italy.** You can sip cappuccino in coffee bars where you may be the only one speaking English, or buy sun-dried tomatoes, real Parmesan, or an espresso machine.

The **East Indian shopping district** is on Main Street around 50th Avenue. Curry houses, sweet shops, grocery stores, and sari shops abound.

A small **Japantown** on Powell Street at Dunlevy Street is made up of grocery stores, fish stores, and a few restaurants.

Department Stores

Among Vancouver's top department stores is **Eaton's** (701 Granville St., ☎ 604/661–4425), which carries everything: clothing, appliances, furniture, jewelry, accessories, and souvenirs. **Holt Refrew** (Pacific Centre, Granville at Georgia, ☎ 604/681–3121) is smaller, focusing more exclusively on high fashion for men and women. Both are Canadian-owned and have stores at most malls as well as downtown.

Flea Markets

A huge flea market (703 Terminal Ave., ☎ 604/685–0666), with more than 360 stalls, is held weekends and holidays from 9 to 5. It is easily accessible from downtown on the SkyTrain, if you exit at the Main Street station.

Auctions

On Wednesday at noon and 7 PM, art and antiques auctions are held at **Love's** (1635 W. Broadway, ☎ 604/733–1157). **Maynard's** (415 W. 2nd Ave., ☎ 604/876–6787) has home furnishings auctions on Wednesday at 7 PM.

Specialty Stores

Antiques
A stretch of antiques stores runs along Main Street from 19th to 35th avenues. **Folkart Interiors** (3715 W. 10th Ave., ☎ 604/228–1011) specializes in whimsical B.C. folk art and Western Canadian antiques. For very refined antiques and decorative arts, see **Artemis** (3050 Granville St.). For Oriental rugs, go to **Granville Street** between 7th and 14th avenues.

Art Galleries
There are many private galleries throughout Vancouver. **Buschlen/Mowatt** (1445 W. Georgia St., ☎ 604/682–1234), among the best of them, is a showcase for Canadian and international artists. **Diane Farris** (1565 W. 7th Ave., ☎ 604/737–2629; call first) also very good, often spotlights hot new artists.

Books
Duthie's (919 Robson St., ☎ 604/684–4496; and 4444 W. 10th Ave., ☎ 604/224–7012), downtown and near the university, is tops of Vancouver's many bookstores when it comes to size and selection. **World Wide Books and Maps** (736A Granville St., downstairs, ☎ 604/687–3320), one of several specialty bookstores in town, offers travel books and maps that cover the world.

Clothing
Fashion is big business in Vancouver, and there are clothing boutiques on almost every corner downtown. If your tastes are traditional, don't miss **George Straith** (900 W. Georgia St., ☎ 604/685–3301) in the Hotel Vancouver, offering tailored designer fashions for both sexes. Handmade Italian suits, cashmere, and leather for men are sold at stylish **E.A. Lee** (466 Howe St., ☎ 604/683–2457); there are also a few women's items to browse through. Buttoned-down businesswomen usually shop at **Wear Else?** (789 W. Pender St., ☎ 604/662–7890), focusing on career women's fashions. For truly unique women's clothing, try **Dorothy Grant** (Sinclair Centre at Hastings and Granville, ☎ 604/681–0201) where traditional Haida native designs meld with modern fashion in a boutique that looks more like an art gallery.

Neto Leather (347 Water St., ☎ 604/682–6424), in Gastown, carries a huge selection of men's and women's leather outfits and accessories. At the architecturally stunning **Versus** (1008 W. Georgia St., ☎ 604/688–8938) boutique, ladies and gents sip espresso as they browse through the fashionable Italian designs of Gianni Versace. **Leone** (757 W. Hastings St., ☎ 604/683–1133) is yet another ultrachic boutique, dividing designer collections in themed areas; there's DKNY, Georgio Armani, and more here. Trendy men's and women's casual wear by Ralph Lauren is available at **The Polo Store** (375 Water St., ☎ 604/682–7656).

Gifts

Want something special to take home from British Columbia? One of the best places in Vancouver for good-quality souvenirs (West Coast native art, books, music, jewelry, and so on) is the **Clamshell Gift Shop** (Public Aquarium, ☎ 604/685–5911) in Stanley Park. The **Salmon Shop** (☎ 604/666–6477) in the Granville Island Public Market will wrap smoked salmon for travel. In Gastown, Haida, Inuit, and Salish native art is available at **Images for a Canadian Heritage** (164 Water St., ☎ 604/685–7046), as is a selection of fine Canadian crafts. Near Granville Island, **Leona Lattimer's** shop (1590 W. 2nd Ave., ☎ 604/732–4556), built like an Indian longhouse, is full of Indian arts and crafts ranging from cheap to priceless.

SPORTS AND THE OUTDOORS

Participant Sports

Biking

Stanley Park (*see* Tour 2 *in* Exploring, *above*) is the most popular spot for family cycling. Rentals are available here from **Bayshore Bicycles** (745 Denman St., ☎ 604/688–2453) or **Stanley Park Rentals** (1798 W. Georgia, ☎ 604/681–5581).

Another popular summer biking route is along the north or south shores of **False Creek.** For bikes, try **Granville Island Bike Rentals** (1496 Cartwright, ☎ 604/669–2453) or **Granville Island Water Sports** (Charter Boat Dock, ☎ 604/662–7245).

Boating

Several charter companies offer a cruise-and-learn vacation, usually to the Gulf Islands. **Sea Wing Sailing Group, Ltd.** (Granville Island, ☎ 604/669–0840) offers a five-day trip teaching the ins and outs of sailing. If you'd rather just rent a speedboat to zip around the bay for a day, contact **Granville Island Boat Rentals** (☎ 604/682–6287) or **Granville Island Water Sports** (☎ 604/662–7245); the latter also rents Jet Skis and offers parasailing for the more adventurous.

Fishing

You can fish for salmon all year in coastal British Columbia. **Sewell's Marina Horseshoe Bay** (6695 Nelson St., Horseshoe Bay, ☎ 604/921–3474) organizes a daily four-hour trip on Howe Sound or has hourly rates on U-drives. **Bayshore Yacht Charters** (1601 W. Georgia St., ☎ 604/691–6936) has a daily five-hour fishing trip; boats are moored five minutes from downtown Vancouver. **Island Charters** (Duranleau St., Granville Island, ☎ 604/688–6625) arranges charters or boat shares and supplies all gear.

Golf

Lower Mainland golf courses are open all year. Spacious **Fraserview Golf Course** (☎ 604/280–8623), with fairways well defined by hills and mature conifers and deciduous trees, is the busiest in the country. Fraserview is also the most central, about 20 minutes from downtown. **Seymour Golf and Country Club** (☎ 604/929–5491), on the south side of Mt. Seymour, on the North Shore, is a semiprivate club that is open to the public on Monday and Friday. One of the finest public courses in the country is **Peace Portal** (☎ 604/538–4818), near White Rock, a 45-minute drive from downtown.

Health and Fitness Clubs

Both the **YMCA** (955 Burrard St., ☎ 604/681–0221) and the YWCA (580 Burrard St., ☎ 604/662–8188) downtown have drop-in rates that let you participate in all activities for the day. Both have pools, weight rooms, and fitness classes; the YMCA has racquetball, squash, and handball courts. **The Bentall Centre Athletic Club** (1055 Dunsmuir St., lower level, ☎ 604/689–4424), has racquetball and squash courts, weight rooms, and aerobics.

Hiking

Pacific Spirit Park (*see* Other Parks and Gardens *in* Exploring, *above*) has 48 kilometers (30 miles) of hiking trails. The **Capilano Regional Park** (*see* Off the Beaten Path *in* Exploring, *above*), on the North Shore, provides a scenic hike.

Jogging

The seawall around **Stanley Park** (*see* Tour 2 *in* Exploring, *above*) is 9 kilometers (5½ miles) long and gives an excellent minitour of the city. You can take a shorter run of 4 kilometers (2½ miles) in the park around **Lost Lagoon.**

Skiing

CROSS-COUNTRY

The best cross-country skiing is at **Cypress Bowl Ski Area** (☎ 604/926–6007).

DOWNHILL

Vancouver is two hours from **Whistler/Blackcomb,** one of the top-ranked ski destinations in the world (*see* Excursion to Whistler, *below*).

There are three ski areas on the North Shore mountains, close to Vancouver, with night skiing. The snow is not as good as at Whistler, and the runs are generally used by novice, junior, and family skiers or those who want a quick ski after work. **Cypress Bowl** (☎ 604/926–5612; snow report, ☎ 604/926–6007) has the most and the longest runs; **Grouse Mountain** (☎ 604/984–0661; snow report, ☎ 604/986–6262) has extensive night skiing, restaurants, and bars; and **Mt. Seymour** (☎ 604/986–2261; snow report, ☎ 604/879–3999) is the highest in the area, so the snow is a little better.

Tennis

Stanley Park has several well-surfaced outdoor courts near English Bay Beach; many of the other city parks have public courts as well. Contact the **Vancouver Board of Parks and Recreation** (☎ 604/257–8400) for other locations. There are no fees for use of public tennis courts.

Water Sports

KAYAKING

Rent a kayak from **Ecomarine Ocean Kayak Center** (☎ 604/689–7575) on Granville Island (*see* Tour 3 *in* Exploring, *above*) to explore the waters of False Creek and the shoreline of English Bay.

WINDSURFING

Boards can be rented at **Windsure Windsurfing School** (Jericho Beach, ☎ 604/224–0615) and **Windmaster** (English Bay Beach, ☎ 604/685–7245).

Spectator Sports

The **Vancouver Canucks** (☎ 604/254–5141) of the National Hockey League play in the Coliseum October–April. The **Canadians** (☎ 604/872–5232) play baseball in an old-time outdoor stadium in the Pacific Coast League; their season runs April–September. The **B.C. Lions** (☎ 604/583–7747) football team scrimmages at the B.C. Place Stadium downtown June–November. The **Vancouver Eighty-Sixers** (☎ 604/299–0086) play soccer in Swangard Stadium from late April through early September. The **Vancouver Grizzlies** (☎ 604/688–5867), members of the National Basketball Association, hoop it up at the new General Motors Place arena near B.C. Place. Tickets are available from Ticketmaster (☎ 604/280–4444).

Beaches

An almost continuous string of beaches runs from Stanley Park to the University of British Columbia. Children and hardy swimmers can take the cool water, but most others prefer to sunbathe; these beaches are sandy, with grassy areas running alongside. Liquor is prohibited in parks and on beaches. For information, call the **Vancouver Board of Parks and Recreation** (☎ 604/257–8400).

Kitsilano Beach. Kits Beach, with a lifeguard, is the busiest of them all —transistor radios, volleyball games, and sleek young people are ever present. The part of the beach nearest the Maritime Museum is the quietest. Facilities include a playground, tennis courts, a heated salt-water pool (good for serious swimmers to toddlers), concession stands, and many nearby restaurants and cafés.

Point Grey Beaches. Jericho, Locarno, and Spanish Banks begin at the end of Point Grey Road. This string of beaches has a huge expanse of sand, especially in summer and at low tide. The shallow water here, warmed slightly by sun and sand, is best for swimming. Farther out, toward Spanish Banks, you'll find the beach becomes less crowded, but the last concession stand and washrooms are at Locarno. If you keep walking along the beach just past Point Grey, you'll hit Wreck Beach, Vancouver's nude beach. It is also accessible from Marine Drive at the university, but there is a fairly steep climb from the beach to the road.

West End Beaches. Second Beach and Third Beach, along Beach Drive in Stanley Park, draw families. Second Beach has a guarded saltwater pool. Both have concession stands and washrooms. The most lively of the West End beaches is English Bay Beach centered at the foot of Denman Street. A water slide, live music, windsurfing outlet, and other concessions located here are jumping all summer long. Farther along Beach Drive, at the foot of Jervis Street, Sunset Beach, surprisingly quiet considering the location, has a lifeguard on duty but no facilities.

DINING

Vancouver offers the visitor a diverse gastronomical experience; restaurants—from the bustling downtown area to trendy beachside neighborhoods—have enticing locales in addition to succulent cuisine. A new wave of Asian immigration and tourism has brought a proliferation of upscale Asian (Chinese, Japanese, Korean, Thai, Vietnamese) restaurants, offering dishes that would be at home in their own leading cities. Restaurants featuring Pacific Northwest fare—including such homegrown regional favorites as salmon and oysters, accompanied by British Columbia and Washington State wines—have become some of the city's leading attractions.

What to Wear

Vancouver dining is usually fairly informal; casual but neat dress is appropriate.

CATEGORY	*COST
$$$$	over $40
$$$	$30–$40
$$	$20–$30
$	under $20

*per person for a three-course meal, excluding drinks, service, and sales tax

American

$ Isadora's. Not only does Isadora's offer good coffee, a menu that includes lox and bagels and children's specials, but there is also an inside play area packed with toys. Rest rooms with changing-tables accommodate families. In summer, the restaurant opens onto Granville Island's water park, so children can entertain themselves. Service can be slow, but Isadora's staff is friendly. The restaurant is no-smoking. ✗ *1540 Old Bridge St., Granville Island,* ☎ *604/681–8816. Reservations required for 6 or more. DC, MC, V. No dinner Mon., Sept.–May.*

$ Nazarre BBQ Chicken. The best barbecued chicken in several hundred miles comes from this funky storefront on Commercial Drive. Owner Gerry Moutal massages his chickens for tenderness before he puts them on the rotisserie and bastes them in a mixture of rum and spices. Chicken comes with roasted potatoes and a choice of mild, hot, extra-hot, or hot garlic sauce. You can eat in, at one of four rickety tables, or take out. ✗ *1859 Commercial Dr.,* ☎ *604/251–1844. No credit cards.*

Cambodian/Vietnamese

$ Phnom Penh Restaurant. A block from the bustle of Keefer Street, the
★ Phnom Penh is part of a small cluster of Southeast Asian shops on the fringes of Chinatown. The simple, pleasant decor consists of potted plants and framed views of Angkor Wat on the walls. The hospitable staff serves unusually robust Vietnamese and Cambodian fare, including crisp, peppery garlic prawns fried in the shell and slices of beef crusted with ground salt and pepper mixed in the warm beef salad. The decor in the Broadway location is fancier, but the food is every bit as good as at East Georgia Street. ✗ *244 E. Georgia St.,* ☎ *604/682–5777; 955 W. Broadway,* ☎ *604/734–8898. Dinner reservations advised for 5 or more. AE, MC. Closed Tues.*

Chinese

$$–$$$ Imperial Chinese Seafood. This elegant Cantonese restaurant in the Art
★ Deco Marine Building offers stupendous views through two-story floor-to-ceiling windows of Stanley Park and the North Shore mountains across Coal Harbour. Any dish featuring lobster, crab, or shrimp from the live tanks is recommended, as is the dim sum served every afternoon from 11 to 2:30. Portions tend to be small and pricey (especially the abalone, shark's fin, and bird's nest delicacies) but never fail to please. *355 Burrard St.,* ☎ *604/688–8191. Reservations advised. AE, V.*

Downtown Vancouver Dining

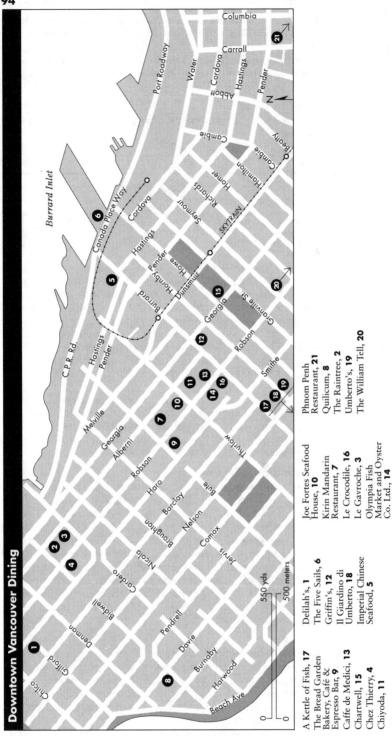

A Kettle of Fish, **17**
The Bread Garden
Bakery, Café &
Espresso Bar, **9**
Caffe de Medici, **13**
Chartwell, **15**
Chez Thierry, **4**
Chiyoda, **11**

Delilah's, **1**
The Five Sails, **6**
Griffin's, **12**
Il Giardino di
Umberto, **18**
Imperial Chinese
Seafood, **5**

Joe Fortes Seafood
House, **10**
Kirin Mandarin
Restaurant, **7**
Le Crocodile, **16**
Le Gavroche, **3**
Olympia Fish
Market and Oyster
Co. Ltd, **14**

Phnom Penh
Restaurant, **21**
Quilicum, **8**
The Raintree, **2**
Umberto's, **19**
The William Tell, **20**

Greater Vancouver Dining

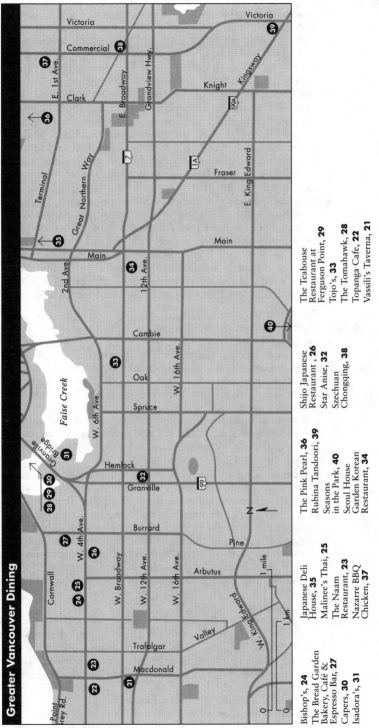

Victoria

Commercial **38**

37

E. 1st Ave.

Clark

36

Terminal

Great Northern Way

E. Broadway

Grandview Hwy.

Victoria

39

Knight

Kingsway

99A

Fraser

E. King Edward

Main

35

2nd Ave.

Main

34

12th Ave.

Cambie

40

W. 16th Ave.

33

Oak

Spruce

W. 6th Ave.

False Creek

Granville Bridge

31

Hemlock

32

Granville

28 **29** **30**

27

W. 4th Ave.

26

Burrard

Pine

Cornwall

25

24

W. Broadway

W. 12th Ave.

W. 16th Ave.

Arbutus

1 mile

The Naam Restaurant, **23**

Malinee's Thai, **25**

Valley

Trafalgar

23

Macdonald

22 **21**

Point Grey Rd.

W. King Edward

1 km

N

Bishop's, **24**
The Bread Garden
Bakery, Café &
Espresso Bar, **27**
Capers, **30**
Isadora's, **31**

Japanese Deli
House, **35**
Malinee's Thai, **25**
The Naam
Restaurant, **23**
Nazarre BBQ
Chicken, **37**

The Pink Pearl, **36**
Rubina Tandoori, **39**
Seasons
in the Park, **40**
Seoul House
Garden Korean
Restaurant, **34**

Shijo Japanese
Restaurant , **26**
Star Anise, **32**
Szechuan
Chongqing, **38**

The Teahouse
Restaurant at
Ferguson Point, **29**
Tojo's, **33**
The Tomahawk, **28**
Topanga Cafe, **22**
Vassili's Taverna, **21**

$$ **Kirin Mandarin Restaurant.** Fish swim in tanks set into the slate-green walls, part of the lavish decorations of this restaurant serving a smattering of northern Chinese cuisines. Dishes include Shanghai-style smoked eel, Peking duck, and Szechuan hot-and-spicy scallops. Kirin is just two blocks from most of the major downtown hotels. *1166 Alberni St.,* ☎ *604/682–8833. Reservations advised. AE, DC, V.*

$$ **Pink Pearl.** This noisy, 650-seat Cantonese restaurant has tanks of live seafood—crab, shrimp, geoduck, oysters, abalone, rock cod, lobsters, and scallops. Menu highlights include clams in black-bean sauce, crab sautéed with five spices (a spicy dish sometimes translated as crab with peppery salt), and Pink Pearl's version of crisp-skinned chicken. Arrive early for dim sum on the weekend if you don't want to be caught in the lineup. *1132 E. Hastings St.,* ☎ *604/253–4316. Reservations advised. AE, DC, MC, V.*

$ **Szechuan Chongqing.** Although fancier Szechuan restaurants can be found, the continued popularity of this unpretentious, white-tablecloth restaurant in a revamped fried-chicken franchise speaks for itself. Try the Szechuan-style fried green beans, steamed and tossed with spiced ground pork, or the Chongqing chicken—a boneless chicken served on a bed of spinach cooked in dry heat until crisp, giving it the texture of dried seaweed and a salty, rich, and nutty taste. ✕ *2808 Commercial Dr.,* ☎ *604/254–7434. Reservations advised. AE, MC, V.*

Continental

$$$–$$$$ **Chartwell.** Named after Sir Winston Churchill's country home (a painting of which hangs over the green marble fireplace), the flagship dining room at the Four Seasons hotel (*see* Lodging, *below*) looks like an upper-class British club. Floor-to-ceiling dark-wood paneling, deep leather chairs to sink back in while you sip claret, plus a quiet setting make this the city's top spot for a power lunch. The chefs cook robust, inventive Continental food with lighter offerings and a variety of low-calorie, low-fat entrées. Favorites, including tomato basil soup with gin, rack of lamb, and a variety of salmon offerings, are repeated on the seasonal menu. ✕ *791 W. Georgia St.,* ☎ *604/844–6715. Reservations advised. AE, DC, MC, V. No lunch Sat.*

$$$–$$$$ **William Tell.** Silver service plates, embossed linen napkins, and a silver flower vase on each table set the tone of Swiss luxury. The William Tell's well-established reputation for excellent Continental food continues at its quarters on the main floor of the Georgian Court Hotel. Chef Christian Lindner offers sautéed veal sweetbreads with red onion marmalade and marsala sauce and such Swiss specialties as *Zürcher Geschnezeltes* (thinly sliced veal with mushrooms in a light white wine sauce) and *Bündnerfleisch* (paper-thin slices of air-dried beef). Make reservations well in advance for the all-you-can-eat "Swiss Farmer's Buffet" on Sunday night. *765 Beatty St.,* ☎ *604/688–3504. Reservations advised. AE, DC, MC, V.*

$$$ **Seasons in the Park.** Seasons has a commanding view over the park gardens to the city lights and the mountains beyond. A comfortable room with lots of light wood and white tablecloths, this restaurant in Queen Elizabeth Park serves a conservative Continental menu with such standards as grilled salmon with fresh mint and roast duck with sundried cranberry sauce. ✕ *Queen Elizabeth Park,* ☎ *604/874–8008. Reservations advised. AE, MC, V. Closed Dec. 25.*

$$$ **Teahouse at Ferguson Point.** The best of the Stanley Park restaurants is perfectly poised for watching sunsets over the water, especially from its glassed-in conservatorylike wing. Although the Teahouse has a less innovative menu than its sister restaurant, Seasons in the Park, certain specialties, such as the cream of carrot soup, lamb with herb crust, and the perfectly grilled fish, don't need any meddling. ✕ *Ferguson Point in Stanley Park,* ☎ *604/669–3281. Reservations required. AE, MC, V. Closed Dec. 25.*

Deli/Bakery

$ **Bread Garden Bakery, Café & Espresso Bar.** What began as a croissant bakery has taken over two neighboring stores and is now the ultimate Kitsilano 24-hour hangout. Salads, quiches, elaborate cakes and pies, giant muffins, and cappuccino draw a steady stream of the young and fashionable. You may be subjected to an irritatingly long wait in line here, or, for that matter, at any of its other locations popping up around the city; quality is suffering with the rapid expansion, but the Garden's following is still strong. *1880 W. 1st Ave.,* ☎ *604/738–6684; 812 Bute St.,* ☎ *604/688–3213. AE, MC, V.*

East Indian

$$ **Rubina Tandoori.** For the best East Indian food in the city, try Rubina
★ Tandoori, 20 minutes from downtown. The large menu spans most of the subcontinent's cuisines, and the especially popular *chevda* (an East Indian salty snack) gets shipped to fans all over North America. Non-smokers get the smaller, funkier back room with the paintings of coupling gods and goddesses; smokers get the slightly more subdued front room. ✕ *1962 Kingsway,* ☎ *604/874–3621. Weekend reservations advised. DC, MC, V. Closed Sun.*

French

$$$ **Le Gavroche.** Time has stood still in this charming, somewhat formal turn-of-the-century house, where a woman dining with a man will be offered a menu without prices. Featuring classic French cooking, lightened—but by no means reduced—to nouvelle cuisine, Le Gavroche's menu also includes such simple listings as smoked salmon with blini and sour cream. Other options may be as complex as smoked pheasant breast on a puree of celeriac, shallots, and wine with a light truffle sauce. The excellent wine list stresses Bordeaux. No reservations are necessary after 9:30, when the late-dessert menu is offered. Tables by the front window promise mountains-and-water views. ✕ *1616 Alberni St.,* ☎ *604/685–3924. Weekend reservations advised. AE, DC, MC, V. Closed holidays. No lunch weekends.*

$$ **Chez Thierry.** This cozy, unpretentious bistro on the Stanley Park end
★ of Robson Street adds pizzazz to a celebration: Charming owner Thierry Damilano stylishly slashes open champagne bottles with a cavalry saber on request. For the past 18 years, he has worked together with chef Francois Launay in creating country-style French fare. Try the signature bouillabaisse; fresh tuna grilled with artichokes, garlic, and tomatoes; or filet mignon with a creamy cognac–Dijon black pepper sauce; and apple *tarte Tatin* for dessert. If you have a favorite French dish, call ahead and Thierry will go all-out to accommodate your particular craving. During the week, the intimate dining room is relaxing; on the weekend, however, the restaurant can be crowded and noisy. ✕ *1674 Robson St.,* ☎ *604/688–0919. Reservations advised. AE, DC, MC, V. Closed Dec. 24–26. No lunch.*

$$ **Le Crocodile.** In a roomy location off Burrard Street, Chef Michael Jacob serves extremely well-cooked, simple food at reasonable prices. His Alsatian background shines with the caramel-sweet onion tart. Anything that involves innards is superb, and even such old standards as duck à l'orange are worth ordering here. ✕ *100-909 Burrard St.,* ☎ *604/669–4298. Reservations required. AE, DC, MC, V. Closed Sun. and holidays. No lunch Sat.*

Greek

$$ **Vassili's Taverna.** The menu in this family-run restaurant in the heart of the city's small Greek community is almost as conventional as the decor: checked tablecloths and mandatory paintings of white fishing villages and the blue Aegean Sea. At Vassili's, though, even standards become memorable due to the flawless preparation. The house specialty is a deceptively simple *kotopoulo* (a half-chicken, pounded flat, herbed, and charbroiled). ✕ *2884 W. Broadway,* ☎ *604/733–3231. Weekend reservations advised. AE, DC, MC, V. Closed Mon. No lunch weekends.*

Health Food

$ ★ **Capers.** Hidden in the back of the most lavish health food store in the Lower Mainland, Capers drips with earth-mother chic: wood tables, potted plants, and heady smells from the store's bakery. Breakfast starts at 8: free-range eggs and bacon with no additives, or feather-light blueberry pancakes crammed with berries. The newer Fourth Avenue location, with its dining room above the store, is by far the nicer of the two; the West Vancouver store is somewhat old and dingy. ✕ *2496 Marine Dr., W. Vancouver,* ☎ *604/925–3316; 2285 W. 4th,* ☎ *604/739–6685. MC, V. Marine Dr. closed Sun. dinner.*

$ **Naam Restaurant.** Vancouver's oldest alternative restaurant is open 24 hours, so if you need to satisfy a late-night tofu-burger craving, rest easy. The Naam also serves wine, beer, cappuccino, and wicked chocolate desserts, along with the vegetarian stir-fries. Wood tables and kitchen chairs provide a homey atmosphere. On warm summer evenings, try the outdoor courtyard at the back of the restaurant. ✕ *2724 W. 4th Ave.,* ☎ *604/738–7151. Reservations required for 7 or more. MC, V.*

Italian

$$$ ★ **Caffe de Medici.** You'll need to shift gears as you leave the stark concrete walls of the Robson Galleria behind and step into this elegant, somewhat formal restaurant with its ornate molded ceilings, rich green velvet curtains and chair coverings, and portraits of the Medici family. But after a little wine, an evening's exposure to courtly waiters, and a superb meal, you may begin to wish the outside world conformed more closely to this peaceful environment. Although an enticing antipasto table sits in the center of the room, consider the *bresaola* (air-dried beef marinated in olive oil, lemon, and pepper) as a worthwhile appetizer. Try the rack of lamb in a mint, mustard, and vermouth sauce. Any of the pastas is a safe bet. ✕ *1025 Robson St.,* ☎ *604/669–9322. Reservations advised. AE, D, DC, MC, V. No lunch weekends.*

$$$ **Il Giardino di Umberto, Umberto's.** First came Umberto's, a Florentine restaurant serving classic northern Italian food, installed in a century-old Vancouver home at the foot of Hornby Street. Then, next door, Umberto Menghi built Il Giardino, a sunny, light-splashed restaurant styled after a Tuscan house. A moneyed, see-and-be-seen crowd goes to Il Giardino for braided breast of pheasant with polenta and reindeer fillet with crushed peppercorn sauce. Fish is treated either Italian style—sea bass or salmon grilled and served with sun-dried tomatoes, black olives, and pine nuts—or with a taste of East Asia, as in yellowfin tuna grilled with wasabi butter. ✕ *Il Giardino, 1382 Hornby St.,* ☎ *604/669–2422. Umberto's, 1380 Hornby St.,* ☎ *604/687–6316. Reservations advised. AE, DC, MC, V. Il Giardino closed Sat. lunch and Sun. Umberto's closed lunch and Mon.*

$$ **Griffin's.** The Sunday brunch ambience here is cheerful, energetic, and kid-oriented: Kids in aprons (provided by the restaurant) whip up their own pancakes and take turns churning ice cream for dessert. The rest of the week the emphasis is on the adult crowd. This brasserie uniquely blends the charm of old Italy with the flair of sophisticated design and fresh, regional ingredients. Squash-yellow walls, bold black-and-white tiles, and splashy food art by Mary Frances Tuck enhance Griffin's liveliness. The brasserie has an open kitchen that prepares inspired cuisine, including such buffet selections as convict bread, a round loaf stuffed with soft, fresh goat cheese, olives, tomatoes, and peppers in olive oil; smoked salmon; chicken pasta al pesto; and baked Pacific black cod with herbed crumbs. ✗ *900 W. Georgia St.,* ☎ *604/ 662–1900. Reservations advised. AE, D, DC, MC, V.*

Japanese

$$$ ★ **Tojo's.** Hidekazu Tojo is a sushi-making legend here. His handsome blond-wood tatami rooms, on the second floor of a modern green-glass tower in the hospital district on West Broadway, provide proper ambience for intimate dining, but Tojo's 10-seat sushi bar stands as the centerpiece. With Tojo presiding, it is a convivial place for dinner and offers a ringside seat for watching the creation of edible art. Although tempura and teriyaki dinners will satisfy, the seasonal menu is more exciting. In fall, ask for *dobbin mushi,* a soup made from pine mushrooms that's served in a teapot. In spring, try salad made from scallops and pink cherry blossoms. ✗ *777 W. Broadway, No. 202,* ☎ *604/ 872–8050. Weekend reservations advised. AE, DC, MC, V. Closed Sun., Dec. 24–26, and Jan. 1 and 2. No lunch.*

$$ **Chiyoda.** The bar curves through Chiyoda's main room: On one side are the customers and an array of flat baskets full of the day's offerings; on the other side are the chefs and grills. There are 35 choices of things to grill, from squid, snapper, and oysters to eggplant, mushrooms, onions, and potatoes. The finished dishes, dressed with sake, soy, or *ponzu* sauce, are dramatically passed over on the end of a long wooden paddle. If Japanese food means only sushi and tempura to you, check this out. ✗ *1050 Alberni St.,* ☎ *604/688–5050. Reservations accepted. AE, DC, MC, V. Closed Sun. No lunch Sat.*

$$ **Shijo Japanese Restaurant.** Shijo has an excellent and very large sushi bar, a smaller robata bar, tatami rooms, and a row of tables overlooking bustling Fourth Avenue. The epitome of modern urban Japanese chic is conveyed through the jazz music, handsome lamps with a patinated bronze finish, and lots of black wood. Count on creatively prepared sushi, eggplant *dengaku* topped with light and dark miso paste and broiled, and shiitake *foil yaki* (fresh shiitake mushrooms cooked in foil with ponzu sauce). ✗ *1926 W. 4th Ave.,* ☎ *604/732–4676. Reservations advised. AE, MC, V. No lunch weekends.*

$ **Japanese Deli House.** The least expensive sushi in town is served in the high-ceilinged main-floor room of a turn-of-the-century building on Powell Street, once the heart of Vancouver's Japantown. This restaurant is not much to look at, but the food is especially fresh and good if you can make it an early lunch: sushi rectangles and rolls are made at 11 AM for the 11:30 opening, and there are all-you-can-eat sushi and tempura lunch specials on weekdays. ✗ *381 Powell St.,* ☎ *604/681–6484. No credit cards. Closed Sun. and Mon. dinners.*

Korean

$ **Seoul House Garden Korean Restaurant.** The shining star in a desperately ugly section of East Broadway, Seoul House is a bright restaurant, decorated in Japanese style, that serves a full menu of Japanese and Korean food. The best bet is the Korean barbecue, which you cook at your table. A barbecue dinner of marinated beef, pork, chicken, or fish comes complete with a half-dozen side dishes—kimchi, salads, stir-fried rice, and pickled vegetables—as well as soup and rice. Service can be chaotic in this very popular restaurant. ✗ *36 E. Broadway,* ☎ *604/ 874–4131. Reservations advised. MC, V. No lunch Sun.*

Mexican

$ **Topanga Cafe.** Arrive before 6:30 or after 8 PM to avoid waiting in line for this 40-seat Kitsilano classic. The California-Mexican food hasn't changed much since 1978, when the Topanga started dishing up fresh salsa and homemade tortilla chips. Quantities are still huge and prices low. Kids can color blank menu covers while waiting for food; a hundred or more of the clientele's best efforts are framed on the walls. ✕ *2904 W. 4th Ave.,* ☎ *604/733–3713. No reservations. MC, V. Closed Sun.*

Nouvelle

$$$$ **Five Sails.** On the fourth floor of the Pan Pacific Hotel, this special-occasion restaurant affords a stunning panoramic view of Canada Place, Lions Gate Bridge, and the lights of the north shore twinkling across the bay. Austrian chef Ernst Dorfler, a past member of the Canadian Culinary Olympic team, has a special flair for presentation, from the swan-shape butter served with breads early in the meal to the chocolate ice-cream bonbon served on a bed of dry ice at the end. Pacific Rim best describes the broad-reaching menu that includes caramelized swordfish, spicy Mongolian-style chicken, and such old favorites as medallions of B.C. salmon or lamb from Salt Spring Island. ✕ *Pan Pacific Hotel, 300–999 Canada Pl.,* ☎ *604/662–8211. Reservations advised. AE, DC, MC, V. Closed Dec. 24 and 26 and Jan. 1. No lunch.*

$$$ **Bishop's.** John Bishop established Vancouver's most influential restaurant in 1985 by serving West Coast Continental cuisine with an emphasis on British Columbia seafood. Penne with grilled eggplant, roasted peppers, and basil pasta cohabit on the menu with medallions of venison, rack of lamb, and roasted duck breast. Seasonal specials such as ravioli filled with crab and mascarpone are enticing. The small white rooms—their only ornament some splashy expressionist paintings—are favored by Pierre Trudeau and by Robert De Niro when he's on location in Vancouver. ✕ *2183 W. 4th Ave.,* ☎ *604/738–2025. Reservations required. AE, DC, MC, V. Closed Dec. 24–26 and 1st wk in Jan. No lunch weekends.*

$$$ **★** **Star Anise.** When Sammy Lalji and Adam Busby, top performers from the highly regarded Bishop's *(see above),* left to open their own restaurant, they built a faithful following in record time. Their superior skills in attentive service, imaginative presentation, and excellent preparation of Pacific Rim cuisine with French flair shine in this intimate, no-smoking location just off Granville on the west side of town. Don't miss the cilantro and Dungeness crab cakes with fried ginger threads, rouille, and potatoes that are often on the seasonal menu; spot prawn ravioli, grilled pork chops, and carrot and ginger mousse are also good choices. The wine list offers an array of fine international and West Coast choices. Weekend brunch is a real treat here. ✕ *1485 W. 12th Ave.,* ☎ *604/737–1485. Reservations advised. AE, D, DC, MC, V. Closed Dec. 25–26 and Jan. 1.*

$$ **★** **Delilah's.** Cherubs dance on the ceiling, candles flicker on the tables, and martini glasses clink in toasts, but this incredibly popular restaurant is simply too crowded and noisy to be romantic. Under the direction of chef Peg Montgomery, the nouvelle California cuisine is delicious, innovative, and beautifully presented. The fresh daily menu lets you choose two- or five-course prix fixe dinners. Try the salmon in strawberry peppercorn sauce and the pecan-crusted pork loin. Reservations are not accepted, and patrons have been known to line up before the restaurant even opens for dinner. ✕ *Buchan Hotel, 1906 Haro St.,* ☎ *604/687–3424. DC, MC, V. Closed Dec 24–27. No lunch.*

Pacific Northwest

$$ Quilicum. Only a few blocks from English Bay, this downstairs "long-house" serves the original Northwest Coast cuisine: bannock bread, baked sweet potato with hazelnuts, alder-grilled salmon, and soapberries for dessert. Try the authentic but odd dish—"oolichan grease"—that's prepared from candlefish. Native music is piped in, and Northwest Coast Indian masks (for sale) peer from the walls. ✕ *1724 Davie St.*, ☎ *604/ 681–7044. Reservations advised. AE, MC, V. No lunch.*

$$ The Raintree. This cool, spacious restaurant has a local menu and a
★ wine list that offers vintages from British Columbia, Washington, and Oregon. Raintree bakes its own bread, makes luxurious soups, and serves up such old favorites as a slab of apple pie for dessert. The kitchen, focusing on healthy cuisine, teeters between willfully eccentric and exceedingly simple. Seasonal specials may include salmon and crab gnocchi with roasted butternut squash cream; roasted Pacific halibut with oregano pesto; smoked Fraser Valley duck breast with gooseberry compote; and rabbit terrine with basil, mint, and blackberry sauce. Main courses change daily depending on market availability. ✕ *1630 Alberni St.*, ☎ *604/688–5570. Weekend reservations advised. AE, DC, MC, V. Closed Dec. 24–26. No lunch weekends.*

$ The Tomahawk. North Vancouver was mostly trees in 1926, when the Tomahawk first opened. Over the years, the original hamburger stand grew and mutated into part Northwest Coast Indian kitsch museum, part gift shop, and part restaurant. Renowned for its Yukon breakfast—five slices of back bacon, two eggs, hash browns, and toast—the Tomahawk also serves gigantic muffins, excellent French toast, and pancakes. The menu switches to oysters, trout, and burgers named for Indian chiefs at lunch and dinner. ✕ *1550 Philip Ave.*, ☎ *604/988–2612. AE, MC, V.*

Seafood

$$ Joe Fortes Seafood House. Reserve a table on the second floor balcony
★ at this Vancouver seafood hot spot to take in the view of the broad wall murals, the mounted blue marlins, and, most especially, the ever-entertaining scene at the noisy bar downstairs. The signature panfried Cajun oysters, the salmon with smoked apple and cider chutney, and the seared sea scallops in sesame and oyster glaze are tasty and filling, but often overlooked in favor of the reasonably priced daily blue-plate special. ✕ *777 Thurlow St.*, ☎ *604/669–1940. Reservations advised. AE, D, MC, V.*

$$ A Kettle of Fish. Since opening in 1979, this family-run restaurant at the foot of Burrard Bridge has developed a strong local following; depend on getting top quality seafood here. The menu varies daily according to market availability, but there are generally 15 kinds of fresh seafood to choose from that are either grilled, sautéed, poached, barbecued, or blackened Cajun-style according to your preference. The B.C. salmon and the seafood combo plate are always good choices. ✕ *900 Pacific St.*, ☎ *604/682–6853. AE, DC, MC, V.*

$ Olympia Fish Market and Oyster Co. Ltd. Some of the city's best fish-and-chips are fried in this tiny shop behind a fish store in the middle of the Robson Street shopping district. The choice is halibut, cod, prawns, calamari, and whatever's on special in the store, served with homemade coleslaw and genuine—never frozen—french fries. It's funky and fun. ✕ *1094 Robson St.*, ☎ *604/685–0716. No reservations. DC, MC, V.*

Thai

$$ Malinee's Thai. The city's most consistently interesting Thai food can
★ be found in this typically Southeast Asian–style room, tapestries adorning the walls. The owners, two Canadians who lived for several years

in Thailand, can give you detailed descriptions of every dish. Steamed fish with ginger, pickled plums, and red chili sauce is on the regular menu; steamed whole red snapper marinated in oyster sauce, ginger, cilantro, red pepper, and lime juice is a special worth ordering when it's available. ✕ *2153 W. 4th Ave.,* ☎ *604/737–0097. Reservations advised. AE, DC, MC, V. Closed Dec. 24–26. No lunch Sat.–Mon.*

LODGING

The hotel industry has become a major business for Vancouver, a fairly young city that hosts large numbers of Asian businesspeople and others who are used to an above-average level of service. Although by some standards pricey, properties here are highly competitive, and you can expect the service to reflect this.

Note: At press time, the new **Wall Centre Garden Hotel** (1088 Burrard St., ☎ 604/331–1000 or 800/663–9255) had just opened and still had many kinks to work out. However, it does look promising.

CATEGORY	COST*
$$$$	over $200
$$$	$150–$200
$$	$100–$150
$	under $100

All prices are for a standard double room, excluding 10% provincial accommodation tax, 15% service charge, and 7% GST.

$$$$ **Four Seasons**. This bustling 28-story hotel adjacent to the Vancouver Stock Exchange is attached to the Pacific Centre shopping mall. Standard rooms are average in size; roomier corner deluxe or deluxe Four Seasons rooms are recommended. Expect tasteful and stylish decor in the rooms and hallways. Service is outstanding, and the Four Seasons has all the amenities. The formal dining room, Chartwell (*see* Dining, *above*), is one of the best in the city. ☎ *791 W. Georgia St., V6C 2T4,* ☎ *604/689-9333; in Canada, 800/268-6282; in the U.S., 800/332-3442;* [FAX] *604/844-6744. 317 rooms, 68 suites. 2 restaurants, bar, indoor-outdoor pool, sauna, aerobics, exercise room. AE, DC, MC, V.*

$$$$ **Pan Pacific Hotel.** Sprawling Canada Place sits on a pier right by the financial district and houses the luxurious Pan Pacific (built in 1986 for the Expo), the Vancouver Trade and Convention Centre, and a cruise-ship terminal; it's very easy to get turned around here. The three-story atrium lobby (once you locate it) has a dramatic totem pole and waterfall, and the lounge, the restaurant, and the café all have huge expanses of glass, so that you are rarely without a harbor view or a mountain backdrop. Earth tones and Japanese detail give the rooms an understated elegance. The hotel's fine-dining restaurant, the Five Sails (*see* Dining, *above*), offers what is arguably the best panoramic view in town and an imaginative menu to match. The health club has a $15 fee that's well worth the price. The busy hotel seems better suited to conventions than an intimate weekend getaway, but they do have pampering down to a science. ☎ *300–999 Canada Pl., V6C 3B5,* ☎ *604/662–8111; in Canada, 800/663–1515; in the U.S., 800/937–1515;* [FAX] *604/685–8690. 467 doubles, 39 suites. 3 restaurants, bar, outdoor pool, massage, sauna, steam room, whirlpool, aerobics, health club, indoor track, paddle tennis, racquetball, squash. AE, DC, MC, V.*

$$$$ **Sutton Place (formerly Le Meridien).** This property feels more like an
★   exclusive guest house than a large hotel: Its lobby has sumptuously thick carpets, enormous displays of flowers, and elegant European furniture. The rooms are even better, furnished with rich, dark woods reminis-

Vancouver Lodging

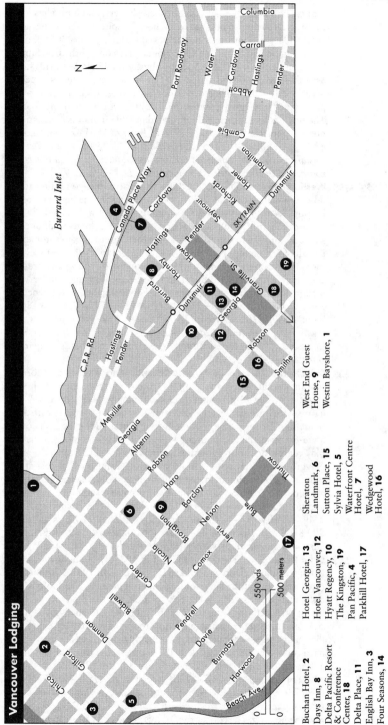

Burrard Inlet

Buchan Hotel, **2**
Days Inn, **8**
Delta Pacific Resort
& Conference
Center, **18**
Delta Place, **11**
English Bay Inn, **3**
Four Seasons, **14**

Hotel Georgia, **13**
Hotel Vancouver, **12**
Hyatt Regency, **10**
The Kingston, **19**
Pan Pacific, **4**
Parkhill Hotel, **17**

Sheraton
Landmark, **6**
Sutton Place, **15**
Sylvia Hotel, **5**
Waterfront Centre
Hotel, **7**
Wedgewood
Hotel, **16**

West End Guest
House, **9**
Westin Bayshore, **1**

cent of 19th-century France. Bathrobes, slippers, and umbrellas in the room attest to the attention to detail here. Despite the size of this hotel, Sutton Place in Vancouver has achieved and maintained a level of intimacy and exclusivity. The Café Fleuri serves one of the best Sunday brunches in town (plus a chocolate buffet on Thursday, Friday, and Saturday evenings), and Le Club, a fine French restaurant, is a special-occasion place. Lots of leather, dark wood, wingback chairs, and a fireplace give the Gérard Lounge the feel of a refined gentlemen's club. The tiny La Boulangerie Bakery, added in 1993, is a hit. An apartment hotel adjoins the Sutton Place. ☎ *845 Burrard St., V6Z 2K6, ☎ 604/ 682–5511, 800/961–7555, ⅀ 604/682–2926. 350 doubles, 47 suites. Restaurant, bar, café, indoor pool, beauty salon, massage, sauna, steam room, health club, business services. AE, D, DC, MC, V.*

$$$–$$$$ **Westin Bayshore.** The closest thing to a resort that you'll find in the downtown area, the Bayshore is perched right on the best part of the harbor. Because it is only a five-minute walk from Stanley Park, because of the truly fabulous view, and because of its huge outdoor pool, sundeck, and grassy areas, it is the perfect place to stay in summer, especially for a family. The new tower has rooms with the best views of the water; rooms in the main wing were updated in 1993 and are now comparable in contemporary style. The café is okay, and Trader Vic's, the hotel's dining room, is a pleasant, Polynesian-style experience. ☎ *1601 W. Georgia St., V6G 2V4, ☎ 604/682–3377 or 800/228–3000; ⅀ 604/687–3102. 484 doubles, 33 suites; 2 floors for persons with disabilities. Restaurant, café, 2 bars, indoor and outdoor pools, massage, sauna, health club, boating, fishing, bicycles, billiards, downtown shuttle. AE, D, DC, MC, V.*

$$$ **Delta Pacific Resort & Conference Center.** It's not a view or a shoreline that makes this place (five minutes from the airport) a resort, it's the facilities on the 14-acre site: three swimming pools (one indoor, with a three-story tubular water slide), four all-year tennis courts with a pro (matching list for partners), an outdoor fitness circuit, squash courts, aqua-exercise classes, outdoor volleyball nets, golf practice nets, a play center for children, summer camps for 5- to 12-year-olds, and a playground. In spite of the hotel's size, the atmosphere is casual and friendly. Guest rooms are modern with contemporary decor and a pleasant blue and green color scheme. The Japanese restaurant is expensive and not the best value. ☎ *10251 St. Edwards Dr., Richmond, V6X 2M9, ☎ 604/278–9611; in Canada, 800/268–1133; in the U.S., 800/877–1133; ⅀ 604/276–1122. 460 doubles, 4 suites. Restaurant, bar, café, saunas, baby-sitting, airport shuttle. AE, DC, MC, V.*

$$$ **Delta Place.** This 18-story hotel built in 1985 by the luxurious Hong Kong Mandarin chain was sold to Delta Hotels in 1987. Although the rates went down, the surroundings did not change: The lobby is still restrained and tasteful—one has to look for the registration desk, which is tucked off to the right. A slight Oriental theme is given to the rich dark-mahogany furnishings. Most rooms have small balconies, and the studio suites—roomier, and only slightly more expensive than a standard room—are recommended. The business and shopping district is a five-minute walk away. ☎ *645 Howe St., V6C 2Y9, ☎ 604/687– 1122; in Canada, 800/268–1133; in the U.S., 800/877–1133; ⅀ 604/ 643–7267. 181 doubles, 16 suites. Restaurant, bar, lap pool, massage, saunas, exercise room, racquetball, squash. AE, DC, MC, V.*

$$$ **Hotel Vancouver.** The copper roof of this grand château-style hotel dom-
★   inates Vancouver's skyline. Opened in 1939 by the Canadian National Railway, the hotel commands a regal position in the center of town across from the art gallery and Cathedral Place. Even the standard guest rooms have an air of prestige with mahogany furniture, TVs in armoires,

attractive linens, and the original, deep bathtubs. Entrée Gold suites, with French doors, graceful wingback chairs, and fine mahogany furniture take up two floors and come with extra services and amenities, including complimentary breakfast in a private, luxurious lounge. Afternoon tea in the lobby lounge is a real treat. ☎ *900 W. Georgia St., V6C 2W6,* ☎ *604/684–3131 or 800/441–1414,* ₣₳ₓ *604/662–1937. 466 doubles, 42 suites. 2 restaurants, bar, lobby lounge, lap pool, health club, exercise room, AE, D, DC, MC, V.*

$$$ Hyatt Regency. The 34-story hotel, which opened in 1973, underwent major renovation in 1992. The Hyatt's standard rooms are spacious and decorated in deep, dramatic colors and dark wood. Ask for a corner room with a balcony on the north or west side. The lobby, with its four-story atrium, can't escape the feel of a large convention hotel. For a small fee, the Regency Club gives you the exclusivity of a floor accessed by keyed elevators, your own concierge, a private lounge with a stereo and large TV, complimentary breakfast, 5 PM hors d'oeuvres, and evening pastries. ☎ *655 Burrard St., V6C 2R7,* ☎ *604/683–1234 or 800/233–1234,* ₣₳ₓ *604/689–3707. 612 doubles, 34 suites. Restaurant, 2 bars, café, outdoor heated pool, sauna. AE, D, DC, MC, V.*

$$$ Waterfront Centre Hotel. This dramatically elegant, 23-story glass hotel opened in 1991 across from Canada Place, the Convention Centre, and the cruise-ship terminal—all of which can be reached from the hotel by an enclosed walkway. Views from the caramel-color lobby and 70% of the guest rooms are of Burrard Inlet. The rooms are attractively furnished with contemporary artwork, minibars, and armoires concealing the TV. A live string quartet entertains in the lobby restaurant, Herons, during a lavish Sunday brunch that includes imaginative dishes and decadent desserts. ☎ *900 Canada Place Way, V6C 3L5,* ☎ *604/691–1991 or 800/441–1414,* ₣₳ₓ *604/691–1999. 460 doubles, 29 suites. Restaurants, heated outdoor pool, massage, steam room. AE, D, DC, MC, V.*

$$$ Wedgewood Hotel. This hotel upholds its reputation as a small, ele-
★ gant property run by an owner who cares fervently about her guests. The intimate lobby is decorated in fine detail with polished brass, beveled glass, a fireplace, and tasteful artwork. All the extra touches are here, too: nightly turndown service, afternoon ice delivery, dark-out drapes, flowers growing on the balcony, terry-cloth robes, and morning newspaper. No tour groups or conventions stop here; the Wedgewood's clients are almost exclusively corporate, except on weekends, when the place turns into a couples' retreat. It's a treasure. ☎ *845 Hornby St., V6Z 1V1,* ☎ *604/689–7777 or 800/663–0666,* ₣₳ₓ *604/688–3074. 60 doubles, 33 suites. Restaurant, bar, exercise room. AE, D, DC, MC, V.*

$$–$$$ Parkhill Hotel. Cool pastel shades echo the colors of Impressionist prints decorating the surprisingly spacious rooms in this West End hotel just a block from the seawall and sandy Sunset Beach. Large, comfortable sitting areas, half-moon balconies with city or bay views, in-room safes, minifridges, hair dryers, and complimentary downtown shuttle services are part of the package. ☎ *1160 Davie St., V6E 1N1,* ☎ *604/685–1311 or 800/663–1525,* ₣₳ₓ *604/681–0208. 191 rooms. 2 restaurants, lounge, pool, sauna, exercise room, travel services. AE, D, DC, MC, V.*

$$–$$$ Sheraton Landmark. The towering Landmark on Robson Street is still the tallest hotel in downtown Vancouver and, since its renovations in 1994–95, contains some of the prettiest guest rooms in town. The Sheraton has turned to the bold jewel tones (emerald, sapphire, and ruby) of paintings by British Columbia's beloved Emily Carr (whose works hang in every room). All rooms enjoy a fine view, but the Cloud Nine revolving restaurant on the top floor is the place to go for an unobstructed vista of all of Vancouver—it's a great place to watch the sunrise over an early breakfast buffet. ☎ *1400 Robson St., V6G 1B9,* ☎ *604/687–0511 or 800/325–3535,* FAX *604/687–2801. 351 rooms, 7 suites. Restaurant, café, sports bar, no-smoking rooms, saunas, exercise room, travel services. AE, DC, MC, V.*

$$ **Days Inn.** For the business traveler looking for a bargain, this location is tops. The six-story hotel, which opened as the Abbotsford in 1920, is the only moderately priced hotel in the business core. Recent renovations of the guest rooms and the lobby have made it even more agreeable. Although it's a basic hotel, rooms are bright, clean, and functional; standard units are very large, but there is no room service and few amenities. Suites 310, 410, 510, and 610 have a harbor view. The Bombay Bicycle Club bar is a favorite with businesspeople. ☎ *921 W. Pender St., V6C 1M2,* ☎ *604/681–4335,* FAX *604/681–7808. 74 doubles, 11 suites. Restaurant, 2 bars, no-smoking rooms, free parking. AE, D, DC, MC, V.*

$$ **English Bay Inn.** This newly renovated 1930s Tudor house is one block
★ from the ocean and Stanley Park in a quiet residential part of the West End. The guest rooms—each with a private bath—have wonderful sleigh beds (in all but one room) with matching armoires, Ralph Lauren linen, and alabaster lighting fixtures. The common areas of this no-smoking inn are generous and elegantly furnished: The sophisticated but cozy parlor has wingback chairs, a fireplace, a gilt Louis XIV clock and candelabras, and French doors opening onto the front garden. A small, sunny English country garden decorates the back of the inn. Breakfast is served in a rather formal room with a Gothic dining room suite, a fireplace, and a 17th-century grandfather clock. ☎ *1968 Comox St., V6G 1R4,* ☎ *604/683–8002. 4 rooms, 1 suite. Free parking. AE, V.*

$$ **Hotel Georgia.** This handsome 12-story hotel, built in 1927, has such Old World features as a dark-wood-paneled lobby, ornate brass elevators, and a subdued, genteel atmosphere. Rooms are small but well furnished, with nothing worn around the edges. Executive rooms have an almost separate seating area; rooms facing the art gallery have the best views. From this hotel (across from the Four Seasons) it's a five-minute walk to the business district. ☎ *801 W. Georgia St., V6C 1P7,* ☎ *604/682–5566 or 800/663–1111,* FAX *604/682–8192. 310 doubles, 3 suites. Restaurant, 3 bars. AE, D, DC, MC, V.*

$$ **West End Guest House.** Judge this lovely Victorian house, built in
★ 1906, by its gracious front parlor, cozy fireplace, and early 1900s furniture rather than by its bright pink exterior. Most of the small but extraordinarily handsome rooms have high brass beds, antiques, gorgeous linens, and dozens of old framed pictures of Vancouver. Avoid the basement rooms, however. The inn's genial host, Evan Penner, makes the difference, with small touches such as a pre-dinner glass of sherry, duvets and feather mattress pads, terry bathrobes, hand-knit slippers, turndown service, and a goodnight tart. The inn is in a residential neighborhood that is a 15-minute walk from Stanley Park and two minutes from Robson Street. Room rates include a full breakfast at this no-smoking establishment. ☎ *1362 Haro St., V6E 1G2,* ☎ *604/681–2889,* FAX *604/688–8812. 7 rooms. Parking. AE, D, MC, V.*

$ **Buchan Hotel.** This three-story 1930s building is conveniently set in a tree-lined residential street a block from Stanley Park, a block from shops and restaurants on Denman Street, and a 15-minute walk from the liveliest part of Robson Street. For the budget price, guests rent tiny, institutional rooms with very basic furnishings, ceiling fans, and color TV, but no telephone or air-conditioning; sadly, recent reports indicate problems with cleanliness. The pension-style rooms with shared bath down the hall are perhaps the most affordable accommodations in downtown. Since 1993, this has been a no-smoking hotel. ⚏ *1906 Haro St., V6G 1H7,* ☎ *604/685–5354 or 800/668–6654,* 𝔽𝔸𝕏 *604/685–5367. 60 rooms, 30 with private bath. Lounge, coin laundry, bike storage. AE, DC, MC, V.*

$ **The Kingston.** The Kingston is a small budget hotel convenient for shopping. It is an old-style, four-story building, with no elevator—the type of establishment you'd find in Europe. The spartan rooms are small and immaculate and share a bathroom down the hall. All rooms have phones and a few have TVs. Rooms on the south side are brighter. Continental breakfast is included. ⚏ *757 Richards St., V6B 3A6,* ☎ *604/ 684–9024. 60 rooms, 7 with bath. Lounge, sauna, coin laundry, free parking. AE, MC, V.*

$ **Sylvia Hotel.** The Sylvia Hotel is perhaps the best bargain in Vancouver, but don't count on staying here June–August unless you've booked six months ahead. What make this hotel so popular are its low rates and near-perfect location: about 25 feet from the beach, 200 feet from Stanley Park, and a 20-minute walk from downtown. Rooms are unadorned and have worn, plain furnishings that have probably been around for more than 20 years; not much to look at, but the view—particularly from the south and west sides—and price make it worthwhile. Suites are huge, and all have kitchens, making this a perfect family accommodation. There is little difference between the old and new wings. ⚏ *1154 Gilford St., V6G 2P6,* ☎ *604/681–9321. 97 rooms, 18 suites. Restaurant, lounge, parking. AE, DC, MC, V.*

THE ARTS AND NIGHTLIFE

For information on events, pick up a free copy of the *Georgia Straight* (available at cafés and bookstores around town), or look in the entertainment section of the *Vancouver Sun* (Thursday's paper has listings in the **"What's On"** column). And there's the Arts Hotline (☎ 604/684–2787). For tickets, book through **Ticketmaster** (☎ 604/280–3311).

The Arts

Dance

Watch for **Ballet British Columbia**'s (☎ 604/669–5954) Dance Alive! series, presenting visiting or local ballet companies (from the Kirov to Ballet BC). Most performances by these companies can be seen at the Orpheum or the Queen Elizabeth Theatre (*see below*). Local modern dance companies worth seeing are **Karen Jamison, Judith Marcuse,** and **JumpStart.**

Film

Two theaters have distinguished themselves by avoiding the regular movie fare: **Ridge Theatre** (3131 Arbutus St., ☎ 604/738–6311), which generally plays foreign films and rerun double-bills, and **Pacific Cinématèque Pacifique** (1131 Howe St., ☎ 604/688–3456), which goes for even more esoteric foreign and art films. The **Vancouver International Film Festival** (☎ 604/685–0260) is held during September and October in several theaters around town.

Music

The **Vancouver Symphony Orchestra** (☎ 604/684–9100) and the **CBC Orchestra** (☎ 604/662–6000) play at the restored **Orpheum Theatre** (601 Smithe St.). Choral groups like the **Bach Choir** (☎ 604/921–8012), the **Cantata Singers** (no ☎), and the **Vancouver Chamber Choir** (☎ 604/738–6822) play a major role in Vancouver's classical music scene. The **Early Music Society** (☎ 604/732–1610) performs medieval, Renaissance, and baroque music throughout the year and hosts the Vancouver Early Music Summer Festival, one of the most important early music festivals in North America. Concerts by the **Friends of Chamber Music** (no ☎) and the **Vancouver Recital Society** (☎ 604/736–6034) are always of excellent quality.

Vancouver Opera (☎ 604/682–2871) stages four high-caliber productions a year, usually in October, January, March, and May, at the **Queen Elizabeth Theatre** (600 Hamilton St.). This theater is also the major venue in Vancouver for traveling Broadway musicals.

Theater

The **Vancouver Playhouse** (Hamilton St. at Dunsmuir, ☎ 604/872–6622) is the most established venue in Vancouver. The **Arts Club Theatre** (1585 Johnston St., ☎ 604/687–1644), with two stages on Granville Island and performances all year, is the most active. Both present mainstream theatrical shows. **Carousel Theatre** (☎ 604/669–3410), which performs off-off Broadway shows at the Waterfront Theatre (1405 Anderson St.) on Granville Island, and **Touchstone** (☎ 604/687–8737), at the Firehall Theatre (280 E. Cordova St.), are smaller but lively companies. The **Back Alley Theatre** (751 Thurlow St., ☎ 604/688–7013) hosts *Theatresports,* a hilarious improv event. The **Vancouver East Cultural Centre** (1895 Venables St., ☎ 604/254–9578) is a multipurpose performance space that always hosts high-caliber shows. The **Starlight Theatre** (West End, ☎ 604/280–3311) is the latest of Vancouver's live performance venues to be refurbished.

Bard on the Beach (☎ 604/875–1533) is a summer series of Shakespeare's plays performed under a huge tent on the beach at Vanier Park. **The Fringe** (☎ 604/873–3646), Vancouver's annual live theatrical arts festival, is staged in September at churches, dance studios, and theater halls around town.

Nightlife

Bars and Lounges

The **Gérard Lounge** (845 Burrard St., ☎ 604/682–5511) at Sutton Place Hotel is probably the nicest in the city because of its fireplaces, wingback chairs, dark wood, and leather. For spectacular views, head up to the **Roof Lounge** (900 W. Georgia St., ☎ 604/684–3131) in the Hotel Vancouver, where a pianist plays nightly. The **Bacchus Lounge** (845 Hornby St., ☎ 604/689–7777) in the Wedgewood Hotel is stylish and sophisticated. The **Gallery Lounge** (655 Burrard St., ☎ 604/687–6543) in the Hyatt is a genteel bar, with lots of windows that let in the sun and provide views of the action on the bustling street. The **Garden Court** (791 W. Georgia St., ☎ 604/689–9333) in the Four Seasons is bright and airy with greenery and a waterfall, plus big soft chairs you won't want to get out of. For a more lively atmosphere, try **Joe Fortes** (777 Thurlow St., 604/669–1940), known in town as the local "meet market." Billiards is now tremendously popular in Vancouver, and the **Soho Café and Billiards** (1144 Homer, ☎ 604/688–1180) is the place to go. Another "hot" pool hall is the **Automotive Billiards Club** (1095 Homer, ☎ 604/682–0040).

On Granville Island, the after-work crowds head to **Bridges** (☎ 604/687–4400) near the Public Market overlooking False Creek. Slightly more upscale is **Pelican Bay** (☎ 604/683–7373), the lounge in the Granville Island Howard Johnson Plaza, at the other end of the island. The **Backstage Lounge** (1585 Johnston St., ☎ 604/687–1354), behind the main stage at the Arts Club Theatre, features one of the largest selections of scotches in town and is the hangout for local and touring musicians and actors.

Casinos

A few casinos have been licensed recently in Vancouver, and proceeds go to local charities and arts groups. No alcohol is served. A good bet is the **Royal Diamond Casino** (535 Davie St., ☎ 604/685–2340) downtown. The **Great Canadian Casino** (2477 Heather St., ☎ 604/872–5543), in the Holiday Inn, is another option for gamblers in downtown Vancouver.

Comedy

Yuk Yuks (750 Pacific Blvd., ☎ 604/687–5233) is good for a few laughs. **Punchlines Comedy Theatre** (15 Water St., ☎ 604/684–3015), another cheerful place, is in Gastown.

Music

DISCOS

Although discos come and go, lines still form every weekend at **Richard's on Richards** (1036 Richards St., ☎ 604/687–6794) for live and taped Top-40 music. **Graceland** (1250 Richards St., ☎ 604/688–2648) attracts a slightly younger dance crowd. The go-go dancers at **Mars** (1320 Richards St., ☎ 604/622–7707) are supposed to be there to get dancers into the swing of things.

JAZZ

A jazz and blues hot line (☎ 604/682–0706) gives you current information on concerts and clubs. The **Alma Street Café** (2505 Alma St., ☎ 604/222–2244), a restaurant, is a traditional venue with good mainstream jazz. The **Glass Slipper** (185 E. 11th Ave., ☎ 604/877–0066) has mainstream to contemporary jazz with a more underground atmosphere.

ROCK

The **Town Pump** (66 Water St., ☎ 604/683–6695) is the main venue for local and touring rock bands. The **Soft Rock Café** (1925 W. 4th Ave., ☎ 604/736–8480) is decidedly more upscale than some other Vancouver rock venues; there's live music with dinner. The **86th Street Music Hall** (750 Pacific Blvd., ☎ 604/683–8687) serves up big-name bands. The **Commodore Ballroom** (870 Granville St., ☎ 604/681–7838), a Vancouver institution, has been restored to its original, Art Deco style and offers live music ranging from B.B. King to zydeco bands.

EXCURSIONS

Victoria

Exploring

Numbers in the margin correspond to points of interest on the Downtown Victoria map.

Victoria, originally Fort Victoria, was the first European settlement on Vancouver Island and is the oldest city on Canada's west coast. It was chosen in 1842 by James Douglas to be the Hudson's Bay Company's westernmost outpost, and it became the capital of British Columbia in 1868. Today it's a compact seaside town laced with tea shops and gardens. Though it's quite touristy during the high summer season, it's also at its prettiest, with flowers hanging from turn-of-the-century lampposts and strollers feasting on the beauty of Victoria's natural harbor.

Downtown Victoria

1 A logical place to begin this tour is at the **Visitors Information Centre** on the waterfront. The bridge immediately south affords a grand view of the inner harbor and, across the water on Songhees Point, the 182½-foot **Welcome Totem** (now the tallest totem pole in the world) erected in 1994 for the Commonwealth Games. *812 Wharf St.,* ☎ *604/382–2127.* ☉ *July and Aug., daily 9–9; May, June, and Sept., daily 9–7; Oct.–Apr., daily 9–5.*

2 Just across the way is the **Empress Hotel,** which originally opened in 1908 and is a symbol of both the city and the Canadian Pacific Railway. Designed by Francis Rattenbury, whose works dot Victoria, the property is another of the great châteaus built by Canadian Pacific, still the owners, who also built the Château Frontenac in Québec City, Château Laurier in Ottawa, and Château Lake Louise in Alberta. The ingredients that made the 483-room hotel a tourist attraction in the past are still here. Stop in for tea—served at hour-and-a-half intervals during the afternoon. *721 Government St.,* ☎ *604/384–8111. No jeans, shorts, or T-shirts in tea lobby.*

A short walk around the harbor leads you to the old CPR Steamship Terminal, also designed by Rattenbury, completed in 1924. Today it **3** is the **Royal London Wax Museum,** housing some 300 wax figures, including replicas of Queen Victoria, Elvis, and Marilyn Monroe. *470 Belleville St.,* ☎ *604/388–4461.* ☛ *$7 adults, $6.25 senior citizens, $6 students, $3 children 6–12.* ☉ *May–Aug., daily 9–9; Sept.–Apr., daily 9:30–5.*

4 Next to the wax museum are the **Pacific Undersea Gardens,** where more than 5,000 marine specimens are on display in their natural habitat. You'll also see a short, rather hokey show of performing scuba divers and a giant Pacific octopus. Unfortunately, there are no washrooms, and the site is not wheelchair accessible. This one is usually a disappointment to all but the youngest tourists. *490 Belleville St.,* ☎ *604/382–5717.* ☛ *$6.50 adults, $6 senior citizens, $4.75 children 12–17, $3 children 5–11.* ☉ *Oct.–May, daily 10–5; summer, daily 9–9. Closed Dec. 25. Shows run about every 45 mins.*

5 Across Belleville Street is the **Parliament Buildings** complex. The stone structure, completed in 1897, dominates the inner harbor and is flanked by two statues: Sir James Douglas, who chose the location of Victoria, and Sir Matthew Baille Begbie, the man in charge of law and order during the gold-rush era. Atop the central dome is a gilded statue of Captain George Vancouver, who first sailed around Vancouver Island; a statue of Queen Victoria stands in front of the complex; and outlining the building at night are more than 3,000 lights. Another of Rattenbury's creations, the complex is a good example of the rigid symmetry and European elegance that characterize much of the city's architecture. The public can watch the assembly, when it's in session, from the galleries overlooking the Legislative Chamber. *501 Belleville St.,* ☎ *604/387–3046.* ☛ *Free. Tours run several times daily and are conducted in at least 4 languages in summer and 3 in winter.* ☉ *Sept.–June, weekdays 8:30–5; summer, daily 8:30–5:30.*

6 Follow Belleville Street one block east to reach the **Royal British Columbia Museum,** easily the best attraction in Victoria. Here you can spend hours wandering through the centuries, back 12,000 years. In the prehistoric exhibit, you can actually smell the pines and hear the calls of mammoths and other ancient wildlife. Other exhibits allow you to explore a turn-of-the-century town, with trains rumbling past. In the Kwakiutl Indian longhouse, the smell of cedar envelops you, while piped-in potlatch songs tell the origins of the genuine ceremonial house before you. *675 Belleville St.,* ☎ *604/387–3014.* ☛*Free Mon., Oct.–Apr.; otherwise $5 adults, $3 students and senior citizens, $2 children 6– 18 and people with disabilities.* ⊙ *Sept.–June, daily 10–5:30; July and Aug., daily 9:30–7. Closed Dec. 25 and Jan. 1.*

Just behind the museum and bordering Douglas Street is **Thunderbird Park,** where totem poles and a ceremonial longhouse constructed by Kwakiutl Chief Mungo Martin stand in one corner of the garden of **Helmecken House,** the oldest house in British Columbia. Built in 1852 by pioneer doctor and statesman John Sebastian Helmecken, it is a treasure trove of history, from the early Victorian furnishings to an intriguing collection of 19th-century medical tools. Audio tours last 20 minutes. For further information on this and other heritage attractions in Victoria (Craigflower Farm and Schoolhouse, Emily Carr House, and Point Ellice House), call 604/387–4697. *Helmecken House, 10 Elliot St.,* ☎ *604/361–0021.* ☛*$4 adults, $3 senior citizens and students, $2 children 6–12, $10 families.* ⊙ *May–Oct., daily 11–5; early to mid-Nov., daily noon–4; mid- to late Dec. by reservation.*

❼ A walk east on Superior Street to Douglas Street will lead you to **Beacon Hill Park,** a haven for joggers, walkers, and cyclists. The park's southern lawns offer one of the best views of the Olympic Mountains and the Strait of Juan de Fuca. There are also lakes, walking paths, abundant flowers, a wading pool, a petting zoo, and an outdoor amphitheater for Sunday-afternoon concerts.

❽ From the park, go north on Douglas Street and stop off at the **Crystal Gardens.** Opened in 1925 as the largest saltwater swimming pool in the British Empire, this glass-roof building—now owned by the provincial government—is home to flamingos, macaws, 75 varieties of other birds, hundreds of blooming flowers, and monkeys. At street level there are several boutiques and Rattenbury's Restaurant, one of Victoria's well-frequented establishments. *713 Douglas St.,* ☎ *604/381–1213.* ☛*$6 adults, $4 senior citizens and children 6–16; discounted admission in winter.* ⊙ *Oct.–Apr., daily 10–5:30; May–Sept., daily 9–9.*

From Crystal Gardens continue north on Douglas Street to View Street,
❾ then west to **Bastion Square,** with its gas lamps, restaurants, cobblestone streets, and small shops. This is the spot James Douglas chose as the original Fort Victoria in 1843 and the original Hudson's Bay Company trading post. Today fashion boutiques and restaurants occupy the old buildings. While you're here, you may want to stop in at
❿ what was Victoria's original courthouse but is now the **Maritime Museum of British Columbia.** Dugout canoes, model ships, Royal Navy charts, photographs, uniforms, and ship's bells chronicle Victoria's seafaring history. A seldom-used 100-year-old cage lift, believed to be the oldest in North America, ascends to the third floor. In 1996, however, a new museum is scheduled to open and replace this facility. *28 Bastion Sq.,* ☎ *604/385–4222.* ☛*$5 adults, $4 senior citizens, $3 students, $2 children 6–11.* ⊙ *Daily 9:30–4:30; closed Dec. 25–26, Jan. 1.*

West of Government Street, between Pandora Avenue and Johnson Street,
⓫ is **Market Square,** which offers a variety of specialty shops and boutiques and is considered one of the most picturesque shopping districts in the city. At the turn of the century this area—once part of Chinatown—provided everything a visitor desired: food, lodging, entertainment. Today the square has been restored to its original, pre-1900s character.

⑫ Just around the corner from Market Square is Fisgard Street, the heart of **Chinatown,** one of the oldest in Canada. It was the Chinese who were responsible for building much of the Canadian Pacific Railway in the 19th century, and their influences still mark the region. If you enter Chinatown from Government Street, you'll walk under the elaborate **Gate of Harmonious Interest,** made from Taiwanese ceramic tiles and decorative panels. Along the street, merchants display fragile paper lanterns, embroidered silks, imported fruits, and vegetables. **Fan Tan Alley,** just off Fisgard Street, holds claim not only to being the narrowest street in Canada but also to having been the gambling and opium center of Chinatown, where mah-jongg, fan-tan, and dominoes games were played.

⑬ A 15-minute walk or a short drive east on Fort Street will take you to Joan Crescent, where **Craigdarroch Castle** stands. This lavish mansion was built as the home of British Columbia's first millionaire, Robert Dunsmuir, who oversaw coal mining for the Hudson's Bay Company. (He died before the castle's completion in about 1890.) Converted into a museum depicting turn-of-the-century lifestyle, the castle is strikingly authentic, with elaborately framed landscape paintings, stained-glass windows, carved woodwork—precut in Chicago for Dunsmuir and sent by rail—and rooms for billiards and smoking. The location offers a wonderful view of downtown Victoria from the fourth-floor tower. *1050 Joan Crescent,* ☎ *604/592–5323.* ☛*$6 adults, $5 students, $2 children 6–11.* ☼ *Mid-June–early Sept., daily 9–7:30; mid-Sept.–mid-June, daily 10–4:30.*

What to See and Do with Children

Anne Hathaway's Cottage, tucked away in a unique English village complex in Victoria, is a full-size replica of the original thatched home in Stratford-Upon-Avon, England. The building and the 16th-century antiques inside are typical of Shakespeare's era. The Olde England Inn, on the grounds, is a pleasant spot for tea or a traditional English-style meal. You can also stay ($76–$198; AE, DC, MC, V) in one of the 50 antiques-furnished rooms, some complete with four-poster beds. *429 Lampson St., V9A 5Y9,* ☎ *604/388–4353.* ☛*$6.50 adults, $4.25 senior citizens and children 8–17.* ☼ *June–Sept., daily 9–9; Oct.–May, daily 10–4. Guided tours leave from inn in winter and from cottage in summer. From downtown Victoria, take Munro bus to door.*

Pacific Undersea Gardens (*see* Exploring, *above*).

Swan Lake Christmas Hill Nature Sanctuary. This 23-acre lake, in 110 acres of open fields and wetlands, is 10 minutes from downtown Victoria. From the 1½-mile chip trail and floating boardwalk, birders can spot a variety of waterfowl in winter and nesting birds in the tall grass. *3873 Swan Lake Rd. (take Bus 70 or 75),* ☎ *604/479–0211.* ☛*Free.* ☼ *Nature House: weekdays 8:30–4, weekends and holidays noon–4.*

Royal London Wax Museum (*see* Exploring, *above*).

Off the Beaten Path

★ **Butchart Gardens,** on the 130-acre Ross estate about 21 kilometers (13 miles) north of downtown Victoria, grows more than 700 varieties of flowers and has Italian, Japanese, and English rose gardens. In summer, many of the exhibits are illuminated at night. Also on the premises are a teahouse and restaurants. *800 Benvenuto Ave., Brentwood Bay,* ☎ *604/652–5256.* ☛*$11 adults, $5.75 children 13–17, $1.50 children under 13, excluding GST; discounted rates in winter. Hrs vary seasonally; call ahead.*

Shopping

Shopping in Victoria is easy: Virtually everything can be found in the downtown area on or near Government Street stretching north from the Empress. You'll smell the sweets well before you get to **Roger's Chocolates** (913 Government St., ☎ 604/384–7021), purveyor of fine chocolates and an array of other candies. If the British spirit of Victoria has you searching for fine teas, head to **Murchie's** (1110 Government St., ☎ 604/381–5451), where they have over 40 varieties to choose from (not to mention blended coffees, tarts, and cakes). Next door, **Munro's Books** (1108 Government St., ☎ 604/382–2464) sells a wide selection of books, and the building itself, with its high ceiling, elaborate moldings, and murals, is worth a peek. **The Best of British Columbia** (910 Government St., ☎ 604/384–7773) focuses on products produced in British Columbia, from maple syrup to original art.

The **Cowichan Trading Co., Ltd.** (1328 Government St., ☎ 604/383–0321) sells native jewelry, moccasins, and Cowichan Indian sweaters. **Hill's Indian Crafts** (665 Fort St. at Government St., ☎ 604/383–8224) has a mixture; you'll have to plow through some schlocky souvenirs to find the good-quality West Coast native art.

The **House of Traditions** (910 Government St., ☎ 604/361–3020) offers frilly lace blouses and skirts, some Victorian in fashion. Men's designer clothes by Ralph Lauren are available at **The Polo Store** (1200 Government St., ☎ 604/381–7656). As the name would suggest, **Irish Linen Stores** (1090 Government St., ☎ 604/383–6812) offers fine linen and lace items—hankies, napkins, tablecloths, and place mats.

For a wide selection, head to the larger shopping centers downtown. **Eaton Centre** (1 Victoria Eaton Centre, at Government and Fort Sts., ☎ 604/382–7141) is a department store and mall with around 100 boutiques and restaurants. **Market Square** (560 Johnson St., ☎ 604/386–2441) has three stories of specialty shops and offbeat stores; there's everything from fudge, music, and comic books to jewelry, local arts, and New Age accoutrements.

A 10-minute drive (or Bus 1 or 2) from downtown out Fort Street to Oak Bay Avenue will take you to one of the few residential shopping areas that is not a mall. **Oak Bay Village** is great for browsing, buying, or an afternoon cuppa'. Start at the corner of Oak Bay and Foul Bay and work your way east toward the water.

At last count, Victoria had 60-plus antiques shops specializing in coins, stamps, estate jewelry, rare books, crystal, china, furniture, or paintings and other works of art. A short walk on Fort Street going away from the harbor will take you to Antique Row between Blanshard and Cook streets. You will also find antiques on the west side of Government Street near the Old Town.

Sports and the Outdoors

GOLF

Though **Victoria Golf Club** (1110 Beach Dr., ☎ 604/598–4321) is private, it's open to other private-club members; the windy course is the oldest (built in 1893) in British Columbia and offers a spectacular view of the Strait of Juan de Fuca. The **Cordova Bay Golf Course** (5333 Cordova Bay Rd., ☎ 604/658–4444), Victoria's newest public course, is an 18-hole, par-72 course set on the shoreline overlooking Haro Strait and the San Juan Islands. The **Olympic View Golf Club** (643 Latoria Rd., ☎ 604/474–3673), 20 minutes from downtown, offers both challenging and forgiving tees and stunning views of the Strait of Juan de Fuca and the Olympic Mountains.

Dining

For price categories, *see* Dining *in* Vancouver, *above.*

$$$-$$$$ **Empress Room.** For that special-occasion dinner, reserve a fireside table in the elegant Empress Room. Innovative and beautifully presented Pacific Northwest cuisine vies for attention with the setting when candlelight dances on the tapestried walls beneath an intricately carved mahogany ceiling. Fresh local ingredients go into imaginative seasonal dishes such as house-cured Pacific salmon with wild blackberry-ginger butter, pan-roasted Arctic char with wild-rice polenta and gooseberry chutney, or peppered Vancouver Island venison with black currant sauce, all perfectly complimented by wines from the Empress Hotel's extensive cellar. ✕ *721 Government St.,* ☎ *604/384–8111. Reservations advised. AE, D, DC, MC, V. No lunch.*

$$$ **Chez Daniel.** One of Victoria's old standbys, Chez Daniel offers dishes that are rich, though the nouvelle influence has found its way into some creations. The interior, following a burgundy color scheme, seems to match the traditional caloric cuisine. The wine list is varied, and the menu has a wide selection of basic dishes: rabbit, salmon, duck, steak. The romantic atmosphere here encourages you to linger. ✕ *2524 Estevan Ave.,* ☎ *604/592–7424. Reservations advised. AE, MC, V. Closed Sun., Mon. No lunch.*

$$-$$$ **Marina Restaurant.** This lovely, round restaurant overlooking the Oak
★ Bay Marina is so popular with the locals that it's always crowded and a bit noisy. While seasonings and presentation often change, best bets on the imaginative menu are warm salmon salad, grilled marlin in citrus sesame vinaigrette, rack of lamb in port glaze, and crab served with drawn butter and Indonesian hot-and-sour sauce. Choose from over 500 wines to complement the meal. If you don't have reservations and the dining room and oyster bar are full, head downstairs to the Café Deli for Mediterranean picnic foods prepared by the chefs upstairs; go early for the best selection. ✕ *1327 Beach Dr.,* ☎ *604/598–8555. Reservations advised. AE, DC, MC, V. Closed Dec. 25.*

$$ **Camilles.** This restaurant is romantic, intimate, and one of the few West Coast–cuisine restaurants in Victoria. Such house specialties as carrot and smoked Gruyère cheese cake (an appetizer), roast loin of venison with wild-rice risotto, rack of lamb stuffed with mint pesto, and hazelnut crepes are all served in generous portions. Camilles also has an extensive wine cellar. ✕ *45 Bastion Sq.,* ☎ *604/381–3433. Reservations advised. MC, V. Closed Mon. No lunch.*

$$ **Il Terrazzo.** A charming redbrick terrace edged by potted greenery, lit by flickering candles, and warmed by fireplaces and overhead heaters make Il Terrazzo, tucked away off Waddington Alley, the locals' choice for romantic al fresco dining in Victoria. Baked garlic served with warm cambozola cheese and focaccia; scallops dipped in roasted pistachios garnished with arugula, Belgian endive, and mango salsa; grilled lamb chops on angel hair pasta with tomatoes, garlic, mint, and black pepper; and other hearty Northern Italian dishes come piping hot from the restaurant's authentic wood oven. Anything from the daily fresh sheet is worth a try here. ✕ *555 Johnson St. (off Waddington Alley),* ☎ *604/361–0028. Reservations advised. AE, MC, V. No lunch Sun.*

$$ **Pagliacci's.** Another fine Italian bistro in Victoria, Pagliacci's is a must. Dozens of pasta dishes, quiches, veal, and chicken in marsala sauce with fettuccine are standard. The pastas are freshly made in-house. You'll dine surrounded by orange walls covered with photos of Hollywood movie stars. *1011 Broad St.,* ☎ *604/386–1662. MC, V.*

$-$$ **Don Mee's.** A large neon sign signals guests to Don Mee's, a traditional Chinese restaurant. The long, red staircase leads to an expansive, comfortable restaurant for Szechuan and Cantonese entrées, such as sweet-and-sour chicken, almond duck, and bean curd with broccoli. Dim sum is served daily during lunch hours. ✕ *538 Fisgard St.,* ☎ *604/383–1032. AE, DC, MC, V.*

$–$$ **Le Petit Saigon.** This intimate café-style restaurant offers quiet dining with beautifully presented meals and fare that is primarily Vietnamese, with a touch of French. The crab, asparagus, and egg swirl soup is a specialty of the house, and combination meals are cheap and tasty. ✕ *1010 Langley St.,* ☎ *604/386–1412. AE, MC, V. Closed Sun. No lunch Sat.*

$ **Barb's Place.** This funky, rainbow-colored take-out shack on Fisherman's Wharf has been around long enough to become an institution in Victoria, and the authentic fish-and-chips are consistently judged to be the best by the locals. Pick up an order before taking a quick ride on the little harbor ferry across the bay to Songhees Point for a picnic. ✕ *310 Lawrence St.,* ☎ *604/384–6515. No credit cards.*

$ **Cafe Mexico.** Hearty portions of Mexican food, such as *pollo chipotle* (grilled chicken with melted cheddar and spicy sauce, on a bed of rice) are served at this spacious, redbrick dining establishment just off the waterfront. Colorful bullfight ads and cactus plants provide a suitably Mexican atmosphere. ✕ *1425 Store St.,* ☎ *604/386–5454. AE, DC, MC, V.*

$ **Periklis.** Standard Greek cuisine is offered in this warm, taverna-style restaurant, but there are also steaks and ribs on the menu. On weekends you can enjoy Greek and belly dancing, but brace yourself for the hordes of people who come for the entertainment. ✕ *531 Yates St.,* ☎ *604/386–3313. AE, MC, V. No lunch weekends.*

$ **Siam.** The Thai chefs at Siam, one block south of the McPherson Playhouse, work wonders with both hot and mild Thai dishes. The *Phad Thai Goong* (fried rice noodles with prawns, tofu, peanuts, eggs, bean sprouts and green onions) and *Panang* (choice of meat in curry and coconut milk) are particularly good options. Mirrored walls give this small, simple restaurant a feeling of space, and there is a well-stocked bar with a variety of beer suited to the spices used here. ✕ *1314 Government St.,* ☎ *604/383–9911. MC, V.*

$ **Six-Mile-House.** While it's a bit of a drive from downtown, this 1855 carriage house is a Victoria landmark. The brass, carved oak moldings, and stained glass set a festive mood for the evening. The menu constantly changes but always includes seafood selections and burgers. Try the cider or one of the many international beers offered. ✕ *494 Island Hwy.,* ☎ *604/478–3121. DC, MC, V.*

Lodging

The Victoria Visitors Information Centre has a lodging reservations service; call 800/663–3883.

CATEGORY	VICTORIA*	OTHER AREAS*
$$$$	over $180	over $125
$$$	$110–$180	$90–$125
$$	$70–$110	$50–$90
$	under $70	under $50

All prices are for a standard double room, excluding 10% provincial accommodation tax, service charge, and 7% GST. Prices are in Canadian dollars.

$$$$ **Bedford Regency.** This European-style hotel in the heart of downtown is reminiscent of San Francisco's small hotels, with personalized service and strict attention to details. Rooms are in earth colors, and many have goose-down comforters, fireplaces, and whirlpool bathtubs. Meeting rooms and small conference facilities are also available, making this a good business traveler's lodging. ☎ *1140 Government St., V8W 1Y2,* ☎ *604/384–6835 or 800/665–6500,* ℻ *604/386–8930. 40 rooms. Restaurant, pub. AE, MC, V.*

$$$$ Chateau Victoria. Wonderful views can be had from the upper rooms and rooftop restaurant of this 19-story hotel across from Victoria's new Conference Centre, near the inner harbor and the Royal British Columbia Museum. Rooms are fairly standard in size, and some have balconies or sitting areas and kitchenettes. ☎ *740 Burdett Ave., V8W 1B2,* ☎ *604/382–4221 or 800/663–5891,* ℻ *604/380–1950. 71 rooms, 107 suites. Restaurant, lounge, indoor pool, meeting rooms, van to ferry, free parking. AE, D, DC, MC, V.*

$$$$ Empress Hotel. This is Victoria's dowager queen with a face-lift. First opened in 1908, the hotel underwent a major renovation in 1989 that enhanced its Edwardian charm, updated existing guest rooms, and added some 45 new ones (opt for one of the new rooms for more space). Stained glass, carved archways, and hardwood floors are used effectively. The Empress dominates the inner-harbor area and is the city's primary meeting place for politicians, locals, and tourists. Afternoon tea has been a tradition here since 1908, but it's so popular today that reservations are a must. The Bengal Lounge is full of colonial charm from British India, including a stuffed Bengal tiger, overhead fans, and mosquito netting. Award-winning Pacific Northwest cuisine is featured in the elegant Empress Room (*see* Dining, *above*). ☎ *721 Government St., V8W 1W5,* ☎ *604/384–8111 or 800/441–1414,* ℻ *604/381–4334. 466 rooms, 17 suites. Restaurant, café, 2 lounges, indoor pool, sauna, health club, convention center. AE, D, DC, MC, V.*

$$$–$$$$ Abigail's. A Tudor country inn with gardens and crystal chandeliers, ★ Abigail's is not only lovely but also conveniently located four blocks east of downtown. The guest rooms are prettily detailed in contemporary colors. Down comforters, together with Jacuzzis and fireplaces in some, add to the pampering atmosphere. There's a sense of elegant informality about this no-smoking hotel, noticeable especially in the guest library and sitting room. Breakfast, included in the room rate, is served from 8 to 9:30 in the downstairs dining room. ☎ *906 Mc-Clure St., V8V 3E7,* ☎ *604/388–5363,* ℻ *604/361–1905. 16 rooms. Dining room, library. MC, V.*

$$$–$$$$ Beaconsfield Inn. Built in 1875 and restored in 1984, the Beaconsfield has retained its Old World charm. Dark mahogany wood appears throughout the house; down comforters and some canopy beds and claw-foot tubs adorn the rooms, reinforcing its Edwardian style. Some of the rooms have fireplaces and whirlpool bathtubs. Added pluses are the guest library and conservatory/sun room. Full breakfast, with homemade croissants or scones, and afternoon tea as well as evening sherry are included in the room rates. This is a no-smoking property. ☎ *998 Humboldt St., V8V 2Z8,* ☎ *604/384–4044,* ℻ *604/721–2442. 10 rooms, 1 suite. Library. MC, V.*

$$$–$$$$ Oak Bay Beach Hotel. This Tudor-style hotel beside the ocean in Oak Bay, on the southwest side of the Saanich Peninsula, is well removed from the bustle of downtown. There's a wonderful atmosphere here, though; the hotel overlooks the Haro Strait and catches the setting sun. The interior decor is as dreamy as the grounds, with antiques and flower prints decorating the rooms. The restaurant, Tudor Room by the Sea, is average, but the bar with its cozy fireplace is truly romantic. ☎ *1175 Beach Dr., V8S 2N2,* ☎ *and* ℻ *604/598–4556;* ☎ *800/668–7758 for reservations. 51 rooms. Restaurant, pub, boating. AE, DC, MC, V.*

$$$ Clarion Hotel Grand Pacific. This is one of Victoria's newest and finest hotels, with a lot of mahogany woodwork and an elegant ambience.

Overlooking the harbor, and adjacent to the legislative buildings, the hotel accommodates business travelers and vacationers looking for comfort, convenience, and great scenery; all rooms have terraces, with views of either the harbor or the Olympic Mountains. The elaborate health club is one of the best in the city. ☎ *450 Québec St., V8V 1W5,* ☎ *604/386–0450 or 800/424–6423,* 𝐅𝐀𝐗 *604/383–7603. 130 rooms, 19 suites. Restaurant, lounge, indoor pool, massage, sauna, aerobics, racquetball, squash, convention center, free parking. AE, D, DC, MC, V.*

$$$ Holland House Inn. Two blocks from the inner harbor, legislative buildings, and ferry terminals, this no-smoking hotel has a sense of casual elegance. Some of the individually designed rooms have original fine art created by the owner, and some have four-poster beds and fireplaces. All rooms have private baths, and all but two have their own balconies. A lavish breakfast is included in room rates. You'll recognize the house by the picket fence around it. ☎ *595 Michigan St., V8V 1S7,* ☎ *604/384–6644,* 𝐅𝐀𝐗 *604/384–6117. 10 rooms. Lounge. AE, DC, MC, V.*

$$$ Mulberry Manor. This Tudor mansion is the last building designed by
★ Victoria architect Simon McClure; the grounds were designed and, until recently, maintained by a gardener at the world-famous Butchart Gardens; and the manor has been restored and decorated to magazine-cover perfection with antiques, sumptuous linens, and tile baths. Charming hosts Susan and Tony Temple provide sumptuous breakfasts with homemade jams and great coffee. ☎ *611 Foul Bay Rd., V8S 1H2,* ☎ *604/370–1918,* 𝐅𝐀𝐗 *604/370–1968. 3 rooms, 1 suite. MC, V.*

$$$ Ocean Pointe Resort. Across the "blue bridge" from downtown Vic-
★ toria, the resort opened in the summer of 1992 on the site of an old shingle mill in an area once claimed by the Songhees natives. Public rooms and half of the guest rooms offer romantic evening views of downtown Victoria and the parliament buildings. Guest rooms are spacious; some come with floor-to-ceiling windows and small balconies. Amenities include several restaurants, extensive fitness facilities, and the best aesthetics spa in town. The housekeeping suites have kitchens. ☎ *45 Songhees Rd., V9A 6T3,* ☎ *604/360–2999 or 800/667–4677,* 𝐅𝐀𝐗 *604/360–5856. 213 rooms, 37 suites. 2 restaurants, lounge, indoor pool, sauna, spa, 2 tennis courts, exercise room, racquetball, squash. AE, DC, MC, V.*

$$$ Victoria Regent Hotel. Originally built as an apartment house, this is now a posh, condo-living hotel that offers views of the harbor or city. The outside is plain, with a glass facade, but the interior is sumptuously decorated with warm earth tones and modern furnishings; each suite has a living room, a dining room, a deck, a kitchen, and one or two bedrooms with bath. It's a good choice for families. ☎ *1234 Wharf St., V8W 3H9,* ☎ *604/386–2211 or 800/663–7472,* 𝐅𝐀𝐗 *604/386–2622. 15 rooms, 32 suites. Restaurant, coin laundry, free parking. AE, D, DC, MC, V.*

$$–$$$ Coast Victoria Harbourside. Built in 1991 on the quieter, more residential
★ section of the harbor front next to Fisherman's Wharf, the hotel enjoys water views while being removed from the bustling traffic and crowds on Government Street. Serene relaxation in modern comfort is a theme here, from the warm mahogany-paneled lobby and soothing shades of blue-gray and pale pink in average-size guest rooms to an extensive health club. Fishing and whale-watching charters and the pudgy little harbor ferries stop at the hotel's marina just outside, and the action of the inner harbor is a leisurely stroll or quick shuttle ride away. ☎ *146 Kingston St., V8V 1V4,* ☎ *604/360–1211 or 800/663–1144,* 𝐅𝐀𝐗 *604/360–1418. 125 rooms, 7 suites. Restaurant, lounge, health club, meeting rooms, downtown shuttle, free parking. AE, DC, MC, V.*

$–$$ Admiral Motel. On Victoria harbor along the tourist strip, this motel is in the center of things, although it is relatively quiet in the evening. If you're looking for basic, clean lodging, the Admiral is just that. The amiable owners take good care of the newly refurbished rooms, and small pets are permitted. ☎ *257 Belleville St., V8V 1X1, ☎ and* FAX *604/388–6267. 29 rooms, 23 with kitchens. Coin laundry, free parking. AE, D, MC, V.*

$ Cats Meow. If you're on a tight budget, you may appreciate this small youth hostel just across the bridges in Victoria West. Operated by bubbly Daphne Cuthill and resident meow Rufus, the hostel offers dorm rooms plus two baths, two showers, two kitchens, and a TV room. Laundry service and breakfast are available at nominal extra cost; Daphne also arranges discounted day trips. It's only a 15-minute walk from downtown. ☎ *422 Wilson St., V9A 3G5, ☎ and* FAX *604/380–1157. 5 dorms with 26 beds. No credit cards.*

The Arts and Nightlife

THE ARTS

Galleries. The **Art Gallery of Greater Victoria,** considered one of Canada's finest art museums, is home both to large collections of Chinese and Japanese ceramics and other art and to the only authentic Shinto shrine in North America. The gallery also hosts a permanent Emily Carr exhibit and numerous temporary exhibitions yearly. *1040 Moss St.,* ☎ *604/384–4101.* ☛*$4 adults, $2 senior citizens and students, children under 13 free; free Thurs. after 5, though donations are accepted.* ☉ *Mon.–Wed., Fri., and Sat. 10–5; Thurs. 10–9; Sun. 1–5.*

Among the numerous commercial galleries, the **Fran Willis North Park Gallery** (200–1619 Store St., ☎ 604/381–3422) is a good bet. In a gorgeously restored warehouse near the waterfront, it shows contemporary paintings and sculpture by local artists; music is performed from time to time. **Eagle's Moon Gallery** (1010 Government St., ☎ 604/361–4184) showcases the totems, serigraphs, and original paintings of renowned Tsimishian artist Roy Henry Vickers. Original art and fine Canadian crafts are the focus at the **Northern Passage Gallery** (1020 Government St., ☎ 604/381–3380).

Music. The **Victoria Symphony** has a winter schedule and a summer season, playing in the recently refurbished **Royal Theatre** (805 Broughton St., ☎ 604/386–6121) and at the **University Centre Auditorium** (Finnerty Rd., ☎ 604/721–8480). The **Pacific Opera Victoria** performs three productions a year in the 900-seat **McPherson Playhouse** (3 Centennial Sq., ☎ 604/386–6121), adjoining the Victoria City Hall. The **Victoria International Music Festival** (☎ 604/736–2119) features internationally acclaimed musicians each summer from the first week in July through late August.

The **Victoria Jazz Society** (☎ 604/388–4423) organizes an annual **JazzFest International** in late June, which in the past has featured such jazz, blues, and world-beat artists as Dizzy Gillespie, Frank Morgan, and Ellis Marsalis.

For listings of clubs and restaurants featuring jazz during the year, call **Jazz Hotline** (☎ 604/658–5255).

Theater. Live productions can be seen at the **Belfry Theatre** (1291 Gladstone Ave., ☎ 604/385–6815), the **Phoenix Theatre** (Finnerty Rd., ☎ 604/721–8000) at the University of Victoria, **Langham Court Theatre** (805 Langham Ct., ☎ 604/384–2142), and **McPherson Playhouse** (3 Centennial Sq., ☎ 604/386–6121).

In addition to live music, darts, and brewery tours, **Spinnakers Brew Pub** (308 Catherine St., ☎ 604/386–2739) features plenty of B.C. microbrewery beer, including eight of their own concoctions on tap. **Harpo's** (15 Bastion Sq., ☎ 604/385–5333) has live rock, blues, and jazz, with visits from internationally recognized bands. For dancing, head to **Sweetwater's** (27-560 Johnson St., ☎ 604/383–7844), where a younger crowd moves on two dance floors to taped techno and Top 40.

Victoria Essentials
ARRIVING AND DEPARTING
By Boat. B.C. Ferries (☎ 604/277–0277 in Vancouver or 604/656-0757 in Victoria for recorded schedule information) provides frequent year-round passenger and vehicle service from Tsawwassen (south of Vancouver) to Swartz Bay (30 minutes by car north of Victoria).

There is year-round passenger service (closed Christmas) between Victoria and Seattle on the **Victoria Clipper** (☎ 604/382–8100 in Victoria or 800/888–2535 in the U.S.).

Washington State Ferries (☎ 604/381–1551 in Victoria, 206/464–6400 in Seattle) cross daily, year-round, between Sidney, just north of Victoria, and Anacortes, Washington. **Black Ball Transport** (☎ 604/386–2202 in Victoria; 206/457–4491 in Port Angeles) operates between Victoria and Port Angeles, Washington.

By Bus. Greyhound (☎ 604/662–3222 in Vancouver, 800/661–8747 in Canada, or 800/231–2222 in the U.S.) connects destinations throughout British Columbia with cities and towns all along the Pacific North Coast.

By Car. The TransCanada Highway, Route 1, runs south from Nanaimo to Victoria. Route 14 connects Sooke to Port Renfrew, on the west coast of Vancouver Island, with Victoria.

By Plane. Victoria is served by **Victoria International Airport** and **Vancouver International Airport.** Domestic airports are in most cities. **Air Canada** (☎ 604/688–5515 in Vancouver, 800/776–3000 in the U.S.) and **Canadian Airlines International** (☎ 604/279–6611 in Vancouver, 800/426–7000 in the U.S.) are the two dominant carriers. **Air B.C.** (☎ 604/688–5515 in Vancouver, 604/360–9074 in Victoria, 800/776–3000 in the U.S.) is the major regional line and runs daily flights between Seattle and Victoria. **Kenmore Air** (☎ 206/486–1257 or 800/543–9595 in the U.S. and Canada) offers direct daily flights from Seattle to Victoria, Nanaimo, Campbell River, and Northeast Vancouver Island. **Horizon Air** (☎ 800/547–9308) provides service between Seattle and Victoria airports.

GETTING AROUND
By Bus. The **BC Transit System** (☎ 604/382–6161) runs a fairly extensive service throughout Victoria and the surrounding areas, with an all-day pass that costs $4 for adults, $3 for students and senior citizens. Passes are sold at many outlets in downtown Victoria, including Eaton Centre and the Tourist Info Centre.

GUIDED TOURS
Tally-Ho Horsedrawn Tours (☎ 604/479–1113) offers visitors a get-acquainted session with downtown Victoria that includes Beacon Hill Park. **Victoria's Carriage Tours** (☎ 604/383–2207) is another option for horse-drawn tours. From April through September it's possible to tour downtown Victoria by pedicab; contact **Kabuki Kabs** (☎ 604/385–4243).

History buffs may prefer looking into Victoria's background on the intriguing guided cemetery tours put together by the **Old Cemeteries Society** (☎ 604/384–0045).

IMPORTANT ADDRESSES AND NUMBERS

Emergencies. Dial **911** for **police, ambulance,** or **poison control.**

Hospital. Victoria General Hospital (35 Helmcken Rd., ☎ 604/727–4212).

Late-Night Pharmacy. McGill and Orme Pharmacies (649 Fort St., ☎ 604/384–1195).

Visitor Information. Contact **Tourism Victoria** (1175 Douglas St., Suite 710, V8W 2E1, ☎ 604/382–2160 or 800/663–3883 for reservations, FAX 604/361–9733).

Whistler

Exploring

If you think of skiing when you hear mention of Whistler, British Columbia, you're thinking on track. Whistler and Blackcomb mountains, part of Whistler Resort, are the two largest ski mountains in North America and are consistently ranked the first- or second-best ski destinations on the continent. There's winter and summer glacier skiing, the longest vertical drop in North America, and one of the most advanced lift systems in the world. At the base of the mountains is Whistler Village—a small community of lodgings, restaurants, pubs, gift shops, and boutiques. With dozens of hotels and condos within a five-minute walk of the mountains, the site is frenzied with activity. Culinary options in the village range from burgers to French, Japanese to deli cuisine; and nightly entertainment runs the gamut from sophisticated piano bars to casual pubs.

In winter, the village buzzes with skiers taking to the slopes, but as the scenery changes from winter's snow-white to summer's lush green landscapes, the mood of Whistler changes, too. Things seem to slow down a bit, and the resort sheds some of its competitive edge and relaxes to a slower pace. Even the local golf tournaments and the triathlon are interspersed with Mozart and bluegrass festivals.

Recent developments in this rapidly growing resort include **Whistler North,** with still more boutiques, condo hotels, and dining outlets; **Glacier Creek Lodge,** a visually stunning addition at Blackcomb that expands the dining options on the mountain; and the new **Meadow Park Sports Centre** (☎ 604/938–3133), with a six-lane pool, a hot tub, a sauna, a steam room, and two squash courts.

Adjacent to the area is the 78,000-acre (31,579-hectare) **Garibaldi Provincial Park,** with dense mountainous forests splashed with hospitable lakes and streams. Even if you don't want to roam much farther than the village, there are five lakes for canoeing, fishing, swimming, and windsurfing, and many nearby hiking and mountain-bike trails.

Whistler Village is a pedestrian-only community. Anywhere you want to go within the resort is at most five minutes away, and parking lots are just outside the village. The bases of Whistler and Blackcomb mountains are also just at the edge; in fact, you can ski right into the lower level of the Chateau Whistler Hotel, and all 3,000 of the village's hotel rooms are less than 1,000 feet from the lifts.

If you are interested in a tour of the area, **Alpine Adventure Tours** (☎ 604/932–2705) has a Whistler history tour of the valley and a Squamish day trip.

Scenic Drives

The **Coast Mountain Circle** links Vancouver to Cariboo Country. This 702-kilometer (435-mile) route takes in spectacular Howe Sound, the deep-water port of Squamish, Whistler Resort, and Pemberton Valley before heading back to Vancouver through scenic Fraser Canyon and Harrison Hot Springs. The loop makes a comfortable two- to three-day journey. For more information contact the **Tourism Association of Southwestern B.C.** (204-1755 W. Broadway, Vancouver V6J 4S5, ☎ 604/739–9011 or 800/667–3306, FAX 604/739–0153).

Sports and the Outdoors

CANOEING AND KAYAKING

You'll see lots of canoes and kayaks at the many lakes and rivers near Whistler. If you want to get in on the fun, rentals are available at Alta Lake at both **Lakeside Park** and **Waside Park.** Another spot that's perfect for canoeing is the **River of Golden Dreams,** either from Meadow Park to Green Lake or upstream to Twin Bridges. Kayakers looking for a thrill may want to try **Green River** from Green Lake to Pemberton. Call **Whistler Outdoor Experience** (☎ 604/932–3389), **Whistler Sailing and Water Sports** (☎ 604/932–7245) or **Sea to Sea Kayaking** (☎ 604/898-5498) for equipment or guided trips.

FISHING

Whistler Backcountry Adventures (☎ 604/938–1410) or **Whistler Fishing Guides** (☎ 604/932–4267) will take care of anything you need—equipment, guides, and transportation. All five of the lakes around Whistler are stocked with trout, but the area around **Dream River Park** is one of the most popular fishing spots. Slightly farther afield, try **Cheakamus Lake, Daisy Lake,** and **Callaghan Lake.**

GOLF

Arnold Palmer designed the par-72 championship **Whistler Golf Course** (☎ 604/932–4544), a "good four-iron shot from the village." The course is very scenic, fairly flat, and challenging for the experienced but pleasant for beginners. The equally scenic **Chateau Whistler Golf Club** (4612 Blackcomb Way, ☎ 604/938–8000), designed by Robert Trent Jones II and nestled at the foot of the mountain on the opposite side of Whistler Village, was ranked the best new course in Canada by *Golf Digest* in 1993.

SKIING

The vertical drops and elevations at **Blackcomb** (☎ 604/932–3141) and **Whistler** (☎ 604/932–3434) mountains are, perhaps, the most impressive features to skiers here. Blackcomb has a 5,280-foot vertical drop, North America's longest, while Whistler comes in second, with a 5,020-foot drop. The top elevation is 7,494 feet on Blackcomb and 7,160 on Whistler. These mountains also have the most advanced ski-lift technology: Blackcomb has a 27,102-skier-per-hour lift capacity, while Whistler's capacity is 22,815 skiers per hour. Blackcomb and Whistler have more than 100 marked trails each and receive an average of 360 inches of snow per year; Blackcomb is open June–August for summer glacier skiing. **Whistler Ski School** and **Blackcomb Ski School** offer lessons to skiers of all levels.

In Whistler, **Mountain Heli-Sports** (☎ 604/932–2070), **Tyax Heli-Skiing** (☎ 604/932–7007), and **Whistler Heli-Skiing** (☎ 604/932–4105) have day trips with up to four glacier runs, or 12,000 vertical feet of skiing for experienced skiers; the cost is about $350.

Dining

Dining at Whistler is informal; casual dress is appropriate everywhere.

For prices *see* Dining *in* Vancouver, *above.*

$$$ **Il Caminetto di Umberto; Trattoria di Umberto; Settebello's.** Umberto Menghi is among Vancouver's best-known restaurateurs because of his fabulously successful Italian restaurants. Now there are three in Whistler. Il Caminetto and the Trattoria are in the village, and Settebello's is in Whistler Creek, about 3 kilometers (2 miles) south. Umberto offers home-style Italian cooking in a relaxed atmosphere; he specializes in such pasta dishes as crab-stuffed cannelloni or a four-cheese lasagna. The Trattoria has a Tuscan-style rotisserie, highlighting a pasta dish served with a tray of chopped tomatoes, hot pepper, basil, olive oil, anchovies, and Parmesan so that you can mix it as spicy and flavorful as you like. Settebello's specialty is lean grilled beef and chicken, and Il Caminetto, perhaps the best restaurant in the Whistler area, is known for its veal, osso buco, and zabaglione. ✗ *Il Caminetto: 4242 Village Stroll,* ☎ *604/932–4442; Trattoria: Mountainside Lodge,* ☎ *604/932–5858; Settebello's: Whistler Creek Lodge,* ☎ *604/932– 3000. Dinner reservations advised. AE, DC, MC, V.*

$$$ **Les Deux Gros.** The name means "the two fat guys," which may ex-
★ plain the restaurant's motto, "Never trust a skinny chef." Portions of the country French cuisine are generous indeed. The Alsatian onion pie, steak tartare, juicy rack of lamb, and salmon Wellington are all superbly crafted and presented, and the service is friendly but unobtrusive. Just southwest of the village, this is the spot for a special romantic dinner; request one of the prime tables by the massive stone fireplace. ✗ *1200 Alta Lake Rd.,* ☎ *604/932–4611. Reservations advised. AE, MC, V. No lunch.*

$$$ **The Wildflower Cafe.** Although this is the main dining room of the Chateau Whistler, it's an informal, comfortable restaurant. Huge picture windows overlook the ski slopes. The rustic effect of the Chateau Whistler lobby continues in the Wildflower—more than 100 antique wood birdhouses decorate the room, and chairs and tables have a farmhouse look. An à la carte menu focuses on Northern Italian cuisine and fresh seafood; the restaurant also offers terrific breakfast, lunch, and dinner buffets that may include fresh crepes and omelets, sweet-potato-and-parsnip soup, barbecued salmon, smoked halibut, artichoke-and-mushroom salad, pepper salad, seafood pâté, pasta in a spicy tomato sauce, and cold meats. ✗ *Chateau Whistler Hotel,* ☎ *604/938–2033. Dinner reservations advised. AE, D, DC, MC, V.*

$$ **La Rúa.** One of the brightest lights on the Whistler dining scene is La
★ Rúa, on the ground floor of Le Chamois (*see* Lodging, *below*). Reddish flagstone floors and sponge-painted walls, a wine cellar behind a wrought-iron door, modern oil paintings, and sconce lighting give the restaurant an intimate, Mediterranean ambience. Favorites from the Continental menu include Asian prawns, rack of lamb, and baked sea bass with fresh herbs. Start with the filling black-bean soup and end with the pleasing tiramisù. ✗ *4557 Blackcomb Way,* ☎ *604/932–5011. Reservations advised. AE, DC, MC, V. No lunch.*

Lodging

All lodgings can be booked through the **Whistler Resort Association** (☎ 604/932–4222 or 800/944–7853); summer rates are greatly discounted.

For price categories, *see* Lodging *in* Vancouver, *above*.

$$$$ **Chateau Whistler.** Whistler's most extravagant hotel is a large and friendly-looking fortress just outside the village. It was built and run by Canadian Pacific and is the same style as the Banff Springs Hotel and the Jasper Park Lodge. The marvelous lobby is filled with rustic Canadiana, handmade Mennonite rugs, enormous fireplaces, and enticing overstuffed sofas. Floor-to-ceiling windows in the lounge, the health club, and the Wildflower Cafe overlook the base of Blackcomb Mountain. The standard rooms, called premier, are average, but the suites are fit for royalty, with specially commissioned quilts and artwork, complemented by antique furnishings. Both the Wildflower Cafe (*see* Dining, *above*) and La Fiesta, a tapas bar, are very good choices for a meal. The resort added an extensive spa facility in late 1993; ask about reasonably priced retreat packages and summer rates that drop by 50%. ☎ *4599 Chateau Blvd., Box 100, V0N 1B0,* ☎ *604/938–8000 or 800/441–1414 in the U.S. and Canada,* ᶠᴬˣ *604/938–2055. 307 doubles, 36 suites. 2 restaurants, bar, indoor-outdoor pool, massage, saunas, steam rooms, golf course, 3 tennis courts, exercise room. AE, D, DC, MC, V.*

$$$$
★ **Le Chamois.** Sharing the prime ski-in, ski-out location at the base of the Blackcomb runs is this elegant luxury hotel. Of the 62 spacious guest rooms with convenience kitchens, the most popular are the studios with Jacuzzi tubs set in front of the living room's bay windows overlooking the slopes and lifts. Guests can keep an eye on the action also from the glass elevators and the heated outdoor pool. ☎ *4557 Blackcomb Way,* ☎ *604/932–8700 or 800/777–0185 in the U.S. and Canada,* ᶠᴬˣ *604/938–1888. 62 suites and studios. Restaurant, deli, pool, hot tub, exercise room, ski storage, coin laundry, village shuttle, free parking. AE, DC, MC, V.*

$$ **Pension Edelweiss.** The Edelweiss, one of several charming and very European bed-and-breakfasts around Whistler, is within walking distance of Whistler Village. Rooms have a crisp, spic-and-span feel, in keeping with the Bavarian chalet style of the house; all have private baths and some have balconies and telephones. Each morning a different breakfast (included in the room rate) is served: Scandinavian, American, French, German. A bus stop just outside provides easy access to Whistler Village. ☎ *7162 Nancy Greene Way, Box 850,* ☎ *604/ 932–3641 or 800/665–1892 (Whistler B&B Inns),* ᶠᴬˣ *604/938–1746. 8 rooms, 1 suite. Hot tub, sauna. AE, MC, V.*

Whistler Essentials

ARRIVING AND DEPARTING

By Bus. Maverick Coach Lines (☎ 604/255–1171, ᶠᴬˣ 604/255–5700) has buses leaving every couple of hours for Whistler Village from the depot in downtown Vancouver. The fare is approximately $26 round-trip. During ski season, the last bus leaves Whistler at 9:45 PM.

Perimiter Bus Transportation (☎ 604/261–2299 or 800/663–4265, ᶠᴬˣ 604/266–1628) has daily service, November–April and June–September from Vancouver Airport to Whistler. Reservations are necessary 24 hours in advance; the ticket booth is on the Arrivals level of the airport. The fare is around $26 one way.

By Car. Driving time from Seattle to Vancouver is about three hours. Whistler is 2–2½ hours north of Vancouver via Route 99, the Sea-to-Sky Highway.

By Train. BC Rail (☎ 604/984–5246) travels north from Vancouver to Whistler along a beautiful route. The Vancouver Bus Terminal and the

North Vancouver Station are connected by bus shuttle. Rates are under $20 one way.

IMPORTANT ADDRESSES AND NUMBERS

Emergencies. Dial 0 for **police, ambulance,** or **poison control.**

Visitor Information. Contact the **Whistler Resort Association** (4010 Whistler Way, Whistler V0N 1B4; in Whistler, ☎ 604/932–4222 or 800/944–7853 in the U.S. and Canada, FAX 604/932–7231). There is an information booth (☎ 604/932–2394) in Whistler Village at the front door of the Conference Center; hours fluctuate, so call before visiting.

A provincial government **Travel Infocentre** (☎ 604/932–5528) is on the main highway, about 1½ kilometers (1 mile) south of Whistler.

VANCOUVER ESSENTIALS

Arriving and Departing

By Bus

Greyhound Lines (☎ 604/662–3222 or 800/661–8747) is the largest bus line serving Vancouver. The Pacific Central Station (1150 Station St.) is the depot. **Quick Shuttle** (☎ 604/244–3744 or 800/665–2122 in the U.S.) bus service runs between Vancouver and Seattle five times a day in winter and up to eight times a day in summer.

By Car

From the south, I–5 from Seattle becomes **Route 99** at the U.S.–Canada border. Vancouver is a three-hour drive from Seattle. Avoid border crossings during peak times: holidays and weekends.

Route 1, the **Trans-Canada Highway,** enters Vancouver from the east. To avoid traffic, arrive after rush hour (8:30 AM).

By Ferry

BC Ferries (☎ 604/277–0277, 24-hour recorded schedule information; 604/669–1211, reservations) operates two major ferry terminals outside Vancouver. From Tsawwassen to the south (an hour's drive from downtown), ferries sail to Victoria and Nanaimo on Vancouver Island and to the Gulf Islands (the small islands between the mainland and Vancouver Island). From Horseshoe Bay (30 minutes north of downtown), ferries sail a short distance across the strait and up the coast to Nanaimo on Vancouver Island.

By Plane

Vancouver International Airport is on an island about 14 kilometers (9 miles) south of downtown. Current expansion of the airport facilities is due for completion in 1996; in the meantime, all departing passengers are charged a $15 improvement fee. **American Airlines** (☎ 800/433–7300), Delta (☎ 604/221–1212), **Horizon Air** (☎ 800/547–9308), and **United** (☎ 800/241–6522) fly into the airport. The two major domestic airlines are **Air Canada** (☎ 800/776–3000) and **Canadian Airlines** (☎ 800/426–7000).

Air BC (☎ 604/688–5515) offers 30-minute harbor-to-harbor service (downtown Vancouver to downtown Victoria) several times a day. Planes leave from near the Bayshore Hotel. **Helijet Airways** (☎ 604/273–1414) has helicopter service from downtown Vancouver to downtown Victoria. The heliport is near Vancouver's Pan Pacific Hotel.

BETWEEN THE AIRPORT AND DOWNTOWN

The drive from the airport to downtown is 20–45 minutes, depending on the time of day. Airport hotels offer free shuttle service to and from the airport.

The **Vancouver Airporter Service** (☎ 604/261–2299) bus leaves the international and domestic arrival levels of the terminal building approximately every half hour stopping at major downtown hotels. It operates from 6 AM until midnight. The fare is $9 one-way and $15 round-trip.

Taxi stands are in front of the terminal building on domestic and international arrivals levels. Taxi fare to downtown is about $24. Area cab companies are **Yellow** (☎ 604/681–3311) and **Black Top** (☎ 604/681–2181).

Limousine service from **Airlimo** (☎ 604/273–1331) costs about the same as a taxi to downtown: The current rate is about $28.

By Train

The **Pacific Central Station** (1150 Station St.) is the hub for rail, bus, and SkyTrain service. The **VIA Rail** (☎ 800/561–8630) station is at Main Street and Terminal Avenue. VIA provides transcontinental service through Jasper to Toronto three times a week. Passenger trains leave the **BC Rail** (☎ 604/631–3500) station in North Vancouver for Whistler and the interior of British Columbia.

Getting Around

By Bus

Exact change is needed to ride **B.C. Transit** (☎ 604/261–5100) buses: $1.50 adults, 75¢ for senior citizens and children 5–13. Books of 25 tickets are sold at convenience stores and newsstands; look for a red, white, and blue "Fare Dealer" sign. Day passes, good for unlimited travel after 9:30 AM, cost $4.50 for adults. They are available from fare dealers and any SeaBus or SkyTrain station. Transfers are valid for 90 minutes and allow travel in both directions.

By Car

Although no freeways cross Vancouver, rush-hour traffic is not yet horrendous. The worst rush-hour bottlenecks are the North Shore bridges, the George Massey Tunnel on Route 99 south of Vancouver, and Route 1 through Coquitlam and Surrey.

By Rapid Transit

Vancouver has a one-line, 25-kilometer (15-mile) rapid transit system called **SkyTrain,** which travels underground downtown and is elevated for the rest of its route to New Westminster and Surrey. Trains leave about every five minutes. Tickets, sold at each station from machines (correct change is not necessary), must be carried with you as proof of payment. You may use transfers from SkyTrain to SeaBus (*see below*) and B.C. Transit buses and vice versa.

By SeaBus

The **SeaBus** is a 400-passenger commuter ferry that crosses Burrard Inlet from the foot of Lonsdale (North Vancouver) to downtown. The ride takes 13 minutes and costs the same as the transit bus. With a transfer, connection can be made with any B.C. Transit bus or Sky-Train.

By Taxi
It is difficult to hail a cab in Vancouver; unless you're near a hotel, you'd have better luck calling a taxi service. Try **Yellow** (☎ 604/681–3311) or **Black Top** (☎ 604/681–2181).

Guided Tours

North Shore tours usually include any or several of the following: a gondola ride up Grouse Mountain, a walk across the Capilano Suspension Bridge, a stop at a salmon hatchery, the Lonsdale Quay Market, and a ride back to town on the SeaBus. Half-day tours cost anywhere from $30–$45 and are offered by **Landsea Tours** (☎ 604/255–7272), **Harbour Ferries** (☎ 604/687–9558), **Gray Line** (☎ 604/879–3363), and **Pacific Coach Lines** (☎ 604/662–7575).

Air
Tour the mountains and fjords of the North Shore by helicopter for around $200 per person (minimum of three people) for 50 minutes: **Vancouver Helicopters** (☎ 604/270–1484) flies from the Harbour Heliport downtown. Or see Vancouver from the air for $65 for 30 minutes: **Harbour Air**'s (☎ 604/688–1277) seaplanes leave from beside the Bayshore Hotel.

Boat
The Royal Hudson, Canada's only functioning steam train, heads along the mountainous coast up Howe Sound to the logging town of Squamish. After a break to explore, you sail back to Vancouver via the MV *Britannia*. This excellent excursion costs about $55, takes 8 hours, and is organized by **Harbour Ferries** (☎ 604/687–9558). Reservations are advised.

The SS *Beaver* (☎ 604/682–7284), a replica of a Hudson Bay fur-trading steamship that ran aground here in 1888, offers two trips. One is the Harbour Sunset Dinner Cruise, a three-hour trip with a barbecue dinner; the other is a three-hour daytime trip up Indian Arm with salmon for lunch. Each is under $50 and reservations are necessary for both.

Harbour Ferries (☎ 604/687–9558) takes a 1½-hour tour of Burrard Inlet in a paddle wheeler; the tour operates Wednesday–Sunday and costs under $20.

Fraser River Connection (☎ 604/525–4465) will take you on a six-hour tour of a fascinating working river—past log booms, tugs, and houseboats. Between May and October, ride from New Westminster to Fort Langley aboard a convincing replica of an 1800s-era paddle wheeler for under $50 (half price for children).

Orientation
Gray Line (☎ 604/879–3363), the largest tour operator, offers the 3½-hour Grand City bus tour year-round. Departing from the Sandman Inn in summer and the Plaza of Nations in winter, the tour includes Stanley Park, Chinatown, Gastown, English Bay, and Queen Elizabeth Park and costs about $31. During the spring, summer, and fall, **Westcoast City and Nature Sightseeing** (☎ 604/451–5581) accommodates up to 24 people in vans that run a 3½-hour City Highlights Tour for $27 (pickup available from any downtown location). Using minibuses, **Vance Tours** (☎ 604/941–5660) offers a similar tour (3½ hours, $33) that includes a visit to the University of British Columbia, and a shorter city tour (2½ hours, $30).

The **Vancouver Trolley Company** (☎ 604/451–5581) runs turn-of-the-century–style trolleys through Vancouver from April to October on a

2-hour narrated tour of Stanley Park, Gastown, English Bay, Granville Island, Queen Elizabeth Park, and Chinatown, among other sights. A day pass allows you to complete one full circuit, getting off and on as often as you like. Start the trip at any of the sights and buy a ticket on board. Adult fare is around $20, children half that. During the rest of the year, the trolley runs the same circuit on a 2½-hour trip, but no on-off option is available. Between June and September, **Gray Line** (☎ 604/879–3363) offers a similar narrated tour aboard double-decker buses; passengers get on and off as they choose and are allowed to ride free the following day if they haven't had their fill. Adult fare is $18, children's $9.

Personal Guides

Early Motion Tours (☎ 604/687–5088) covers Vancouver in a Model-A Ford convertible. For about $60, up to four people can take an hour-long trip around downtown, Chinatown, and Stanley Park.

AAA Horse & Carriage (☎ 604/681–5115) has a 50-minute tour of Stanley Park, along the waterfront, and through a cedar forest and a rose garden for about $10.

Individualized V.I.P. tours are available from personal guide **Marcel Jonker** (☎ 604/261–9169).

Opening and Closing Times

Banks traditionally are open Monday–Thursday 10–3 and Friday 10–6, but many banks have extended hours and are open on Saturday, particularly outside of downtown.

Museums are generally open 10–5, including Saturday and Sunday. Most are open one evening a week as well.

Department store hours are Monday–Wednesday and Saturday 9:30–6, Thursday and Friday 9:30–9, and Sunday noon–5. Many smaller stores are also open Sunday.

Important Addresses and Numbers

Radio Stations

CFOX-FM (99.3), contemporary rock; **CFUN-AM (1410)/FM (100.1),** oldies and hits; **CBU-AM (1370),** CBC Radio—news and features; and **CJJR-FM (93.7),** country music.

Consulates

United States (1075 W. Pender St., ☎ 604/685–4311); **United Kingdom** (800–1111 Melville St., ☎ 604/683–4421).

Dentist

The counterpart to Medicentre (*see below*) is **Dentacentre** (1055 Dunsmuir St., lower level, ☎ 604/669–6700), which is next door and is also open weekdays.

Emergencies

Call 911 for **police, fire** department, and **ambulance.**

Hospital and Clinic

St. Paul's Hospital (1081 Burrard St., ☎ 604/682–2344), a downtown facility, has an emergency ward. **Medicentre** (1055 Dunsmuir St., lower level, ☎ 604/683–8138), a drop-in clinic on the lower level of the Bentall Centre, is open weekdays.

Late-Night Pharmacy

Shopper's Drug Mart (1125 Davie St., ☎ 604/685–6445) offers 24-hour service daily.

Road Emergencies

BCAA (☎ 604/293–2222) has 24-hour emergency road service for members of AAA or CAA.

Travel Agencies

American Express Travel Service (1040 W. Georgia St., ☎ 604/669–2813), **Mirage Holidays** (14–200 Burrard St., ☎ 604/685–4008), and **P. Lawson Travel** (409 Granville St., Suite 150, ☎ 604/682–4272).

Visitor Information

Vancouver Tourist Info Centre (200 Burrard St., ☎ 604/683–2000) provides maps and information about the city and is open July and August daily 8–6; the remainder of the year, weekdays 8:30–5, Saturday 9–5. A kiosk in Pacific Centre Mall is open daily in summer, Monday–Saturday 9:30–5, Sunday noon–5; in winter, Monday–Saturday 9–5. Eaton's department store downtown also has a tourist information counter that is open all year. **Discover B.C.** (☎ 800/663–6000) is available year-round to assist with tourist information and reservations.

4 Portrait of Seattle and Vancouver

In the Footsteps of the First Settlers

More Portraits

IN THE FOOTSTEPS
OF THE FIRST SETTLERS

THERE'S A SORT OF PRIMEVAL MYSTERY about the majestic landscapes of the Pacific Northwest Coast, something elemental and ancient that can give you a strange sense of being dislocated in time. Drive along the coastal roads of Washington's Olympic Peninsula, for example, and you'll pass magnificent rain forest, pounding surf, and partially submerged chunks of headland stranded at sea. Every bridge you cross takes you over an ancient fishing stream where prehistoric Indians harvested salmon. The oldest trees along the road bear scars where these Indians pulled off bark strips dozens of feet long, which they used for clothing, construction work, and rope making. Stop to look out over the water, and you feel the presence of ancient whale hunters scanning the horizon for spouts among the waves.

It isn't just a question of landscape, either. Elders in the Eskimo (Inuit is the preferred term in Canada) and Indian communities along the coast still pass on stories told to them by their ancestors, stories that can sometimes be traced as far back as 1,000 years, and their tribal art is a living expression of cultures whose origins are lost in the mists of prehistory.

Despite a lack of hard evidence, many archaeologists believe the first people to inhabit the New World arrived by way of the Pacific North Coast. Unlike Columbus and the seafaring Vikings, Polynesians, Chinese, and Japanese, all of whom crossed oceans to arrive at different points in North and South America, it is believed that the first Americans came on foot. If these pioneers had boats at all, they were small ones, not designed for long-distance travel across oceans. They came via Alaska and traveled through Canada into the western United States.

Although these assertions sound feasible, there aren't any known archaeological sites to support them. The oldest documented sites in the New World are believed to be 20,000–13,000 years old; the oldest known sites in the Pacific Northwest are Indian settlements that fall at the younger end of this range, at about 13,000 years old. Why then is the Pacific Northwest Coast believed to be the point of entry for the earliest settlers? Because it's the only place where people could have walked into the New World or used their small boats to travel along the coast without excessive danger. The last Ice Age tied up so much water that ocean levels probably dropped by hundreds of feet around the world. On certain winter days today, a person can walk between Alaska and the Soviet Union on ice when the oceans freeze over. But during the Ice Age the oceans were so reduced that the seabed was temporarily exposed as dry land, supporting vegetation and game, with fish in the rivers and sea mammals on the coast. So much ground was exposed, in fact, that the Old World and the New were connected by dry land. And though their languages and blood types differ, evidence strongly suggests that both the Eskimos and Indians have their roots somewhere in Asia. As one Eskimo friend of mine once said, "You know, those Chinese look an awful lot like us. They must be descended from Eskimos."

Why then aren't there any sites to prove this migration theory? All human activity may have been confined to lower ground levels now hidden under the ocean, reason the archaeologists. Or people may have traveled in small numbers, so their remains aren't easily detected. Or we may have already found these sites without recognizing them as such. Even though the two American continents were not inhabited with people at the outset, they did have abundant herds of large game, animals that had no fear of humans. Hunters with such easy prey wouldn't stay in one place for long; as they killed off their local supply of meat, or as the animals learned how to avoid people, the hunters moved on. So it is possible that the settlers arrived in the Pacific Northwest, lived a nomadic life there for a while, and then roamed on to other parts of North America and into South America.

THE FIRST AMERICANS came to a land we wouldn't recognize today. Most of Canada, Alaska, and the northern United States were still under ice. Arctic weather and the forests, animals, and plants that are found in today's far north were prevalent halfway down the lower 48 states. Then the weather changed: The ice sheets melted and the ice receded north. The animal and plant distributions we see today started to become established about 10,000 years ago. Rivers and streams that were previously frozen started to run fast and clear at low temperatures. Conditions for pioneering salmon became so ideal that by 5,000 or so years ago, there were huge runs extending hundreds of miles inland.

For hunters it was a revolutionary time. Herds of large animals started to diminish or disappear, and the big-game hunters were increasingly confronted with more work and less to show for their efforts. Many hunters in the Pacific Northwest Coast, particularly those in Washington, British Columbia, and southeastern Alaska, turned to fishing instead. Their nomadic life following the herds became a more settled one as they switched to fishing. And as they started to settle down, they were able to accumulate more material things.

The first Americans moved north to south, from Alaska to Canada and then to the lower 48 states and finally into Central America and South America. The more recent inhabitants who made their living from salmon fishing, however, headed in the opposite direction, from the lower Pacific Northwest up into Canada and Alaska. The art and culture of these people spread and flourished in the Pacific Northwest and continued to do so in the centuries preceding their contact with European explorers. Archaeological sites of these fishing peoples date back 2,500 years and more.

Native Americans often moved when they felt their villages had grown too big. According to stories told by Indian elders, entire clans would depart and make new settlements along the Pacific Coast. Battles between Indian tribes, and warfare between the Eskimos and Indians, also prompted the relocation of some villages. And eventually, as the native and Euro-American economies became entwined, some Indians and Eskimos abandoned their villages. Many of these villages can still be seen today: Houses may have fallen, totem poles may have been reduced by museum acquisitions, and the forest is once again dense, but the villages are there. Not only can archaeologists find and excavate the abandoned sites of these people, they also can talk to their descendants. When an archaeologist is puzzled by an object he digs out of the ground, he can consult the elders of various Indian and Eskimo groups, who can often identify it and describe its use. And when the elders can't identify an object, they can often point researchers in the right direction.

During this prehistoric fishing era, the most prosperous natives were those of Washington, British Columbia, and southern Alaska. They had the good life, and they flaunted it. Their art was larger than life, while their potlatches (celebratory feasts) gave new meaning to the words conspicuous consumption. The success of the fishing peoples led to imitation. The natives of Kodiak Island were Eskimo, for example, and their ancestors came to the New World to fish and hunt sea mammals along the coast, rather than hunt the big land-bound game as the Indians' ancestors did. Surprising enough, however, the Kodiak people achieved a society in many ways remarkably similar to that of Indian tribes living to the east and south. Their art, archaeology, and legends demonstrate the connections.

Indian groups were open to the ways of others too. In the far north of Alaska, where trees don't grow and fish runs can be counted in dozens instead of millions, Eskimo hunters had great success in capturing large whales. Indian groups of the lower Pacific Northwest did the same, using many of the whale-hunting techniques and rituals employed by people as far away as Point Barrow on the Arctic Coast.

Although the native groups along the Pacific Northwest Coast were lucky enough to avoid outright war with the European and American settlers, they did suffer some adversity. The natives of Kodiak, for example, were viciously attacked by Russians, and many natives eventually lost land in Canada and the United States. All the natives suffered when commercial fishing and river dams reduced salmon runs, and again when Yankee whalers destroyed whales in huge numbers. Despite these setbacks, however, both the Indians and Eskimos have retained much of their culture and way of life into the present.

One of the best-known archaeological sites of these settlers is Ozette, located on the Makah Reservation in Washington's Olympic Peninsula. The finds of the site can be viewed by the public, and visitors can request permission to visit the site itself. Call the Makah Reservation (tel. 206/645–2711) for information. The village of Ozette was partially covered by a mud slide several hundred years ago. This apparent catastrophe ironically turned out to preserve the village, however, for the wet mud provided an anaerobic environment hostile to most decay-causing organisms. As a result, the mud-covered section of Ozette was preserved in its entirety, a kind of New World Pompeii.

ARCHAEOLOGISTS USUALLY EXCAVATE with masons' trowels because they generally dig up stone and ceramics, objects that a skillfully handled trowel won't harm. But at Ozette in the 1970s, there was a delightful obstacle to overcome. Basketry, cordage, clothing, and all kinds of soft materials had been preserved, but since they were preserved wet, they were particularly soft, and the trowels cut through them like mud. Even experienced excavators couldn't feel the damage they were doing to the objects.

A whole new excavation approach was undertaken, called "wet site" archaeology. Using water hoses to excavate the village, the archaeologists discovered that mud and debris could be washed away, leaving artifacts intact. During the handlers' first clumsy attempts at hosing down the mud, artifacts could be seen tumbling downhill with the water, but after some

trial and error, the workers were able to keep even small finds in place.

One of the most exciting aspects of the Ozette excavation was the support archaeologists received from Indians living in the region. The Makah tribe encouraged archaeologists to excavate Ozette and assisted in the fieldwork; tribal members provided logistical support and helped interpret finds. And the tribe even built a museum based on the artifacts on its grounds at Neah Bay.

The Indians also helped prepare artifacts for public display, which turned out to be quite a challenge. Generally, archaeological finds of stone and ceramic pieces are preserved simply by being cleaned first in water and then glued together. But Ozette produced all kinds of perishable artifacts, objects that quickly started to deteriorate once they were removed from their muddy entombment. So the Makah tribe provided laboratory space and helped the archaeologists preserve and stabilize the finds.

These descendants of the ancient Indians went one step further and created a living experiment on the site. The Makah people worked outside to build a plank house, like those in Ozette, and then attempted to use the interior in the same ways their ancestors did. Life in the house was set up based upon the directions of tribal elders, historic accounts, and archaeological interpretations. In the end, the house looked as if one good mud slide would turn it into another ruined Ozette home. After this experimental period, the tribe dismantled the house and rebuilt it inside the Makah museum.

A large dugout canoe was also built for the museum. The art of making canoes had almost died out, but it was revived to capture an important part of life in Ozette. Young and old worked together to build the boat and to pass on these ancient skills.

Other archaeological sites in the area require a bit more effort to explore. From southern Alaska to Oregon, you can find hundreds of petroglyphs (rock carvings) and pictographs (rock paintings). Only a handful of them can be dated, however, so they can't be attributed to any particular group of people. Some are easily accessible, and seen by the public every day. Others are so hidden you can only find them if you happen to stumble upon them. Still other carvings are positioned at the tidal zone and consequently are under water at high tide. One worthwhile guide to the many accessible rock carvings is Beth and Ray Hill's *Indian Petroglyphs of the Pacific Northwest*.

Prehistoric Indians also carved petroglyphs on land, although mostly facing the ocean, or else overlooking a river or waterway. Pictographs, on the other hand, can be seen throughout the Northwest Coast. Some of these detailed rocks have been jackhammered from their embedded frames and carted away; others have eroded, and still others lie beneath reservoirs. But the vast majority are right where they were created, and with permission from native or nonnative landowners, or government agencies, visitors can examine them. More than 500 sites are known. One protected site open to the public is Petroglyph Park in the town of Nanaimo, a Vancouver Island. Petroglyphs at Wrangell, Alaska, are also open to the public.

The ancient craft of carving giant totem poles out of trees has survived as a living art form, with plenty of demand for new poles. Carvers today often work in public throughout the Pacific Northwest, at museums or on the grounds of institutions that have commissioned their artwork. Young workers aspire to apprentice with master carvers, and gift shops all over the region offer miniature reproductions.

The totem pole is the best-known example of current Northwest Coast tribal art, but masks, tools, and a variety of paintings and prints also continue the artistic tradition of the area. Artwork can be purchased at local galleries, many of which are located on Indian lands and are run by Indians. The choices are broader and the prices lower here than they are in the native art galleries of New York and California. The Dukuah Gallery (1971 Peninsula Rd., Ocluelet, B.C., V0R 3A0, ☎ 604/726–7223) is run by native Lillian Mac and her husband, Bert Mac, the hereditary Chief of the Toquant tribe. Native artists visit and work in the gallery year-round.

The British Columbia Provincial Museum in Victoria, with its unique collection of prehistoric fish bones, is an outstanding research center, with representation from all five species of salmon and almost every other fish that might have been harvested by prehistoric natives. Each fish skeleton has been mounted on wires, with all the bones together in proper anatomical order. While this is a scientific collection, it verges on being a work of art in itself, with skeletal fish elongating and compressing into fantastic shapes.

In Vancouver, at the University of British Columbia's Museum of Anthropology, there's an excellent archaeological collection that's very accessible to the public. Visitors can open any of the Plexiglas-covered drawers to examine even the most delicate artifacts. Other artifacts can be seen at the Thomas Burke Memorial Washington State Museum at the University of Washington in Seattle, and at the Alaska State Museum in Juneau, where they also have a first-rate collection of historic baleen (fibrous plates that hang from the roof of the whale's mouth) baskets. Only native hunters and artisans are legally permitted to own unprocessed baleen.

Any overview of Northwest Coast archaeology inevitably leaves out more than it includes. Paleo-Indian sites, Russian fur-hunting activities, cave sites in Washington's channeled scablands, mastodons and mammoths, and cairns dug up 100 years ago can all be found along the Pacific Northwest Coast. And if you visit the area searching for a glimpse of the past, native people will share their stories, researchers may invite you to observe their work, artisans will explain their ancient crafts, and the museums will let you view even the most fragile artifacts. For here, one thing remains constant: the people's eagerness to document and understand the past.

By Glenn W. Sheehan

MORE PORTRAITS

Fiction & Memoirs

Recommended novels and stories of the Northwest include the imaginative and sometimes surreal creations of novelist Tom Robbins; bittersweet short fiction by Raymond Carver; the Jack London classic, *Call of the Wild*; and works by such writers as Annie Dillard, Ursula LeGuin, Aaron Elkin, Frank Herbert, J. A. Jance, W. P. Kinsella, Jack Hodgin, Willo Davis Roberts, William Stafford, Walt Morey, and Norman Maclean. *At the Field's End,* by Nicolas O'Connell, features interviews with 20 leading writers who are all closely connected to the Pacific Northwest and reflect the character of the region. The *Journals of Lewis and Clark* can also make for interesting reading as you follow in the explorers' path.

History & Travel Essays

The late Bill Spiedel, one of Seattle's most colorful characters, wrote about the early history of the city in books replete with lively anecdotes and legends; *Sons of the Profits* and *Doc Maynard* are two of his best. Timothy Egan's *The Good Rain* uses history to explore what the Northwest means. *Washingtonians, A Biographical Portrait of the State,* edited by David Brewster and David M. Buerge, is a series of essays on well-known and influential residents who have left their mark on the state. *Whistlepunks and Geoducks—Oral Histories from the Pacific Northwest,* by Ron Strickland, is a collection of stories told by old-timers from all walks of life in Washington State.

Short History of Canada, by Desmond Morton, is a recent historical account of the country. Stephen Brook's *The Maple Leaf Rag* is a collection of idiosyncratic travel essays. *Why We Act Like Canadians: A Personal Exploration of Our National Character,* by Pierre Burton, is one of his many popular nonfiction books focusing on Canada's history and culture. *Local Colour—Writers Discovering Canada,* edited by Carol Marin, is a series of articles about Canadian places by leading travel writers.

Nature & the Outdoors

Gloria Snively's *Exploring the Seashore* offers a guide to shorebirds and intertidal plants and animals in Washington and British Columbia. The *Northwest Sportsman Almanac,* edited by Terry W. Sheely, provides an in-depth guide to fishing and hunting in the Pacific North Coast.

Television & Movies

The Pacific Northwest has provided the setting for a number of television series—*Frasier, Northern Exposure,* and *Twin Peaks,* not to mention the many syndicated series shot (if not set) in Vancouver. For a glimpse of the region on the big screen, check out such recent films as *Sleepless in Seattle, The Hand that Rocks the Cradle, Singles,* and *White Fang.* Idiosyncratic filmmaker and Portland native Gus van Sant has set a number of his movies in the Northwest, including *Drugstore Cowboy* and *My Own Private Idaho.*

INDEX

NOTES

NOTES

NOTES

NOTES

NOTES

NOTES

NOTES

NOTES

NOTES

NOTES

Fodor's Travel Publications

Available at bookstores everywhere, or call 1–800–533–6478, 24 hours a day.

Gold Guides
U.S.

Alaska	Florida	New Orleans	Santa Fe, Taos, Albuquerque
Arizona	Hawaii	New York City	
Boston	Las Vegas, Reno, Tahoe	Pacific North Coast	Seattle & Vancouver
California		Philadelphia & the Pennsylvania Dutch Country	The South
Cape Cod, Martha's Vineyard, Nantucket	Los Angeles		U.S. & British Virgin Islands
	Maine, Vermont, New Hampshire	The Rockies	
The Carolinas & the Georgia Coast	Maui	San Diego	USA
			Virginia & Maryland
Chicago	Miami & the Keys	San Francisco	Waikiki
Colorado	New England		Washington, D.C.

Foreign

Australia & New Zealand	Egypt	London	Provence & the Riviera
Austria	Europe	Madrid & Barcelona	Scandinavia
The Bahamas	Florence, Tuscany & Umbria	Mexico	Scotland
Bermuda	France	Montréal & Québec City	Singapore
Budapest	Germany	Moscow, St. Petersburg, Kiev	South America
Canada	Great Britain		South Pacific
Cancún, Cozumel, Yucatán Peninsula	Greece	The Netherlands, Belgium & Luxembourg	Southeast Asia
Caribbean	Hong Kong		Spain
China	India	New Zealand	Sweden
Costa Rica, Belize, Guatemala	Ireland	Norway	Switzerland
Cuba	Israel	Nova Scotia, New Brunswick, Prince Edward Island	Thailand
The Czech Republic & Slovakia	Italy		Tokyo
	Japan	Paris	Toronto
Eastern Europe	Kenya & Tanzania	Portugal	Turkey
	Korea		Vienna & the Danube

Fodor's Special-Interest Guides

Branson	Fodor's London Companion	Kodak Guide to Shooting Great Travel Pictures	Walt Disney World for Adults
Caribbean Ports of Call	France by Train		Where Should We Take the Kids? California
The Complete Guide to America's National Parks	Halliday's New England Food Explorer	Shadow Traffic's New York Shortcuts and Traffic Tips	
		Sunday in New York	Where Should We Take the Kids? Northeast
Condé Nast Traveler Caribbean Resort and Cruise Ship Finder	Healthy Escapes	Sunday in San Francisco	
	Italy by Train		
Cruises and Ports of Call		Walt Disney World, Universal Studios and Orlando	

Special Series

Affordables

Caribbean

Europe

Florida

France

Germany

Great Britain

Italy

London

Paris

Fodor's Bed & Breakfasts and Country Inns

America's Best B&Bs

California's Best B&Bs

Canada's Great Country Inns

Cottages, B&Bs and Country Inns of England and Wales

The Mid-Atlantic's Best B&Bs

New England's Best B&Bs

The Pacific Northwest's Best B&Bs

The South's Best B&Bs

The Southwest's Best B&Bs

The Upper Great Lakes' Best B&Bs

The Berkeley Guides

California

Central America

Eastern Europe

Europe

France

Germany & Austria

Great Britain & Ireland

Italy

London

Mexico

Pacific Northwest & Alaska

Paris

San Francisco

Compass American Guides

Arizona

Chicago

Colorado

Hawaii

Hollywood

Las Vegas

Maine

Manhattan

Montana

New Mexico

New Orleans

Oregon

San Francisco

Santa Fe

South Carolina

South Dakota

Southwest

Texas

Utah

Virginia

Washington

Wine Country

Wisconsin

Wyoming

Fodor's Español

California

Caribe Occidental

Caribe Oriental

Gran Bretaña

Londres

Mexico

Nueva York

Paris

Fodor's Exploring Guides

Australia

Boston & New England

Britain

California

Caribbean

China

Egypt

Florence & Tuscany

Florida

France

Germany

Ireland

Israel

Italy

Japan

London

Mexico

Moscow & St. Petersburg

New York City

Paris

Prague

Provence

Rome

San Francisco

Scotland

Singapore & Malaysia

Spain

Thailand

Turkey

Venice

Fodor's Flashmaps

Boston

New York

San Francisco

Washington, D.C.

Fodor's Pocket Guides

Acapulco

Atlanta

Barbados

Jamaica

London

New York City

Paris

Prague

Puerto Rico

Rome

San Francisco

Washington, D.C.

Rivages Guides

Bed and Breakfasts of Character and Charm in France

Hotels and Country Inns of Character and Charm in France

Hotels and Country Inns of Character and Charm in Italy

Short Escapes

Country Getaways in Britain

Country Getaways in France

Country Getaways Near New York City

Fodor's Sports

Golf Digest's Best Places to Play

Skiing USA

USA Today The Complete Four Sport Stadium Guide

Fodor's Vacation Planners

Great American Learning Vacations

Great American Sports & Adventure Vacations

Great American Vacations

National Parks and Seashores of the East

National Parks of the West

Your guide to a picture-perfect vacation

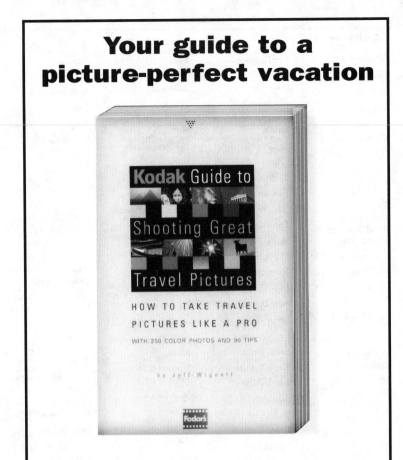

Kodak and Fodor's join together to create the guide that travelers everywhere have been asking for—one that covers the terms and techniques, the equipment and etiquette for taking first-rate travel photographs.

The most authoritative and up-to-date book of its kind, **The Kodak Guide to Shooting Great Travel Pictures** includes over 200 color photographs and spreads on 100 points of photography important to travelers, such as landscape basics, undersea shots, wildlife, city streets, close-ups, photographing in museums and more.

$16.50 ($22.95 Canada)

At bookstores everywhere, or call 1-800-533-6478.